social activities, and level of living of more than 700 rural Cuban families. This material is combined with historical background, census analyses, and on-the-spot observations for a comprehensive study that fills a gap in the available literature on the subject. The volume includes appendixes providing a description of the geography of the survey area and a verbatim sample report of a survey interviewer, together with a glossary of Spanish words, a bibliography, and tables.

In this book rural Cuba's problems are thoroughly discussed, present-day progress toward their solution is reported, and suggestions are offered for future agricultural policies that could help enrich the lives of Cuba's people.

Rural Cuba

Rural Cuba

BY

Lowry Nelson

PROFESSOR OF SOCIOLOGY, UNIVERSITY OF MINNESOTA

THE UNIVERSITY OF MINNESOTA PRESS, *Minneapolis*
LONDON · GEOFFREY CUMBERLEGE · OXFORD UNIVERSITY PRESS

Preface

This book is the result of a year of investigation and observation. The author was appointed rural sociologist in the United States Department of State in September 1945 and remained in Cuba until September 1946. Under the technical guidance of the Office of Foreign Agricultural Relations of the Department of Agriculture, he was given the general responsibility of making a study of rural life in the Caribbean.

It soon became clear that one year was little enough to spend in even one country of the "ocean sea," without attempting to range over such a vast social, political, economic, and geographic complex as the Caribbean represents. Visits of one to two weeks were made to the Dominican Republic, Puerto Rico, the Virgin Islands, and Trinidad, but they were of insufficient duration to do more than gather a few data and make general observations. The visits proved valuable, however, in helping the writer to see Cuba in better perspective, while observing some of the variations in culture among the countries of the Antilles.

When it had been decided to center attention upon Cuba, an analysis was first made of the population censuses of the island. Fortunately these are reasonably adequate, particularly those made since 1898. The most important undertaking at the next stage was the development of a cooperative plan with the Cuban Ministry of Agriculture for a series of local community surveys.[1]

---

[1] Referred to throughout this work as the Special Surveys.

v

A word of explanation regarding these Special Surveys is appropriate at this point. Shortly after my arrival in Havana, I discussed with Dr. Paul G. Minneman, the agricultural attaché of the American Embassy, the desirability of proposing to the Cuban government a cooperative survey of at least four rural community types in the island. He approved the idea, and I drew up a memorandum embodying our suggestion which was duly submitted to the Minister of Agriculture. He in turn discussed it with the President of the Republic. All officials were agreeable to the idea of cooperating on such a study, but regarded the outline I submitted as too limited in scope. They felt it would be necessary to include about eleven areas if we were to sample the varied types of farming of the country. A brief description of the areas finally agreed upon will be found in Appendix A.

It was further agreed that I should provide general direction of the project with an associate director, Sr. Casto Ferragút, named by the Ministry of Agriculture. The field interviewing was done by the agricultural inspectors in Pinar del Río, in the Cienfuegos-Trinidad area, and in Alto Songo. The balance of the schedules were taken by three girls who had had training in the school of social service of the University of Havana and were employed in the Ministry of Agriculture.[2] They had had some experience in field interviewing and their work generally was of good quality. Appendix B consists of a translation of the field report of Sr. Alejandro Fernández de Cueto, who did the interviewing in the Cienfuegos-Trinidad area.

While the field work was under way, Sr. Ferragút and I, together with my son, made a trip throughout the island in a truck provided by the ministry. We traveled a total of 1,800 miles by truck, railway, and horse, visiting all the survey localities. At each place we interviewed local leaders, farmers, school teachers, and agricultural inspectors roughly equivalent to county agricultural agents in the United States as general background for our interpretation of the survey data.

The Ministry of Agriculture also provided for the machine tabulation of the data collected from the 742 families interviewed. The schedule was seven pages long, covering such subjects as

---

[2] Señoritas Graciella Llarena, Elsa Mallea, and Aida Alonso.

family composition, education, housing, recreation, farming, land
tenure, diet, family expenditures, and the like. It was longer than
is ordinarily desirable, but there were so many items on which
we wanted information that the temptation to include them all
was greater than we could resist. After all, this was the first systematic study ever attempted of rural life in Cuba, and we hoped
to get badly needed data to make the report substantial and
factual. Nevertheless, there are many aspects of Cuban life still
awaiting study.

For example, I would have preferred to spend a few additional
months on the island to finish my investigation of organized
groups among farm workers and farm operators. All but one of
the sugar plantations was unionized at the time this study was
made. Farm labor unions are comparatively new in Cuba. A
national federation of farmers was also recently formed, and its
activities deserve careful study. The analysis of vital statistics
was only partially done when the year's leave came to an end.
The same situation was true for the study of health and welfare
agencies.

In spite of the many notes and materials accumulated on these
and other subjects, I could not feel that I was prepared to give
an adequate treatment of them in this report. Perhaps in the
course of academic time, opportunity for further leave may permit another visit to this fascinating and pleasant land. Meanwhile,
this book must be regarded in a very real sense as an *introduction*
to the study of Cuban society.

The excellent support of Cuban officials, from President Grau
San Martín to the field interviewers, and of the families themselves, who submitted patiently to the long list of questions, assured the success of this initial venture in social-survey technique
in Cuba. The author is deeply indebted to them all for their help
and appreciation. He can only hope that the published report will
not fall too far below their expectations.

Officials in the American Embassy, including Ambassador R.
Henry Norweb, Counsellor of Embassy Robert F. Woodward,
Economic Counsellor Albert F. Nufer, John T. Reid, cultural attaché, and Paul G. Minneman, agricultural attaché, along with
many other staff members, gave assistance at various times which

is gratefully acknowledged. Special mention should be given Dr. Minneman, without whose helpfulness throughout the year, in numerous ways, the work could not have progressed as it did. His detailed knowledge of Cuban agriculture made him an invaluable consultant.

Sr. Casto Ferragút of the Ministry of Agriculture was a constant and efficient collaborator. He assumed major responsibility in connection with the field surveys and the tabulation of the data, and has advised in the preparation of the manuscript.

There are, of course, innumerable persons other than those already mentioned to whom I am indebted, not only for direct assistance given, but for many courtesies extended. Sr. Jorge Clark, on whose cafetal I was a guest for three days, was a considerate host and a helpful friend. Sr. Antonio Guerra, who wrote the text for the population census of 1943, gave generously of his time and counsel. Mrs. S. A. Neblett, American-born resident of Cuba for over twenty years, assisted in arranging the field trip to San Blas reported in Chapter I and helped in other ways. Señora Elena Mederos de González of Havana was a most helpful friend. The "new Cuba" will be profoundly influenced by her work and that of her associates. Various ministries in addition to the Ministry of Agriculture gave complete cooperation when called upon for information.

Finally, Lowry Nelson, Jr., has assisted with some of the translations and acted at times as interpreter and recorder of interviews during the field work. His sister, Janet, helped with typing and preparation of the index.

Nevertheless, the author is inevitably responsible for any shortcomings or mistakes which the work contains. He trusts the reader will appreciate the fact that the book is based upon material gathered five years ago and that changes have taken place in the years since 1945. If the book adds something to the understanding of Cuba, by people of the United States as well as by Cubans themselves, its major purpose will have been achieved.

LOWRY NELSON

Minneapolis, Minnesota
June 6, 1950

Table of Contents

ix

Rural Cuba

CHAPTER I

Rich Land—Poor People

"The land is very rich and the people very poor," said José Fariñas Castro, operator of a two-thousand-acre livestock ranch in central Cuba. I was sitting on the porch of their relatively good ranch home with Señor and Señora Fariñas and their two charming daughters, asking questions which I hoped would bring forth expressions of opinion and attitudes that might help me to a better understanding of the life and aspirations of Cuban farm people. I had come to Cuba for a year of study and investigation as rural sociologist in the United States Department of State, and I wanted to visit as many different farmers and types of farms as possible.

Señor Fariñas was an immigrant from Galicia who arrived in Cuba a half-century ago. He has done well over the years in spite of the agricultural hazards and calamities he has experienced. He now has upward of five hundred head of cattle with a monthly milk check of from $1,000 to $1,500, as well as additional income from part of the ranch which is rented to tobacco farmers; but only a year previous to our visit, a hurricane had passed over the country destroying thirty-three houses on his ranch, valued at $1,000 each and uninsured. Other losses, too, particularly from starvation among his cattle during the dry season, are sometimes very heavy.

Cuban people do not love the land and are careless in its management, according to Señor Fariñas, and so the land does not

3

reward them. "The field is the mother of the poor," says a proverb he quoted. He thinks it might help if more young people from Cuban farms could be given a chance to go abroad and see other countries. Instead of drafting them into the army, for example, he would give each young person $50 and transportation to a foreign country where he would be expected to remain for two years, after which he would be given his passage home. He thinks the returning youths would see their own country with new appreciation, and would have acquired a determination to improve it.

Other Cuban farmers with whom I talked tended to agree that Cubans are careless of the land. A tobacco farmer near Santa Clara who came from the Canary Islands claimed to be the only man in the neighborhood who fertilized his land. "In the Canary Islands," he went on to say, "where water is very scarce, they care for it and their land as much as they care for their children. In Cuba there is much water, much land, but it is poorly managed."

And, said Señor Díaz, a tobacco farmer of Cabaiguán, "The wealth of the nation comes from the land; if the farmers are unprotected, the nation suffers." Perhaps the word "unprotected" could be extended to mean unprosperous, uneducated, and all of the other conditions associated with a low status in society. Señor Díaz is a tenant on land owned by a large landholder whose combined rentals in 1945 amounted to $40,000. An intelligent father, Señor Díaz had aspirations for his children; he wanted them to have an education and opportunity to get ahead in the world. Yet there was no school in this area because, he said, the owner would not give the land on which to build it. An itinerant teacher came to the farm homes and taught the children, and for this the parents paid $1.00 a month for each pupil. In all his fifty years, Señor Díaz said, he has never needed a soldier or a policeman, but of these there are plenty. What are really needed, he thought, are teachers for the children of the people, and of these there are few.

There is much that is unsightly and unpleasant in the human landscape of Cuba, just as there is in the United States and in practically every country. As we rode horseback through the countryside toward San Blas, my guide and friend, Jesús Martínez Moreno, kept pointing out to me the miserable habitations of the *precaristas*, the squatters who have settled on other people's land,

Cuba's Provinces

and he would say, "Very bad!"—an overworked phrase, I thought, in his limited English vocabulary. "Very bad" were the *bohíos*, the peasant houses, with their dirt floors, thatched roofs, and improvised walls of bark from royal palm trees. "Very bad" were the trails over which we rode, where in places the horses sank almost to their bellies in mud during the rainy season. "Very bad" were the naked children, their swollen stomachs testifying to an unbalanced diet and infection from parasitic worms—in rural Cuba parasitism is practically universal. "Very bad" was the evidence of great poverty everywhere on the part of large numbers of people, the absence of schools, medical care, and up-to-date methods of agriculture. "Very bad" also, in my friend's eyes, were the large concentrations of land in the hands of a few, and the politicians who took for themselves money which should have been spent for the benefit of the people.

The attitude of most Cubans toward these many problems is best understood in the light of Cuba's political history since liberation from Spanish control. A country that has passed through a period of colonial existence is likely to be distrustful of government and anxious to be as free as possible from restraints. The people are likely, also, to have little feeling of responsibility for their government and little or no sense of democratic participation in public affairs.

Cuba has had a special reason for being sick and tired of being ruled. It knew at first hand the corruption and ineptitude of a colonial government at its worst, since it was one of the last remnants of Spain's empire to gain its independence. The Spanish colonial officials were more interested in the personal gain they could realize through being officials than they were in providing services for the people under their charge. Yet this evil pattern of government was the ideal which all too many Cubans clasped to their political bosoms. The example set by four centuries of colonial rule, the latter years of which were the weakest and most corrupt of all, could not be expected to disappear by magic in favor of patterns of upright and responsible democracy.

Nevertheless, the first years of the Republic were good ones. After the military occupation by the United States, at first under General John Rutter Brooke (1899) and later under General Leonard Wood (1900–2), the Republic of Cuba was launched in 1902. Under its first president—honest, conscientious, incorruptible, democratic Thomas Estrada Palma—the new nation saw what most historians would agree were its "best years." He established schools, built roads, improved sanitation, and generally tried to carry on the projects already launched under General Wood for the welfare of the people. Besides carrying out these laudable programs, Estrada Palma was able to accumulate a surplus of twenty-six million dollars in the treasury.

This handsome sum played an important part in his undoing, for greedy politicians were determined to get their hands on it. Before the end of his first term of office, Estrada Palma had a revolution on his hands. Threatened by armed revolt, he finally called upon President Theodore Roosevelt to intervene with military force. The historians of this period seem generally agreed that it was the bungling of William Howard Taft, whom Roosevelt sent to Cuba to try to pacify the situation, that made military intervention inevitable.

There followed the administration of Charles E. Magoon as governor from 1906 until 1909. Succeeding Magoon, Cuban government was restored under the presidency of José Miguel Gómez, who served from 1909 to 1913. He was undoubtedly the most popular president the country ever had, but he brought back into prominence the old political evils of the Spanish tradition. He did not try to establish a new pattern of political morality for Cuba as Estrada Palma had done; he let the latent tendencies toward corruption have their way. By the time he left office, Cuba was on the downgrade politically.

The administrations that followed—of President Mario García Menocal from 1913 to 1921, and Alfredo Zayas, elected in the fraudulent and violent election of 1921—were noted for nothing so much as their unprecedented and steadily increasing political corruption. The high hopes of many Cubans for honest and competent government were frustrated as nepotism, graft, election frauds, and other corrupt practices became common. Furthermore, the postwar depression of 1921, after the war-induced prosperity, left the Cuban economy prostrate. The financial problems improved somewhat as business recovery set in and a loan from the United States was negotiated; but Cuban political life had sunk to a new moral low.

Nor was the unhappy island benefited by the president who followed Zayas, General Gerardo Machado, who was elected in 1924. Machado borrowed heavily from the United States banks on the theory, it is said, that if he were heavily indebted to these institutions, he would enjoy the protection of the United States government. He was also careful to see to it that the army was strengthened in numbers and equipment, and the morale of the soldiers bolstered by improved salaries and living conditions.

Following the brief boom from 1921 to 1924, known locally as the "dance of the millions," the sugar market again declined and scarcely recovered at all until the outbreak of World War II. Machado, therefore, governed during times which were far from prosperous. Unemployment and poverty were widespread. With borrowed American money, he began a program of public works, including the construction of the capitol building in Havana, and the Central Highway, a concrete road the full length of the island. The highway was constructed by a company which President Machado owned, and the graft involved in this project is said to have totaled around thirty million dollars. Of the twenty million spent on the new capitol, twelve million is estimated to have been graft.

As his critics became more active and the rumblings of the people more articulate, Machado resorted to repressive measures to protect his regime. Press censorship was established, the University of Havana was closed, opposition leaders were imprisoned and tortured when they were not murdered outright, and labor organizations were driven underground. Such measures only hastened the day of final reckoning, which came in August 1933. A general strike and the rebellion of the army compelled Machado to flee the country.

The immediate successor to Machado as provisional president was Dr. Carlos Manual de Céspedes, who served only twenty-four days when a revolutionary junta, with Dr. Ramón Grau San Martín at its head, demanded his surrender of power. Dr. Grau, a professor of the University of Havana, was made president, but after four months of intermittent violence and failure to gain recognition by the United States, he retired from office. On January 17, 1934, all parties agreed upon Colonel Carlos Mendieta for the presidency. Disorder and strikes continued, however, until one Fulgencio Batista, an army sergeant, organized a successful coup d'état, ousted the commissioned officers, and made himself chief of staff and master of Cuba. He suppressed the strikes, established and maintained order, albeit with strong measures, and ruled as the strong man of Cuba through a succession of presidents until 1940. He became president in that year by defeating ex-president Grau San Martín. Batista in turn was defeated by Grau in 1944 and went into exile in the United States.

The governments that followed the overthrow of Machado all veered to the left and sought to improve conditions in one way or another. Batista, for example, did a good deal for rural education by establishing a normal school for the training of rural teachers and regional schools where rural children are maintained and taught at the expense of the public treasury. Cuba's new constitution, approved in 1940, is very liberal and incorporates most of the political ideals represented in the Western democratic tradition. Promises are freely made, by candidates and by party platforms, of land for the landless peasantry, rural schools, rural roads, and numerous other reforms for the benefit and welfare of the population. Such promises have led the rural people to expect much of the government of Dr. Grau San Martín, and it is to be hoped that the rural problems discussed in the chapters to come will gradually find solution.

Cuba presents a paradox on a grand order. Nature is bountiful. Climate and soil combine to provide extraordinary fruitfulness with even nominal care. True, the dry season with its insufficient rain is a problem, but through most of the year, food crops can be grown. Yet the masses of Cuba's rural population are impoverished, ill housed, ill fed, and poorly clothed. "The land is very rich, but the people are very poor."

Not all of rural Cuba presents such a discouraging picture, however. There are prosperous small farms and farmers, too, and many of the families working on the large plantations and ranches are quite well off. In the course of a field trip into the farm areas of the municipality of Cienfuegos,[1] I visited a number of well-kept farms and inspected a public orphanage as well. The orphanage is located at Cuanao, a small town on the outskirts of Cienfuegos, and maintained by the Ministry of Health and Public Assistance. It seems to be reasonably well maintained and managed, caring for about seventy-five children between the ages of six and fourteen. At the time of our visit, a class was being conducted by the teachers who are part of the staff. We visited the dormitory, the kitchen, and the shower and locker rooms, all of which were orderly and clean. The director of the orphanage, a woman of about thirty who trained in home economics at the University of Havana, expressed her ambition—and a worthy one indeed—to have the land planted to crops so that the children could be given some experience in gardening and farming.

Leaving the orphanage, Señor Martínez[2] and I drove on into farming country. At Cuanao we left the paved highway and went into the fields over a road which once had been paved with cobblestones, but, as is frequently the case in Cuba, had apparently never had any repair work. As a consequence, the road was in worse condition than it probably would have been if no effort had ever been expended on it. It was no place for an automobile! However, I nudged the car slowly over the small boulders and around the high centers, and we traversed several miles in the course of the afternoon.

[1] The Cuban *municipio* corresponds roughly to a county in the United States.

[2] The mayor of Cienfuegos, Dr. Bustamante, kindly placed at my disposal the services of Jesús Martínez Moreno as guide and interpreter, to whom I am deeply indebted for a pleasant companionship for four days.

En route we visited four or five farms. The first visit was to a truck gardener. A native of China, he came to Cuba over fifty years ago as part of the great Chinese "importation" which is one of the remarkable features of Cuban history. Like so many of his fellow-Chinese he fought in Cuba's War of Independence of 1895 to 1898; also like so many of them, he became a truck gardener. His tract was small, but he owned it himself and it was intensively utilized. His beds were planted to onions and lettuce, while in the bottom of an *arroyo* he grew water cress. In his little storehouse, he showed us two large bags of commercial fertilizer—from the United States. He complained of the limited market for his products, because so few Cubans consume this type of vegetable as part of their regular diet. Although he said he had a wife and two children in China, he lived alone in a little bohío.

The next farm, also operated by its owner, contained four *caballerías*—a caballería is equal to about thirty-three acres—devoted to diverse crops, but with beef cattle as a major source of income. Most of the farm, therefore, was in pasture. The cultivated portion was devoted to fruits—grapefruit, limes, and bananas—and vegetables—*boniatos* (sweet potatoes), *yuca* (cassava), and some maize. There were two bohíos on the farm, one of which was the home of a married son and his family. The next farm, of two caballerías, was also devoted to diversified crops. One caballería was rented to a son.

The best farm visited on this trip was that of a colored family, consisting of husband, wife, one daughter, and a niece and nephew. We entered the bohío and found it had a dirt floor but was neatly kept. In the kitchen the mother proudly showed us a large sack of rice which they had produced, and the husband took us over part of his farm, where we saw a patch of upland rice—produced without irrigation—a plot of Irish potatoes, some yuca and boniatos, and a patch of corn. They also had several trees of limes, grapefruit, and bananas, and at least one of papaya. A plot of land had also been prepared for planting vegetables for winter production. This man is one of eighteen brothers who live in the neighborhood and who are similarly small farmers, owning their land and growing diversified crops, some of which are sold in the Cienfuegos market. At the same time they provide themselves with an abundance of diverse foods.

Later in the afternoon we returned to the city of Cienfuegos and I was taken to the home of Jorge Clark, where arrangements were made for us to leave with him early the next morning for several days' visit at his *cafetal*, or coffee farm. I did not have much of an idea what to expect, since my guide spoke little English and I understood less Spanish. Clark spoke no English at all, for although his grandfather had come from England, the family had become completely Cubanized.

We drove the car about fifteen miles to Central Soledád, a large sugar plantation, over a paved road in good condition. There I met Mr. Reed, the manager, and arranged to leave my car until I returned. Then we boarded a small "bus" which the sugar company operates over its narrow-gauge railway line during the "dead season"—that is, before the sugar cane is ready to harvest. This took us through the plantation to a point about twenty minutes distant, where the railroad crosses the main road to La Sierra and San Blas, our destination. Here we mounted saddle horses for the remainder of the journey.

The "terminal" of the railroad was interesting. There were a large number of saddle horses and pack horses, the latter being used to bring milk in five-gallon cans from the farms in the neighborhood. The packsaddle is constructed of wood in such a way that two of the cans can be put on either side of the horse, and is sufficiently rigid to protect the horse from direct contact with the cans. At the terminal the milk from the smaller cans is transferred to ten-gallon cans, and the latter are loaded on the "bus" for transport to the *central*, the big sugar mill. From there they are taken by truck to Cienfuegos.

Our horses were late in arriving, having been brought from San Blas; but by about eleven o'clock we were mounted and on our way. About three or four kilometers up the country, we visited the Finca Arena, a farm owned by one Antonio González Rodríguez. To his welcome "*desmonte*," we complied and entered his house. It was a commodious farm home, the living room neatly furnished with "store" furniture. The floors were cement, and the entire establishment gave evidence of considerable prosperity and progressive management. Señor González owns seven caballerías, devoted to diversified crops and livestock. He also produces some cane, which he sells to Central Soledád. His main source of income, however, is his 160 head of cattle, 80 head of which are used as milk cows. Forty cows were in production at the time, but the amount of milk produced seemed to be rather small, judging from the fact that it could be taken on two or three horses to the railroad. The usual field crops—yuca, boniatos, *limones* (lemons), and *plátanos*, or plantain, a starchy vegetable—were also produced on the farm.

This farm had a running water system installed. Water was pumped by hand from a well located about one hundred feet from the house into a tank, from which running water was supplied to the kitchen sink and to a shower bath off the kitchen. One of the farm buildings, previously used by the farmer for a shop and storage place, was being enlarged and improved for use as a schoolhouse for the neighborhood. The schoolteacher was there, but the building was not yet ready for use. There were to be sixty-one pupils when the school was in session.

From Finca Arena we proceeded to the village of La Sierra, a place of about 800 inhabitants and the administrative seat of the *barrio*, or township, of the same name. Here there is the inevitable "bar," five grocery stores, two general stores, a restaurant, a saddlery shop, quarters for the military, a Catholic church in process of construction, and the club, which provides the meeting place for the community. The club is the most imposing building of the village, with the military quarters coming next. The church is a stone structure, and at present is only completed up to the square. There is also a hospital here, although there is no doctor or nurse.

After lunch at La Sierra, we went on toward San Blas, stopping on the way out of town to greet the mayor, whose office is in his home. As we rode along through the mudholes and over the rocky outcroppings, it seemed incredible that this road was ever traversed by automobiles. However, during the dry season the road is made passable for the trucks which transport the coffee from San Blas to Cienfuegos.

San Blas is about eight kilometers from La Sierra. About one kilometer from our destination, we called on another family. The husband was not at home, being at work in San Blas, but the wife, a young woman of about twenty-five, her young child, and a sister who was engaged to be married all received us. The house was attractive, with a cement floor in the living quarters, although none in the kitchen. The grounds outside were almost a solid bank of flowers, and between the highway and the house was a rather large plot of yuca and other vegetables. There was also a patch of cane used for feeding livestock. In a small pen a hog was kept, one of the finest I saw in Cuba, being fattened for slaughter. As the young wife spoke in Spanish with my companions, she had a disconsolate look, and I wondered why, in view of her unusually attractive home and surroundings. I learned that it was because of the isolation imposed by the terrible roads. As I was to discover later, this is the heaviest burden that weighs upon many rural Cuban people. They may be well fed and fairly well housed— better than the average *campesinos,* or farmers, of Cuba; but their hunger is for social contact, for the improved highway that would make accessible the city and the towns with their social advantages and markets.

This hunger for improved transportation facilities amounts almost to a passion, and the people look with enthusiastic expectancy upon any Cuban government that shows any interest in their welfare and any evidence of intentions to improve the roads. It was understandable, therefore, that there was great trust in the present government. We saw a poignant expression of this faith in the home just described, where the wife had taught her pet parrot to say *"Viva* Grau San Martín!"

We arrived in San Blas about six in the evening, and I was introduced all around. This was Cuba's coffee country. San Blas itself is a mere hamlet, the geographical center of one of the early circular *corrales,* the original Spanish grants of land. The structures there at present are the Clark home—headquarters of the large cafetal of eighty caballerías—and two small general stores which handle groceries, tobaccos, and liquors mainly, but also such supplies as machetes, axes, leggings, patent medicines, sugar, salt, spices, and the like. In addition there are the residences of the two storekeepers, the residence and shop of the blacksmith, residences of two other farm families, the schoolhouse, and one residence in process of construction.

San Blas is located in the bottom of a valley. Actually, it is at the head of the valley; from the hamlet, the mountains rise sharply in a semicircle, north, east, and south. The Clark cafetal occupies the eastern portion of the valley or mountain cove, extending from a point well up on the north side of the valley to the top of the mountain on the south and east. It is operated by a partnership of five brothers, who inherited the property from their father. The father in turn had inherited it from his father, so that the present owners represent the third generation on the place. Bordering the Clarks on the south side of the valley is Finca Romero, fifty caballerías, owned originally by Don Romero, a friend of the grandfather Clark. The elder Romero, then ninety-two, was still in apparently good health and in possession of all his faculties, but he had divided his cafetal equally among his twelve children.

Bordering Clark on the north side of the valley is Finca Días of twelve caballerías, now occupied by twelve colored families. Since coffee grows only in the shade, the fincas on the north slope of the valley are not very suitable for its cultivation, and the families on Finca Días grow little or none. They occupy the rural slums of this area, and their standard of living, as reflected in their homes and surroundings, in their dress and general appearance, is in sharp contrast with that on the neighboring cafetals. The Días folk, according to a local informant, are lacking in industry, prone to drink and gamble, and seem to have no other aspirations beyond simple existence.

A few hundred yards from the hamlet of San Blas is a hydroelectric plant, constructed during the Machado regime. (President Machado was said to be president of the company which installed the plant.) The current generated, amounting to some 850 kilowatts, is transmitted to Cienfuegos over thirty-two kilometers of high-tension line, but it enables some of the farm homes in San Blas hamlet to enjoy electric lights, refrigerators, and other conveniences. The Clark home, for example, has electricity, as do five Romero homes in and near the hamlet. So also do the stores and the homes of the storekeepers. The Clark home and some nineteen other families also have running water, with some having showers and flush toilets.

I spent the major portions of two days on horseback visiting the bohíos scattered through the two cafetals of Clark and Romero. About one-third of all the houses have cement floors. All have thatched roofs, and most of them have lumber or adobe walls. Only five had walls made of palm, which is very common in other parts of Cuba. The furnishings of the houses also were considerably above average. Chairs were almost universally the *taburete,* a sturdy kitchen chair constructed of a native hardwood, with seat and back of rawhide. Of twenty houses for which the number of rooms were reported, five had one room; four, two rooms; three each had three and four rooms; two each had five and six rooms; and one house had seven rooms. Generally, the larger the family, the larger the house, although there were two families of five living in one room.

Food appeared to be ample, but most families' diets were composed predominantly of starchy vegetables and meat. The latter was mainly chicken and pork. The absence of green stuff in the diet is noticeable. All of the families reporting in the survey said they had two meals each day—at eleven in the morning and at six at night. I was told that for breakfast—which they do not count as a meal—there is usually coffee and bread. During the day *café solo* is frequently drunk. Judging by my own experience, no visitor leaves a home before being served a small cup of sweet black coffee. Usually it is served in small cups, but lacking these, the housewives serve it in any cup available. I was served at one home in a sherbet glass. At the two meals, huge quantities of food are consumed. If soup is served, it is not uncommon for people to add heaping quantities of rice, plátanos, or corn meal. At one place, I saw a woman add two fried eggs to her serving of soup, stirring the yolks carefully into the liquid. The amount consumed of these various items, by men and women alike, seemed to me prodigious.

Four tenure groups prevail in this area—owners, cash renters, share renters, and wagehands. The cash renters are called *arrenda- tarios,* while the share renters are called *partidarios,* locally translated as "sharecroppers." The wagehands (*jornaleros*) work as coffee-pickers mainly and are paid on a piecework basis, twenty-six cents per can. The use of the *lata* (can) as the standard measure is derived from the earlier use of five-gallon oil cans as receptacles in which the pickers carried the coffee beans. The can itself has been replaced by a well-designed basket which hangs at the picker's waistline, but it is still called a "lata." Some jornaleros work by the month, earning $25 to $30 a month, with board and room as perquisites, during the two-month picking season, and $21 during the other months. The usual share paid by share renters for the use of the land is one-third. All of the farm families on Cafetal El Infierno, the Clark cafetal, are either arrendatarios or partidarios. There are some partidarios on Romero's place, the twelve owner families renting part of their land to them. On Finca Días the twelve families are proprietors, but are no more than subsistence farmers living on land inherited from the father.

On the Clark cafetal there is a complete set of the most modern mechanical equipment for processing the coffee bean in preparation for the market, including machines for de-pulping the bean, removing the shell, artificial drying, separating the bean, and sorting. Only eight cafetals in all of Cuba were as fully equipped. The machinery is driven by a Diesel engine, and this motive power is used to operate a corn-sheller and corn-meal grinder in addition. For the services of the coffee-treating machinery, the Clarks charge the farmers fifty cents per hundred pounds, but make no charge for shelling and grinding corn for the renters. A small sawmill is also operated from the same motor, and the construction of the bohíos and other buildings in the area reflects its existence in their window and door frames, shutters and doors, and the lumber sides of most of the dwellings. Also, there have been many tables and taburetes made by the campesinos themselves from lumber sawed at this small mill. The Clarks are now constructing a water wheel to be installed near the shop, which they hope will have sufficient power to generate enough electricity to light their buildings. The stream of water available, however, is rather small, and the output in kilowatts may be disappointingly low.

After dinner at the Clarks' on the first evening of my visit, we went to the home of one of the farm families where about thirty or

forty people from the neighborhood were assembled in the combined living and dining rooms. They were campesinos from the
mountain bohíos who wanted to hear about farm life in the United
States. I was agreeably surprised to find present a young man who
had studied English for six years in the Methodist school at Cienfuegos and had a fair command of the language. One of the storekeepers also spoke English fairly well, having spent about three
years in New York, so between the two I had a satisfactory team
of interpreters. Again the second evening the group assembled in
the same place, anxious to hear more about United States farms
and farmers.

I told the group about many things, but the points which
seemed to interest them most were the farm credit system and
rural electrification. The comparatively low interest rates of the
former and the low kilowatt-hour charges for the latter seemed to
impress them very much. I was repeatedly advised that this group
of farm families is considerably above the average for Cuba, and
from general observation I know this to be true. They manifested
a lively interest in rural improvement. It was apparent that they
have many aspirations which they cannot at present satisfy. They
want above all, I think, to be connected with the outside world by
a good road. They are hungry, not for food for the physical body
—of which they seemed to me to have an abundance—but for
food for the spirit. They were anxious for lectures, for reading
material, for an opportunity to visit the city without having to
negotiate part of the distance by horse or on foot, part by rail, and
part by bus.

What this means to them in a very personal way was dramati-
cally shown in one of the most isolated homes I visited. This home
was reached only after a horseback ride of two or three hours up
a steep mountain trail which only a sure-footed animal could
negotiate. The house itself was on a par with the best farm homes
in Cuba. The floors were of cement; the living room was furnished
with "store" furniture. (How they got the chairs and settee up
there one can only imagine!) An eight-year-old daughter was
carrying her arm in a sling, and we were told that it had been
broken. In order to get it attended to, the father had to take the
child by horseback down this steep trail to San Blas, thence to

Central Soledád, and from there to Cienfuegos by bus. In other words, the nearest doctor was in Cienfuegos, some forty-five to fifty kilometers away.

The cost of marketing the farmers' coffee could of course be greatly reduced if better roads were provided, but, more important for some of them, they would be able to get some of their other products to the market, especially fruits and vegetables which now are not marketed at all, except during the period when roads are passable.

But life is not all drab and arduous for these people, even though they obviously suffer many frustrations. A considerable number of their children are sent "outside" to school, mainly to Cienfuegos; and one is impressed at meeting several boys and girls who speak English. I had an opportunity to witness the group at play on my final evening, when a "fiesta" was staged in the same farmhouse where the meetings had been held the previous evenings. It was primarily a dance, but at my urging there was also some singing of folk songs. The orchestra consisted of a bass fiddle, two guitars, the inevitable *maracas*, the *bongó*, and the *claves*, two hardwood sticks about ten inches long. The musicians played well, and the boy on the bongó was, I should say, superb. The dances were the *dansón*, the *son*, the *conga*, and the *guaracha*. *"El americano"* was urged to participate and needed no urging beyond the invitation. If he danced "like a camel" it was worth it to him to see the immense amusement and enjoyment of the campesinos.

Among the folksongs was the *décima*. In this song the singer sits pensively on a chair facing the guitarist, who idly strums the melody. The singer has in his hands the claves, which he clacks in rhythm with the guitar. He first sings a few conventional verses of the song, after which he makes up words as he goes along. A line is sung and then there is a pause, sometimes long, sometimes short, depending on how soon the singer thinks up a new line. Meanwhile the guitarist continues to strum the simple melody until the singer is ready again.

There is obviously much musical talent in the community, for the various members of the group rotated in playing the instruments—even the bongó, which consists of two small drums held between the knees and played with the bare hands. I am told that it requires considerable skill to play this instrument properly, and I can well believe it after trying it myself and getting no "drum" sound from it at all.

My return to Cienfuegos was negotiated on muleback to the narrow-gauge railway. This would have been all right had it not been for the fact that we were late in leaving San Blas and it was necessary, as my guide continually warned me, to make speed if we were not to miss the "cucaracha"—the bus—which left the crossroads at one o'clock. My companion was on a horse, which travels faster than a mule, and was always out ahead by at least half a kilometer and sometimes out of my sight entirely. All of which meant that for most of the distance my mule was on a gallop.

At Central Soledád a brief visit was made to the Harvard Botanical Garden, a two-hundred-acre tract given to the university by the Atkins family of Boston which owns the central. The garden naturally is devoted to tropical and semitropical plant life, with some two hundred species of palm, many species of bamboo, and over one hundred species of cactus. It was interesting to see a building labeled "Harvard House" located thus remotely from Cambridge.

On the evening of our return to the city, we went to the city council meeting where we listened to a discussion of roads. Later I read in the local paper that the city council had demanded of the government that the projected road to Santa Clara, the provincial capital, by way of Camunayagua be completed. One can truthfully say that it needs to be, for the absence of passable roads is one of the great tragedies of Cuba. Another is that after they do construct roads, they fail to keep them in repair and they again become impassable. The great Central Highway is a case in point. The pavement was for long stretches pitted and broken, with no apparent effort having been made at repairs nor any warning signals posted to caution the driver. A great deal of road construction and repair work is now in progress in all parts of the island, however, and it is expected that the Central Highway and other roads will be put in better shape.

The Cienfuegos farming region I have described is one of the more favorable rural areas of Cuba so far as the standard of living is concerned. But en route to San Blas, as well as on Finca Días, I saw something of the other side as well. Not far from the terminal where the sugar company bus goes, we passed the crude dwellings of a considerable number of guajiros, constructed right on the highway. These people are called *desalojos*—people who have been dislodged from a farm that is the property of someone else. Their dislodgment is important to the landowner, for by Cuban law if he allows them to remain for twenty years—if they have some semblance of right there—or thirty years if they have no right at all—they can acquire title to the land under the statute of limitations. Therefore, landowners give considerable attention to keeping squatters off their premises.

The seriousness of the squatter problem to landowners and to squatters alike is indicated by an item in the Havana newspaper *El Mundo* under date of December 2, 1945, a rough translation of which follows. "Santiago de Cuba (Oriente Province), December 1. The American landowner H. S. Chefey applied for and obtained a commitment from the court that a special judge would be named to look into the complaint against 1,200 peasants, residing on the farms of Sevilla, Bayamita, and Peladeros, of 10,000 caballerías, situated in the municipio of El Cobre, many of whom had lived more than thirty years on said lands, which they had assessed and registered as their own property." There are several other cases similar to this one which are pending final settlement. But the plight of the desalojos is pathetic in the extreme. Having no other place to go, those whom I saw had encamped on the public highway, fencing off a portion of it at the side of the road and building their bohíos in the enclosure. Inside the fence passersby can see the naked children, some chickens, a goat or two for milk, and occasionally some scrawny pigs.

Self-criticism on the part of Cubans—of their own ways of doing things, of their shortcomings as a society, and of their political ineptitude—is one of the surprising, as it is one of the most hopeful, characteristics they possess; and while there is much truth to the observation that Cubans who get elected to public office expect to operate the government for their private benefit rather than in the service of the people, one does not have to look far to find examples of faithful, disinterested public servants who constitute one of the bright hopes for the future of the country. For example, the agricultural inspector of the municipio of Cienfuegos, Señor de Cueto, comes to mind. Inadequately paid by United States standards, with few or no facilities for transportation to get over the country and visit the farms, except as he makes such available on his own initiative and frequently at his own expense, he nevertheless works diligently day in and day out to improve the agriculture of his region. Not many county agricultural agents in the United States work more conscientiously for the good of their people than this man. Another competent, underpaid civil servant, Señor Casto Ferragút, supervised the agricultural census of Cuba, taken in 1946. He has the spirit of the civil service at its best, loyally devoted to the ideals of serving the people of the state, rather than working primarily for self-aggrandizement.

One remembers, too, the able schoolmaster of Florencia. Here was a rural school of which any community anywhere in the world might well be proud. Under the initiative of the teacher, the school had been constructed by volunteer contributions and volunteer labor. It was too small for the community as it later developed, but the limited space was put to very effective use by the ingenuity of the teacher. In addition to the main schoolroom and a small workshop, it contained an apartment of two rooms which housed the schoolmaster and his wife. Woodworking tools were kept in a case which could be let down from the wall when in use and could be taken up out of the way when the tools were not needed. The outdoor toilet facilities were kept immaculately clean. In each of the toilets a washbasin, a bucket of water, soap, and a roller towel were provided. Students had their individual drinking cups neatly arranged on a wall near the door. There was even a small library, kept in a cabinet hung on the wall. There were books of special interest to children, including a number of translations from popular foreign books, such as *Bambi*. There was a small collection of biological specimens, some kept in alcohol, others mounted. There are undoubtedly other equally competent schoolmasters in Cuba, but it is well known that there are many less able ones. Multiply this Florencia teacher a thousandfold and rural society in Cuba would be profoundly and beneficially modified.

Then, too, there are the public-spirited women of Cuba, of whom

Señora Elena Mederos de González is a brilliant example, who are slowly but surely emancipating themselves from feudal tradition and striking out for a better Cuba. They are promoting as best they can the idea of better educational facilities, medical service, and recreation and welfare agencies.

Men like Ramiro Guerra, manager of one of Havana's leading newspapers and an eminent historian, and H. Portell Vilá, professor of history in the University of Havana, visualize the possibilities that are within the reach of the Cuban people if they can be inspired and organized around a feasible plan and learn to work together for the common good. Such men represent the Cuban conscience at its best—fighting corruption and inefficiency in government, promoting understanding of public problems, and planning ways for their solution; critics who, though criticized by many of their countrymen, still carry on their fight for a better Cuba.

CHAPTER II

The Cuban People

Columbus discovered Cuba on Sunday, October 28, 1492, and took possession of the island "in the name of Christ, Our Lady, and the reigning sovereigns of Spain." He named the island Juana in honor of the Infante Don Juan, son of Ferdinand and Isabella, but the name failed to take hold; Cuba, the name by which the natives had called their land, persisted. For four centuries Cuba was a colony of Spain, the last of her possessions in the New World to win its independence (in 1898). The first *conquistadores* readily overcame the feeble resistance of the native inhabitants, and the survivors of the conquest were subjugated and used as slaves under the system of *encomiendas,* grants made by the Crown to Spanish colonists conferring the right to use the native Indians for labor.

Records of the number of inhabitants before the census of 1774 are few and fragmentary. It is generally considered, however, that the growth of population was very slow during the sixteenth and seventeenth centuries. The conquest of Peru and Mexico, with their rich treasures of gold and silver, attracted most of the immigrants from the mother country. Cuba, being primarily an agricultural country, had no such wealth to offer the newcomer. Even to the middle of the eighteenth century, the development of Cuba's resources was not on a scale to warrant a significant increase in the population. During the latter half of the eighteenth century,

23

however, the sugar industry began to expand, and it can be assumed that the population increased correspondingly. This increase was perhaps a result more of the importation of Negro slaves than of white immigration.

Since 1774, when the first official census of the island was taken, there have been enumerations at irregular intervals which make it possible to chart the curve of population growth with some degree of accuracy. These data indicate three periods of time in which there were varying rates of growth (see Table 1 and Figure 1). The first period was roughly from 1774 to 1861, when the population rose at a fairly rapid rate, particularly during the early years of the period. From 1861 to 1900 there was very little growth, owing to the chronic unrest and periodic wars incident to the struggle for independence, the suppression of the slave trade, and severe epidemics of cholera and yellow fever. The third period, from 1900 to the present time, has been one of very rapid growth in total numbers, with a rate of growth about equal to that of the early part of the nineteenth century, as will be seen from the slant of the curve during the two periods.

The rapidity of population growth in the early part of the nine-

TABLE 1. TREND OF POPULATION GROWTH IN CUBA
BY COLOR, 1774–1943

	Population		
Year	Total	White	Colored
1774	171,620	96,440	75,180
1792	272,301	133,559	138,742
1817	553,033	239,830	313,203
1827	704,487	311,051	393,436
1841	1,007,624	418,291	589,333
1861	1,396,530	757,603	638,927
1877	1,521,684	988,624	533,060
1887	1,631,687	1,102,889	528,798
1899	1,572,797	1,052,397	520,400
1907	2,048,980	1,428,176	620,804
1919	2,889,004	2,088,047	800,957
1931	3,962,344	2,883,238	1,079,106
1943	4,778,583	3,553,312	1,225,271

SOURCES: *Report of the Census of Cuba, 1899* (Washington: Government Printing Office, 1900), p. 97; *Cuba: Population, History, Resources, 1907* (Washington: United States Bureau of the Census, 1909), p. 236; *Censo de 1943* (Havana: P. Fernandez y Cia, 1945), p. 736.

POPULATION (OOO)

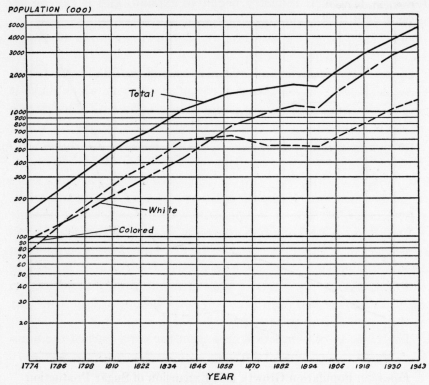

YEAR

Figure 1. Population Growth in Cuba since 1774, by Color

teenth century was largely due to the heavy importation of
Negroes. From 1790 to 1850 the colored population exceeded the
white. However, their numbers declined during the last half of the
century until there were actually fewer reported in 1899 than in
1837. The importation of slaves was for the most part terminated
after the middle of the nineteenth century. Officially, slavery was
banned very much earlier by the Treaty of Vienna (1815), a
treaty with England in 1817 and another in 1835, and by the
Spanish law of 1845; but contraband traffic continued until 1880,
although at an insignificant rate during the latter part of the
period. Actually it is unlikely that any large number of slaves
found their way into Cuba after 1850.

During the political unrest of the latter part of the eighteenth
century, which culminated in the final War of Independence of

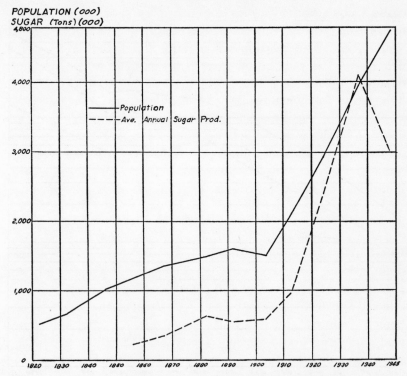

POPULATION (000)
SUGAR (Tons)(000)

Figure 2. Population Growth and Expansion of Sugar Production
Have Been Closely Associated in Cuba until the Depression
of the 1930's

1895–98, the Negro population appears to have suffered much
more severely than the white. For one reason, it was mostly located
in rural areas where the ravages of war were most heavily felt;
besides, Negroes themselves made up a large part of the army of
revolutionaries. Cholera and yellow fever epidemics during this
period also weighed more heavily on the impoverished colored
group than on the whites. Since 1900 the increase of both white
and colored groups has been rapid. The successful conquest of
yellow fever, the restoration of political stability, and the rapid
economic expansion provided the basis for this remarkable growth.

Since Cuba is primarily an agricultural country with only minor
quantities of other natural resources, its population growth has
been largely correlated with its agricultural expansion. Moreover,

because Cuba's agriculture is dominated by sugar cane, the fortunes of this crop have been a determining factor in the growth of population. The relationship is well illustrated in Figure 2, which shows the population growth since 1774 and cane sugar production in tons since 1850.[1] The marked increase in population in the period following the War of Independence (1895–98) follows closely the rise in sugar production in the same period. The conclusion of the war also set the stage for a spectacular increase in sugar output. Capital flowed into the island from abroad, new technological improvements were made in production, and control and management were centralized and made more efficient.

DIFFERENTIAL RATES OF GROWTH OF WHITE AND COLORED POPULATIONS

One-fourth of the population in 1943 was colored, representing a slight decline from the nearly 30 per cent reported in 1907 and the 27 per cent reported in the censuses of 1919 and 1931 (see Table 2). Those of the yellow race (who are included in the census category "colored") declined by some 8,000 in the intercensal period, and thus would account for part of the loss.[2] The Negro population increased only 5.8 per cent, and the *mestizos*[3] 15.9 per cent during the twelve-year interval. Both rates of increase fell far short of that registered by the native whites, which was 56.1 per cent, although as we have just explained (note 2, page 27), this figure is partly fictitious. Nevertheless, the rates of increase for the two colored groups are considerably below that for the total population, which was 20.6 per cent. If the enumerations can be relied upon as approximately accurate, there appears reason

[1] Records of total production of sugar in tons are not available previous to this date. Guerra y Sánchez has compiled data on exports of sugar beginning with the year 1550, as measured in *arrobas* (an *arroba* equals twenty-five pounds), but gives production figures only since 1850. *Azúcar y población en las Antillas* (3rd ed.; Havana: Cultural S.A., 1944), pp. 255f.

[2] On the other hand, the foreign whites in the country in 1943 amounted to only about one-fifth the number reported in 1931, a reduction of about 500,000. The decline in foreign whites is only nominal, however, brought about by a change in the definition of citizenship as incorporated in the Constitution of 1940. In censuses previous to 1940, persons born in Cuba of foreign parents were classed as foreign unless they chose later to become Cubans. The constitution reversed this definition, declaring all persons born in Cuba to be Cuban citizens regardless of the nationality of the parents. The 500,000 who were "foreigners" in 1931 automatically became "native white" in 1943.

[3] The word *mestizo* usually connotes a mixture of Indian and white, but in Cuba it is used to refer to a Negro-white combination, that is, a mulatto.

TABLE 2. COMPOSITION BY COLOR OF THE CUBAN POPULATION, 1931 AND 1943

Color and Nativity	1931		1943	
	Number	Per Cent	Number	Per Cent
All classes	3,962,344	100.0	4,778,583	100.0
Native white	2,185,991	55.2	3,412,242	71.4
Foreign white	670,965	16.9	141,070	3.0
Negroes	437,769	11.0	463,227	9.7
Yellow	26,282	0.7	18,931	0.4
Mixed	641,337	16.2	743,113	15.6

SOURCE: *Censo de 1943*, p. 855.

to believe that the pure Negro population is headed for relative decline in importance.[4] Even the mestizo population appears to be reaching a statistical plateau, while the native whites show much higher rates of growth. The increase in Negroes and mestizos since 1900 has been limited quite largely to the provinces of Havana and Oriente. The increase in Havana is due to migration from other sections of the island and immigration from Jamaica and other Caribbean areas. The increase in Oriente, however, is due largely to the high birth rate among the colored population of that province. Then too, since Oriente is but a few miles across the Windward Passage from the great colored nation of Haiti, there has been considerable immigration, legal or otherwise, of colored people from the neighboring island.

The Chinese also appear to be on the way to extinction through amalgamation. Their total numbers declined from 26,282 in 1931 to only 18,931 in 1943. Moreover, the group has always been composed predominantly of men; the importation of Chinese women has been practically nil. Of the 34,834 Chinese reported in the island in 1861, only 57 were women, and of the 18,931 in 1943, only 1,337 were women. It is highly probable that many of these women are in reality a mixture of Chinese and Negro or white blood.[5] The number of pure Chinese in the population is probably somewhat less than the census enumeration would indicate, and

---

[4] On the question of accuracy there is no way of checking except by a systematic sampling procedure, which has not been undertaken. No census is completely accurate. The Cuban census is taken in a manner similar to that followed in the United States. The censuses of 1899, 1907, and 1919 were taken either directly by United States authorities or under the technical supervision of United States personnel.

[5] The classification of racial groups by the census was left to the enumerators to judge from the physical appearance of the individuals.

without further immigration the group appears bound to continue its decline. Also, there are some who return to China from time to time, tending to accelerate the decrease in Cuba's Chinese population. Those who remain and marry will of necessity choose white or colored women, with consequent diffusion of the blood.

The future of the Negro in Cuba is difficult to predict. It is apparent from the census data that the pure Negro is increasing at a relatively slower rate than the native white or the mestizo. The mestizo population is also decreasing in relative importance to the total, although its decline from 1931 to 1943 was less than that for the Negro. On the other hand, however, the "colored" group, which includes Negro, Chinese, and mixed, had a higher fertility ratio than whites in both the 1931 and 1943 enumerations. Table 3 shows that among the whites in 1943, there were 533 children under 5 years of age for each 1,000 women aged 14 to 44 inclusive, compared with 589 in 1931. The corresponding figures

TABLE 3. NUMBER OF CHILDREN UNDER 5 YEARS OF AGE PER 1,000 WOMEN AGED 14–49, BY COLOR FOR PROVINCES, 1931 AND 1943, WITH RATES FOR 1943 CALCULATED ALSO FOR WOMEN AGED 14–44*

Province	Native White		Colored	
	1943	1931	1943	1931
Children under 5 per 1,000 Women 14–49†				
All provinces	518	542	559	559
Pinar del Río	632	624	686	593
Havana	318	365	312	345
Matanzas	532	516	534	498
Las Villas	551	544	541	500
Camagüey	535	581	513	585
Oriente	700	702	730	714
Children under 5 per 1,000 Women 14–44‡				
All provinces	533	589	572	612
Pinar del Río	665	...	722	...
Havana	410	...	312	...
Matanzas	522	...	580	...
Las Villas	579	...	580	...
Camagüey	567	...	556	...
Oriente	737	...	739	...

* Women in the age group 14–44 were not given by provinces in the published tables of the 1931 census. In order to make provincial comparisons for 1943 and 1931, it was necessary to use the 14–49 group for both years.

† *Censo de 1943*, p. 862, Table 9.

‡ *Ibid.*, p. 870, Table 10. The age group 14–44 has been used when data were available because it represents a better approximation of the childbearing period.

for the colored group are 572 and 612. The percentage decline is
slightly greater for the native whites.

It is important to note the differences between white and
colored in the various provinces in respect to fertility. Except for
Pinar del Río, Havana, and Matanzas there is little difference,
using the 14 to 44 age group as the base. The white group has
higher ratios than the colored in Havana and Camagüey. This
holds true also when the age group for women is 14 to 49. In this
age group in 1943, the big differences in favor of the colored group
are in Pinar del Río and in Oriente. In 1931, the colored people
had higher ratios in Camagüey and Oriente. These differentials
are important because nearly half the total colored population of
the island is found in Oriente Province, where 35 per cent of the
Negroes and 48 per cent of the mestizos reside. The other major
concentration is in Havana Province, which contains 24 per cent
of the Negroes and 21 per cent of the mestizos. Oriente is largely
a rural province, with high birth rates among both white and
colored but with a higher fertility ratio among the colored group.
This, together with the numerical superiority of the colored in
Pinar del Río and Matanzas, is more than sufficient to counter-
balance their comparatively lower fertility in Havana, Las Villas,
and Camagüey.

One trend that augers ill for the Negro is his tendency to migrate
to the cities. Since 1907 there have been proportionately more
whites in the rural population than in the urban, which indicates
a disproportionate urbanization of the Negro. Negroes generally
show higher death and lower birth rates under urban conditions
than do whites. In Cuba, the colored population in Havana
Province shows a lower fertility ratio than do the whites, although
both of them are comparatively low. Moreover, the death rate of
the urban Negro appears to be higher than that for urban whites,
although Cuban data are not at hand to verify the statement.

Whatever hope the Negroes may have for competing with the
whites in the march of population lies primarily in Oriente. Here
they have shown their ability to more than hold their own in the
competition. But the migrants from Oriente to the other provinces
very likely go into the cities, where they fall short of equality
in natural increase with the whites. The fact that for the island

as a whole, whites generally constitute a greater proportion of the rural population, where fertility rates tend to be high, gives that group a long-run advantage over the colored.

Finally, the apparent freedom with which whites and colored intermarry as compared, say, with the United States, where such unions are legally barred in so many of the states, makes for more rapid assimilation and the formation of a hybrid race. This amalgamation in general should not be viewed with misgivings. There is no anthropological evidence to indicate that any weakening of future generations, physically or mentally, results from interracial mixture. On the contrary, the result is frequently a stronger race. From a sociological standpoint, the gradual elimination of color differences would solve a host of problems which now are among the most baffling mankind has to face.

REGIONAL DIFFERENTIALS IN GROWTH

In comparative numbers of people, the six provinces fall into two main groups. The three most populous provinces in order of size are Oriente, Havana, and Las Villas, all in the neighborhood of one million inhabitants. The three smaller ones, also in order of size, are Camagüey, Pinar del Río, and Matanzas, with fewer than 500,000 each. At least two of the provinces, Matanzas and Pinar del Río, seem to have approached the saturation point so far as population growth is concerned, having increased but little in the past sixty years (see Figure 3). The heavy increases in Oriente and Las Villas especially, and to some extent in Camagüey, foreshadow a gradual shifting of the center of population toward the eastern end of the island. Unless some new economic release is found for the provinces of Matanzas and Pinar del Río, the populations of these areas appear to have approximated their maximum growth. It is important to note also that in both Havana and Oriente, the two largest provinces in population, only minor increases were registered in the twelve-year period from 1931 to 1943. The most important increases took place in Las Villas and in Camagüey.

The changes in numbers of the colored population show some differences from the changes in the total population when provinces are compared (see Table 4). In Camagüey and Matanzas

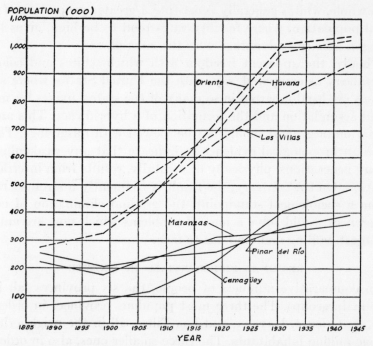

POPULATION (000)

Figure 3. Cuban Population Growth by Provinces, 1885–1943

the number of colored people declined during the twelve-year interval, due in part to the deportation of persons of Haitian or Jamaican citizenship during the depression years. Only small gains were registered in Las Villas and Pinar del Río—less than enough to balance the loss in Camagüey and Matanzas. Thus the net gains were accounted for by the relatively large increases in Oriente and in Havana.

RURAL-URBAN DISTRIBUTION

The differentiation of rural and urban segments of the population of Cuba on the basis of census data can be only approximate. The boundaries of cities are not definitely marked as they are in the United States. The entire island is divided into six provinces and 126 municipios, and the municipios in turn are divided into *barrios*. The municipio corresponds roughly to the county in the United States, and the barrio to the township. A municipality is composed of several barrios, some of which extend into the rural

TABLE 4. GAIN OR LOSS IN POPULATION, TOTAL AND COLORED, OF VARIOUS PROVINCES, FROM 1931 TO 1943

Province	Number Gained or Lost (−)	
	Total	Colored
Pinar del Río	55,314	4,707
Havana	250,439	61,859
Matanzas	23,960	−5,855
Las Villas	123,169	4,984
Camagüey	78,625	−12,372
Oriente	283,732	66,560

SOURCE: *Censo de 1943.*

TABLE 5. PROPORTION OF POPULATION WHICH WAS RURAL, 1943 AND 1931, BY PROVINCES *

Province	Rural Population			
	1943		1931	
	Number	Per Cent of Total	Number	Per Cent of Total
All provinces	2,174,803	45.5	2,029,576	51.2
Pinar del Río	276,750	69.4	249,750	72.7
Havana	151,266	12.2	161,953	16.4
Matanzas	152,836	42.3	160,436	47.6
Las Villas	509,581	54.3	449,631	55.1
Camagüey	260,825	53.5	231,844	56.8
Oriente	823,545	60.7	775,962	72.3

*Figures were supplied by the director of the Office of the National Census, Dr. Juan M. Alfonso Piña, in a letter of November 17, 1945, to the author. The figure for all provinces for 1943 compares with that reported in the census volume, page 722, of 2,171,093. The 1931 figure for all provinces is somewhat at variance with that reported in the official volume, which was 1,927,310. The published census did not report the rural population by provinces, giving merely the rural population density for each province.

TABLE 6. POPULATION IN CUBAN VILLAGES, TOWNS, AND CITIES BY SIZE OF PLACE, 1943 AND 1931

Size of Place	1943			1931		
	Number of Places	Population	Per Cent	Number of Places	Population	Per Cent
Total	*892*	*2,607,490*	*100.0*	*646*	*2,044,747*	*100.0*
Less than 1,001..	611	236,676	9.0	407	167,330	8.2
1,001–4,000	200	401,636	15.5	175	370,802	18.1
4,001–8,000	40	206,072	7.9	28	146,302	7.2
8,001–25,000	27	381,310	14.4	26	364,970	17.8
25,001–100,000 ..	11	478,729	18.6	8	366,092	17.9
100,001 or more.	3	903,067	34.6	2	629,251	30.9
Open country		2,171,093			1,917,597	

SOURCE: Censuses of 1931 and 1943.

33

hinterland, and therefore the population reported for the cities (municipios) usually includes persons who are actually living on farms. In the 1943 census, the families who reported no street or house number on their dwellings were regarded as rural, and the balance of the population urban.[6] However, no tables were presented giving details of population characteristics or distribution by provinces or minor civil divisions on this basis. Only the total rural population was reported in the printed volume, although the provincial figures were available at the census office (see Table 5 on the preceding page).

Estimates of the proportion of the population which was rural in earlier censuses were as follows: in 1899, 52.9 per cent; in 1907, 56.1 per cent; and in 1919, 55.3 per cent. Urbanization has been steadily increasing during the present century. The somewhat smaller percentage of rural inhabitants in 1899, as compared with 1907 and 1919, is due to the War of Independence, which had a more severe impact upon the rural population than upon the urban. Moreover, General Weyler's tragic reconcentration policy of herding great numbers of country people into the cities took a frightful toll of life. This Spanish general was ruthless in his attempts to quell the rebellion. In order to deprive the rebel army of the support of rural noncombatants, who might have provided it with food, shelter, and supplies, he drove the rural Cubans— mostly women, children, and old people—into garrisoned towns or concentration camps surrounded by trenches and stockades. Scores of thousands fell victim to starvation and disease. It has been estimated that 50,000 perished in Havana alone.

The rapidity of urbanization is also apparent in the distribution of the population by size of place, shown in Table 6. Especially noteworthy is the increase in the proportion of the urban population living in cities of 100,000 or over, an increase from 31 per cent in 1931 to 34.6 per cent in 1943. There was also an increase in the proportion of the population living in places under 1,000, but it is not certain whether it represents a real increase or only the identification of more "places" in 1943 than had been listed in 1931. It seems hardly likely that there would be over 200 new villages of under 1,000 inhabitants established—an increase of over 50 per

[6] *Censo de 1943*, p. 1017.

cent! The rapid urbanization of recent years is further demonstrated by the fact that of the total population increase of 816,000, 563,000 were in populated centers, amounting to nearly 70 per cent of the increase, although the urban population in 1931 was only 48.7 per cent of the total.

AGE AND SEX COMPOSITION

The composition of Cuba's population in 1931 and 1943 as regards age and sex is revealed graphically in Figure 4. The arrangement by five-year age groups reveals a true pyramid shape, which is characteristic of a population that has a high rate of growth. However, a comparison between 1931 and 1943 shows that the proportion of children is slightly smaller in the latter year, while the proportion of older people is somewhat larger. This is a trend that is also familiar to students of population in other countries. The present population of Cuba is similar in age composition to that of the United States at about 1900, although the United States population pyramid for 1940 had changed to look more like a rectangle than a cone.

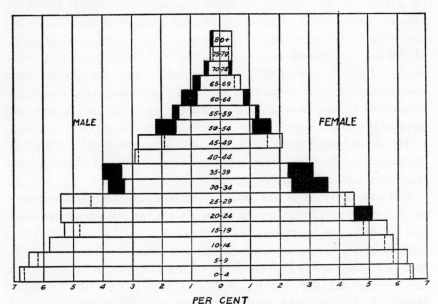

Figure 4. Age and Sex Composition of the Cuban Population, 1931 and 1943 (Dotted Lines and Black Areas Show the 1943 Pyramid)

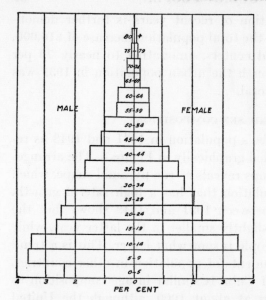

Figure 5. Age and Sex Composition of the Cuban Population in 1899

Marked differences are seen to exist between the 1931 and 1943 pyramids and that for 1899 (Figure 5). The latter is characterized by a remarkably small proportion of children under 5 years of age, unmistakably a result of the War of Independence which had just come to a close when the census was taken. The high mortality of children was the result in large measure of the policy, previously noted, of the Spanish General Weyler of herding the women and children from rural areas into concentration camps in the cities. The effect of this mortality of infants is revealed in the age-sex pyramids of subsequent periods. Note, for instance, the comparatively short bars in the 1931 pyramid for ages 30 to 34 and in 1943 for ages 40 to 44, representing the survivors of the children who were under 5 years of age in 1899.

Unfortunately, it is not possible to compare population pyramids for the rural and urban populations; but an approximation can be arrived at by comparing Havana, the most urban province, with Oriente, the most rural (Figures 6 and 7). These pyramids had to be constructed on the basis of ten-year age intervals, since the census did not report provincial populations by five-year classes. In Havana, the small proportion of children under 20 and the relatively large proportions of adults are a prominent charac-

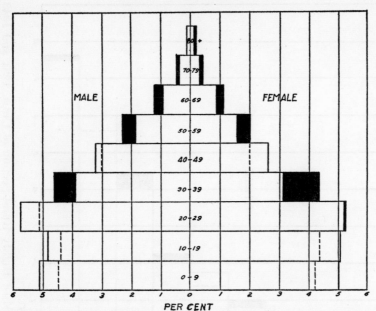

MALE

FEMALE

80 +

70-79

60-69

50-59

40-49

30-39

20-29

10-19

0-9

6 5 4 3 2 1 0 1 2 3 4 5 6

PER CENT

Figure 6. Age and Sex Composition of Havana Province, the Most Highly Urban Section of Cuba, 1931 and 1943 (1943 Data Indicated by Dotted Lines and Black Areas)

teristic. The unusual shape of this pyramid—small at the bottom and wide in the center layers—is similar to that of urban populations in the United States. The deviation from the pyramid for the country as a whole (Figure 4) is the result of two factors: the lower birth rate of the cities, and the cityward migration of persons 20 years of age and over, mostly from rural areas.

The population of Oriente, predominantly rural, presents a marked contrast to that of Havana. Here the age group 0–9 is very large in proportion to the total, as is also that from 10 to 19. Even the group from 20 to 29 is relatively large. The group from 20 to 59, representing the main working population, is relatively small as compared with that of Havana. In other words, the number of dependent children in proportion to working adults is very much greater in Oriente than in Havana. This difference is also evident between rural and urban segments of population in the United States.

The ratio of men to women in Cuba is still comparatively high

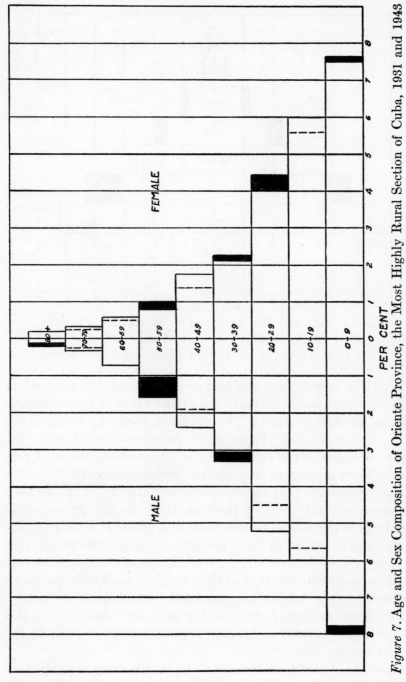

Figure 7. Age and Sex Composition of Oriente Province, the Most Highly Rural Section of Cuba, 1931 and 1943

(1943 Data Indicated by Dotted Lines and Black Areas)

(110 men per 100 women), and has changed but little since 1899 (Table 7). Interestingly, the ratio was higher in 1943 than in 1899. The usual downward trend, found consistently in the United States, has not yet occurred in Cuba, although there was a decline from 1931 to 1943 and it is probable that since 1943 further decline has taken place. In 1899, however, the ratio was lower than it has been at any time since. This was no doubt a consequence of the losses of men in the War of Independence. The subsequent rise to 113 in 1919 was probably due to immigration which consisted predominantly of men. During the depression of the 1930's there was a heavy outward migration, quite largely of men also, which has tended to depress the ratio since (to 110 in 1943). Present restrictions on immigration mean that this factor will not influence the future trend to any marked degree.

TABLE 7. TRENDS IN SEX RATIOS BY PROVINCES, 1899–1943

Province	Number of Males per 100 Females				
	1943	1931	1919	1907	1899
All provinces 110		113.0	113	110.3	107.6
Pinar del Río 112		109.6	107	115.0	112.7
Havana 104		107.4	110	112.4	109.6
Matanzas 111		109.7	112	106.3	105.1
Las Villas 110		111.0	113	112.5	112.9
Camagüey 122		137.6	131	110.6	103.6
Oriente 109		113.8	112	105.6	100.0

SOURCES: Census reports for the years indicated.

There are differences among the provinces, as will be seen from Table 7, Camagüey ranking highest in sex ratio and Havana lowest. The explanation of the low ratio in Havana is simple. City populations always have larger proportions of women, and this province is quite largely urban. The high ratio in Camagüey is not so easy to explain. It may be due to the great number of very large sugar centrals, with their resident populations of machinists and other workers who are largely men, and to the existence of numerous livestock ranches, likewise run by men. However, these are merely hypothetical explanations which require further investigation. In general, it has been found that rural populations have higher sex ratios than do urban, and since Camagüey is less rural than Oriente, the latter should have a higher sex ratio. However, this is not true. Some other factor is evidently present in the case of Camagüey, exercising a peculiar influence on the sex ratio.[7]

PROSPECTS FOR FUTURE POPULATION GROWTH

There can be no doubt that the *rate* of population growth in Cuba will continue to decline in the future, although such decline does not mean that, for some time to come, the population will fail to grow in total numbers. Among the factors tending toward further growth are the following: (a) the present relatively high birth rates, as indicated by the ratio of children to women in the population; (b) the progress being made to reduce death rates, especially among children; and (c) the high proportion of the population living on farms and in rural places with a comparatively low standard of living, lack of educational opportunities, and in relative social isolation.

There are no adequate birth registration statistics available for Cuba. Registration is voluntary and may be made any time within a year after birth, after which a court order is required for registering. At the time of the census of 1943, not more than two-thirds of the children under 5 years of age were reported as registered. A recent report[8] using data for 1936 shows a birth rate of 18.9 per thousand based on the registered births. Assuming that the figures represent not more than two-thirds of all births, the true birth rate at that time would be over 25 per thousand. The same report gives the death rate for 1936 in Cuba as 10.23 per thousand. This figure, which is based upon death registrations, is regarded as fairly accurate, since no cemetery will accept a body for burial without a certificate. It is not unreasonable to postulate a natural increase of upward of 15 per thousand annually. The figure can be checked roughly by taking the difference between the populations of 1935 and 1936 as estimated by interpolation, dividing it by the population for 1935, and multiplying the result by 1,000. The result is a figure of 16.3 per thousand, which is a rough verification of the natural increase rate as derived above. Immigration and emigration are ignored in the calculation, but they are not of very great consequence.

[7] For further discussion of sex ratios and their social significance, see Chapter X.
[8] *Salubridad y asistencia social*, XLVI (October–December 1944), pp. 92–94.

A more satisfactory basis for estimating the vitality of the population is to use the ratio of children under 5 years of age to the number of women in the childbearing ages of from 14 or 15 to 44, inclusive. The use of this "fertility ratio" has an advantage over birth and death statistics in that it can be computed for any population groups for which data on age composition by sex are available, and permits comparison with earlier census enumerations.

The fertility ratios—the number of children under 5 per thousand women of childbearing age—for the Cuban population by various census years are as follows:[9] 1943—549; 1931—588; 1919—711; 1907—722; 1899—353. As indicated earlier, the very low ratio of children to women in 1899 is a reflection of the combined scourges of war and disease which prevailed during the final years of the century. It is probably reflected twenty years later in the sharp drop of over 100 in the fertility ratio from 1919 to 1931, although the difference in age grouping of the women is also a factor.[10] It is clear that the fertility of the population is declining, but it is also true that the 1943 ratio of 549 is relatively high when compared with the ratio of about 330 for the United States in 1940.

The relatively large proportion of the Cuban population living on farms and in small communities may contribute to future population growth. It is a well-established principle that rural populations generally have a higher birth rate than do urban. In Cuba the difference is highly significant, the rural population showing a fertility ratio more than double the ratio for places of 5,000 or more (Table 8). The differences are fairly consistent for all the provinces. Moreover, the rural population of Cuba is generally characterized by a low standard of living, also a factor generally associated with high fertility. The further fact that large proportions of the rural population are without easy communication with the outside world contributes to the continuation of a high fertility rate, inasmuch as they are less likely to be influenced by the small-family pattern which characterizes urban civilization.

[9] The age groups of women are 14–44, inclusive, for 1931 and 1943, and 15–44, inclusive, in 1919, 1907, and 1899. The change accounts for much of the difference between 1919 and 1931. See censuses for the years indicated.
[10] See note 9.

TABLE 8. NUMBER OF CHILDREN UNDER 5 PER 1,000 WOMEN AGED 14–49
BY PROVINCES, RURAL AND URBAN, 1943*

Province	Number of Children (0–5) per 1,000 Women (14–49)		
	Total	Urban†	Rural†
All provinces	515	317	680
Pinar del Río	639	371	696
Havana	301	250	479
Matanzas	525	366	625
Las Villas	541	386	618
Camagüey	518	319	621
Oriente	704	427	829

SOURCE: *Censo de 1943*, p. 863, Table 9.

*It was necessary to use women in the age group 14–49, since those between 14 and 44 were not given separately for the provinces.

†"Urban" includes places of 5,000 or more inhabitants; the remainder of the population is included in "rural."

Educational facilities are still poor or wanting in many rural sections of Cuba. In most countries a rising educational level is associated with declining family size, although by itself it cannot be regarded as a deterrent to population increase. It is, however, usually associated with higher living standards and with aspirations of parents for better opportunities for the children they bring into the world. Increased use of contraceptive devices or other voluntary limitation of births is likely to occur only when the educational level is raised and communication facilities developed so that the rural population is brought under the sway of urban influence.

Finally, the general progress being made in Cuba toward the control of disease and the better care of mothers during pregnancy and after childbirth cannot but operate to raise the rate of natural increase. In 1935 about 21 per cent of all deaths registered in Cuba were children under one year of age; this figure was reduced slightly, to 20 per cent, in 1936. In 1936 the number of infant deaths per 1,000 registered births was 107, or about 80 per thousand of total estimated births.[11] This figure, it will readily be admitted, can be reduced by at least 50 per cent in the space of a few years if known methods of infant care are applied.[12] Cuba is giving attention to the problem, and in all likelihood the efforts

[11] *Salubridad y asistencia social, op. cit.*, p. 96.
[12] Infant mortality in the United States in 1943 was about 40 per 1,000 live births.

will result in a decline in the infant as well as the maternal death rate.

On the other hand, among the factors which may be expected to contribute to further decline in the rate of population growth are the following: (a) the doubtful prospects for expansion in the Cuban economy; (b) the continued urbanization of the population; and (c) the improvement in the standard of living, degree of education, and means of communication. The spread of contraceptive techniques is not listed as a special factor because it is not of primary importance, though it admittedly plays a secondary role. It is related only in a superficial manner to the restriction of the birth rate. Natural increase in a population responds basically to the outlook for economic expansion, to the degree of rurality or of urbanism, and to the level of living. The three factors are in reality very closely related.

It is not within the competence of the present writer to predict the economic future of Cuba. However, it may be safely assumed that it is going to be geared, in the future as it has been in the past, to the fortunes of the sugar industry. With about one-third of the arable land devoted to sugar cane, it cannot well be otherwise unless radical readjustments occur. However, other agricultural opportunities are not lacking in Cuba. There are considerable areas, not now being used for production of crops, which might well be devoted to supplying the country with more of the products which are now imported in large quantities, such as rice, beans, and fresh fruits and vegetables. The Cuban diet, which is deficient generally in the protective foods, can be modified in time by education to encourage more healthful eating habits, at the same time creating new or better markets for many products of the soil. When compared with other islands of the Caribbean— Puerto Rico, Jamaica, Barbados, and the Republic of Haiti— Cuba, with a population density of approximately 110 per square mile, is not to be regarded as overpopulated in the absolute sense. Certainly it is possible for more people to subsist on the island. Nevertheless, in relation to the available job opportunities, there is a chronic surplus of manpower.

Only during the *zafra* (the sugar cane harvest) can there be anything approximating full employment. The 1943 census, which was taken during the "dead season" before the harvest, reported only 856,000 employed out of a labor force of 1,521,000, a little over half the total. In other words, 665,000 were reported either as unemployed or "unknown." There were 321,000 definitely reported as unemployed, about 20 per cent, and this was a relatively prosperous war year. About half (155,000) of the definitely unemployed were in agriculture, although farm workers make up only about 40 per cent of the labor force. Cuba therefore has the serious problem of finding jobs for a labor force which at present seems to exceed by far the number of available positions.

Moreover, the mechanization of agriculture and other enterprises may be expected to increase, tending to reduce the demand for hand labor. This fact is recognized by Cuban labor, which is opposing the introduction of cigar-making machinery because of the technological unemployment that would result. At the same time, Cuba is finding it increasingly difficult to compete in the tobacco markets of the world because of the greater cost of the hand-made article. Technically, it would also be simple to mechanize the handling of sugar cane to a much greater extent than at present. But if machinery were introduced, it would deprive a large number of the cane workers of the few months of employment which they now have.

Thus Cuba is faced with a serious dilemma. Already possessing a surplus of human labor, it can ill afford to add to its unemployment rolls by the introduction of labor-saving machinery. The alternative which the country will face, however, is increasingly difficult competition in the world markets. The present policy seems to be to subsidize labor through mandatory labor legislation, through tariffs on manufactures and on agricultural products. The country appears to be trying to raise itself by its own bootstraps. Improved technological efficiency of labor with correspondingly greater output per worker would seem to be the only feasible way in which to raise the level of living of the workers in the long run. And raising that standard will probably tend to produce a decline in the rate of population growth.

There exist without doubt some possibilities for the expansion of employment in nonagricultural pursuits, but as yet on a rather limited scale. Cuba has considerable deposits of iron, estimated at over three billion tons, 90 per cent of which are reportedly held as reserves by American steel companies.[13] The exploitation of iron is at present on a relatively small scale. Shipments of iron ore reported for 1939 amounted to approximately 400,000 tons. The absence of coal or oil in quantity on the island makes it impractical to process the ore there and means, for the future, scant prospect of developing the heavy industries on any scale. Many other minerals are found in Cuba, the most important of which, from the point of view of present exploitation, are chromium, manganese, and barium. Oil deposits are largely unknown at present, although a small quantity is being produced.[14]

Cuba's forest resources have been seriously depleted in the process of expanding sugar cane production. The original forest cover was burned off to provide land for cane, or was cut down for fuel for steam boilers when steam power was introduced in the sugar mills during the latter part of the eighteenth and especially during the nineteenth century. While woodworking industries now employ a considerable number of people, there is a possibility that many more could be utilized by the application of initiative and imagination in the development of wood products for export. A well-planned and executed reforestation program would add greatly to the national wealth and at the same time provide employment for the large numbers of unemployed and underemployed workers in the rural areas.

Nevertheless, the nonagricultural resources seem to afford only limited opportunities for growth. Much depends, however, upon the degree of imagination which the Cuban people, and particularly their leaders, can bring to the task of finding and developing new products from their natural resources and new skills among the population.

Nothing has been said as yet regarding the prospects for immigration and emigration. What the future holds in this respect is extremely uncertain, but present restrictions upon immigration by the various countries of the world are such as to discourage international movement. Restrictions of other countries will tend

[13] *Statesmen's Yearbook, 1942,* p. 814.
[14] See *Censo de 1943,* pp. 372–80, for a brief review of the production of mineral resources of the island.

to limit the emigration of Cubans, while the present laws in Cuba tend effectively in their turn to discourage immigration. It is hardly likely, therefore, that such movements will be factors of any importance in population growth or decline in the near future.

It should be emphasized that lack of economic opportunities does not bring about a reduction in the birth rate. But if persistent unemployment is associated with a steadily rising level of literacy, education, and social contact, then it is likely to have a depressing effect on population growth. Marriages will be postponed, many persons may fail to marry at all, and judicious parents will question the desirability of bringing into the world children for whom they cannot adequately provide. Although literacy has not been increasing in Cuba in recent years, it is unlikely that present conditions will continue for long. The more reasonable expectation is that programs of education will expand, both for adults and children, and that desires for a higher level of living will increase as a result of increase in education and greater opportunities for social contact. Finally, it is important to note that the church in Cuba probably has less influence than in any other Spanish-American country, and cannot be regarded as an important factor in maintaining a high birth rate.

┌─ CHAPTER III ─┐

The Land, Climate, and
Seasonal Rhythms

Every society has to face the problem of adapting to the physical environment, including the climate, the topography, the quality of the soil, and other natural resources. Human beings, like all other forms of life, subsist upon and owe their existence to the beneficence of nature. But while people are dependent upon the physical world for sustenance, they are able to add greatly to the natural productivity of the earth through intelligent control over natural forces. Their level of culture or civilization largely determines the manner of their utilization of natural resources. Indeed, resources can scarcely be said to exist at all until people begin to make use of them. People create society and culture, of which they are also the raw material. Culture consists of organizations and institutions, folkways and mores, customs and traditions, all of which arise from the interaction of persons and groups of persons, from the process of adaptation of one to the other, and to the physical environment.

The five million Cubans discussed in the previous chapter inhabit what is without question one of the most favorable spots for human existence on the earth's surface. Cuba is blessed with an equable climate and a fertile soil, a combination that permits the production of a great diversity of crops and plants with a minimum of effort and expense. Mere survival is a much simpler matter here than it is in the temperate zone. Little is required in the form of shelter or clothing since there is no season of severe cold. Only the rains constitute an exposure hazard, and they come in the warmer months.

A few facts about the geography of Cuba and its land and climate should be kept in mind while considering other aspects of its national life. The island, largest of the Antilles, lies only 90 miles south of Key West, Florida. Its western reaches guard the mouth of the Gulf of Mexico on a direct line between Yucatán and the Florida peninsula. The exact area of Cuba is not known, but authorities seem to agree that it is approximately 41,660 square miles, or 26,662,563 acres. The Isle of Pines, containing 1,197 square miles, and other small though numerous offshore islands and keys, containing 1,351 square miles, bring the total area of the Republic to 44,208 square miles (114,500 square kilometers) or 28,293,452 acres.[1] Although it is the largest island in the Caribbean, the total area is only about the size of the state of Pennsylvania or Louisiana.

The island is long and narrow. From tip to tip it extends 696 miles (1,140 kilometers); its average width is about 60 miles, ranging from about 25 miles in the narrowest part to 120 in the widest. The elongated shape of the island means that there are few rivers of sufficient size to be used for power or irrigation. Its shape also creates a problem in communication between the eastern and western parts. For example, the capital city, Havana, located in the western—or one might say the midwestern—part of the island, and Santiago de Cuba, capital of Oriente Province and the second largest city on the island, are 604 miles apart. In the state of Pennsylvania, comparable in area to Cuba, the two most important cities, situated at opposite ends of the state, are only 250 miles apart.

LAND RESOURCES

Of the 28 million acres in Cuba, 22,429,480 were reported as included in farms in the census of 1946.[2] Of the area in farms, only 4,867,197 acres or 21.7 per cent were cultivated. An additional

---

[1] The Cuban Constitution of 1940 required of Congress that it make provision for a national property census, "the exact measurement of the national territory and the effecting of the complementary topographic studies." (Transitory Provisions, Title Sixth, section second, first paragraph.) However, no such work has yet been accomplished.

[2] National Agricultural Census, 1946, preliminary release.

42.9 per cent of the area in farms was in pastures, about 14 per cent in forests, 3 per cent in *marabú* (a tough shrub of little economic value which is invading the country), and 18.2 per cent in "other uses."[3] The average size of the 159,958 farms was 140 acres.

Concerning the 4,233,083 acres not included in farms, no information is given. Obviously part of it is accounted for by cities, towns, villages, highways, roads and railroads, and military and other reservations. A large area is included in the Zapata Swamp, the uninhabited small islands off the coast, and in mountainous terrain. The remainder is apparently public land. The truth is that nobody knows how much land the state can legitimately claim as public domain, or how much is in forests or otherwise used. Much of what is called public domain (*realenga*) is claimed by private individuals. No cadastral survey has ever been made of the island.

However, the census of agriculture taken in 1946 gave the areas devoted to the principal crops and to other uses. It is the first comprehensive census of agriculture ever undertaken by the Cuban government.[4] The harvested acreage reported in various crops is shown in Table 9. The dominance of sugar cane in the land-use pattern of Cuba is immediately apparent, occupying as it does well over half of the 4,867,197 acres of cultivated land. Moreover, the land in sugar cane is generally the best land on the island. Since the depression of the 1930's, Cuba has been attempting to diversify its agriculture and thus protect itself against the hazard of undue reliance on a single crop. Although some progress has been made in this program, it is clear that the country is far from its goal of a diversified farm economy.

Crops which have been expanding in acreage and production in recent years include rice, peanuts, and corn. In 1940, Paul G. Minneman[5] estimated the rice acreage at 50,000, and in 1946 the census reported 134,000 acres. Similarly, the corn acreage in 1940, estimated at 300,000, had expanded to 602,000 in 1946. Comparative acreages for peanuts are 80,000 in 1940 and 318,000 in 1946.

[3] Includes buildings, roads, and wasteland.

[4] A quite inadequate census of agriculture was made in 1931 along with the population census of that year, but the data have never been regarded as complete.

[5] Paul G. Minneman, "The Agriculture of Cuba," *Foreign Agriculture Bulletin No. 2*, U.S. Department of Agriculture, December 1942, p. 16.

TABLE 9. ACREAGE OF PRINCIPAL CROPS HARVESTED IN CUBA, 1945

Crop	Acres
Sugar cane	2,470,000
Tobacco	162,820
Coffee	219,524
Rice	133,901
Corn	602,186*
Beans	139,891
Peanuts	317,779
Sweet potatoes	128,124
Yams	16,322
Yuca	136,989
Malanga	79,317
Potatoes	20,671
Bananas	199,339†
Calabaza	53,535
Tomatoes	18,189
Other vegetables	8,107
Henequen	24,028
Citrus fruits	35,956‡
Pineapple	28,168
Total cultivated land	4,867,197§

SOURCE: National Agricultural Census, 1946, preliminary release.

* Represents 2 crops, summer and winter.

† Area planted.

‡ In regular plantations. About a third of the citrus trees of the island are dispersed in pastures and cultivated fields.

§ This is not the sum of the acreages listed here, but includes other miscellaneous and minor acreages devoted to crops. Moreover, the acreages of some crops listed here represent two plantings and therefore double the actual amount of land devoted to the crops concerned.

Cassava (yuca) and sweet potatoes appear to have increased as well, but it is not safe to make comparisons between earlier estimates and the 1946 census on these crops, because of the unreliability of the former. Most of these crops are consumed locally and do not find their way into the market. When the next census of agriculture is taken, it will be possible to observe more accurately the trends toward diversification.

The production of milk and milk products has also increased.[6] At one time Cuba was dependent upon outside sources for almost all of the milk and dairy products consumed on the island, but in 1946 it was largely self-sufficient as far as fresh milk was concerned.

Diversification has been stimulated by a protective tariff policy, begun in 1927 and continued since with extremely high duties on

[6] Raymond Leslie Buell, ed., *Problems of the New Cuba* (New York: Foreign Policy Association, 1935), p. 58.

some commodities. The high duties greatly increased the cost of food to the consumer, with the result that consumption of some commodities tended to decline. Importations fell off not so much because the local supply was increased, but because people could not afford to pay the higher prices.[7] There can be no doubt, however, that the protective tariff effected increased production in some crops at least, including rice and coffee, both of which are staples in the Cuban diet. Although Cuba was at one time a heavy exporter of coffee, its production declined after the middle of the nineteenth century to a point where large quantities were imported to supply the population. In 1927, for example, coffee imports amounted to 28 million pounds.[8] Shortly after the tariff was imposed in 1927, the imports fell to 12 million pounds. This could hardly have been due to increased production entirely, although undoubtedly coffee beans were now harvested which had been left on the trees when low prices had prevailed earlier. It takes several years for coffee trees to reach production, and such increase in the harvest as took place in the years immediately following the imposition of the tariff would of necessity come from trees already mature. By 1935, Cuban coffee production had reached 50 million pounds, and by 1942 almost 79 million pounds.[9] Cuba is now generally self-sufficient in regard to coffee and in some years has a small excess for export.

TOPOGRAPHY AND REGIONAL PATTERNS

The topography of Cuba is characterized by three main series of mountains in the west, central, and eastern parts which parallel each other in echelon fashion. There are several other lesser ranges of hills which also are in parallel formation. The most important ranges are the Sierra Maestra on the southern coast of Oriente Province, the highest peak of which rises to 7,872 feet; the Trinidad Mountains of the central part of the island in Las Villas Province; and the Sierra de Los Organos in the western end of the island. Otherwise the island consists of broad plains and valleys, with much low, rolling country.

[7] *Ibid.*, p. 58.
[8] Levi Marrero, *Elementos de geografía de Cuba* (Havana: Editorial Minerva, 1946), p. 199.
[9] *Ibid.*

It is difficult to find any physiographic and natural regions in Cuba since the climatic conditions vary so little throughout the island. Nevertheless, according to J. Brodermann, there are three regions based upon geological structure—the occidental, central, and oriental.[10] To develop a regionalization according to cultural factors, however, would require more data than are now available. Roughly speaking, the provinces themselves serve rather well as cultural regions, not only from a political or governmental standpoint, but in other ways as well. There are differences in the population characteristics among the provinces which distinguish them one from another, as we have seen in Chapter II. It would be possible to combine Havana and Matanzas into a single region, but the other four provinces might well stand as culturally homogeneous units.

There are few if any crops which could be used as a means of delineating cultural regions. Sugar cane is grown throughout the island. The major coffee-producing sections are the three mountain areas of Pinar del Río, Las Villas, and Oriente, although minor quantities are grown in the other provinces. Altitude is the primary factor in determining the coffee regions. Tobacco likewise is grown in all the provinces, but is rather highly concentrated in limited subregions. In the case of tobacco, it is primarily the character of the soil which determines the crop area. Nor are the vegetable crops, except for those grown on a commercial basis, much help in defining regions. In other words, the delineation of type-of-farming areas can be made only when detailed census data on various aspects of agriculture become available. Moreover, the data must be analyzed by barrios and municipios. Until such a census is achieved, only a few of the well-known major crop areas can be identified.

THE SEASONAL RHYTHMS

Climatically, Cuba is on the geographic fringe of the tropics, variously referred to as the "border tropics," "trade-wind tropics," and "dry tropics."[11] All three phrases are expressive. The first

[10] Quoted by L. Marrero, *op. cit.*, p. 43.

[11] Charles M. Pepper, in his book, *Tomorrow in Cuba* (New York: Harper, 1899), uses the phrase "border tropics." Raymond Crist, formerly economic geographer of the Institute of Tropical Agriculture, Mayaguez, Puerto Rico, in conversation with the author used the phrase "trade-wind tropics," while Dr. Walsingham of the Harvard Gardens at Central Soledád, Cuba, prefers the phrase "dry tropics."

suggests the geographical location, on the frontier of the tropical zone; the second refers to one of the most striking climatic characteristics, the almost never-failing winds that blow from the northeast; and the third implies the moderate rainfall which contrasts with the heavy precipitation usually associated with the tropics in the minds of dwellers in temperate zones. Actually, the rainfall in Cuba is comparatively low, less than that found in many portions of the United States. Most of the precipitation comes during the summer months, the winter months being the dry period (*la seca*).

In Cuba, as in all the Caribbean countries, there are only two seasons—the wet and the dry. Temperature changes are little noted from month to month or from winter to summer, but the periods of rainfall and lack of it are well marked. The wet season usually begins in May and extends through November. While there is scarcely a month when there is no rainfall at all, the amount is seldom sufficient during the dry season to keep plant life in a healthy state, and often is not enough to keep it alive. During January, February, and March the precipitation is especially scanty. During late March or early April, the island viewed from an airplane looks parched and brown. Here and there the expanse of brown is broken by patches of bright green, the fields of unharvested cane. The harvested cane fields blend well into the remainder of the landscape, covered as they are with the leaves trimmed from the cane stalks which have dried to a musty brown. Indeed, what would be the spring months in the northern latitudes exhibit in Cuba many of the aspects of a northern autumn.

WEATHER HAZARDS

Drought. The slight oscillation of the temperature from season to season means at least one less hazard for the Caribbean farmer to contend with, that of killing frosts. What he does fear is the failure of the rains. In this respect he shares the anxieties of farmers on the Great Plains of the United States and Canada. Droughts of extreme severity are not common, but occur often enough to be a source of worry. In the winter of 1944–45 Cuba had its worst drought in almost a century. Between October 18, 1944, when a destructive hurricane swept the western part of the island, and the latter part of June 1945, only a few scattered rains occurred, and many localities had none at all for periods of two months at a time. For the five months from November through March the average rainfall was only 0.5 of an inch, which was about one-fourth of normal.[12]

The losses due to the drought in terms of reduced production are not known exactly. P. G. Minneman, agricultural attaché of the American Embassy, reported that milk production fell to a point "40 per cent below normal" for the winter months while "beef cattle lost weight rapidly," and "many animals died for lack of food and water." Even more seriously, the sugar crop had been reduced by about one million tons as a result of the drought, the tobacco crop reduced by an unestimated quantity, and food crops had "suffered extensively."[13]

Normal rainfalls for the various months, based upon data from the Cuban National Observatory, are as follows:

January	1.74	July	5.54
February	1.48	August	6.47
March	2.05	September	6.87
April	3.60	October	6.77
May	7.31	November	3.44
June	8.16	December	1.62

Hurricanes. Another dread of the Cuban population, whether urban or rural, is the hurricane. They occur mostly in the months of August, September, and October. J. C. Millás in a special study of one hundred hurricanes found that none occurred in the months from January to April inclusive, only one in May, three each in June and July, twenty-six in August, twenty-six in September, thirty-four in October, four in November, and three in December.[14] While a particular storm usually covers a restricted zone of only a few miles in width, the damage within that zone is often very serious. For example, on the farm of José Fariñas Castro near

[12]Paul G. Minneman, "Cuba Has Worst Drought of 86 Years," Special Report of the Agricultural Attaché, American Embassy, Havana, June 19, 1945. The statement used as the title of the despatch is the opinion of the director of the Belen Observatory in Havana.

[13]As summarized by Paul G. Minneman in his despatch of January 29, 1946, American Embassy, Havana. The estimate of sugar damage was revised later when heavy rains in July improved the prospects.

[14]J. C. Millás, "Un ensayo sobre los huracanes de las Antillas," *Boletin del observatorio nacional,* Vol. XXIV, quoted by Marrero, *op. cit.,* p. 155.

Sancti-Spíritus, thirty-three houses were blown down at an estimated loss of $33,000. This is a large farm on which dairying is
combined with tobacco growing. Most of the houses were in the
tobacco-producing part of the farm, but two rather large dairy
barns as well as residences were demolished in the dairy section.
Only one house was left standing. Señora Fariñas, aged fifty-nine,
gave a dramatic description of this harrowing experience:

There were fourteen of us in this house when the hurricane came.
It began about ten o'clock in the morning and the force of the wind
was greatest between ten and eleven. Suddenly the roof of the house
began to tear loose, and it appeared that we would be in danger if we
remained, so we all went outside. The downpour of rain was almost
enough to drown us as we crawled on hands and knees into the pasture. The wind was too strong for us to stand up. Nothing could stand
up. The cows and horses even were blown over. Then the barn roof
blew off, and the wall of the house came down and fell in on the beds,
the chairs, and the tables. The rain soaked everything we had. There
was nothing dry to put on after the rain. There was no shelter either.
We stayed out in the rain for three days. Never in my life did I see
such a storm as that one.

When I visited the section around Sancti-Spíritus eight months
after the hurricane, most of the homes had been repaired, but on
many of them the work was still not complete.

In this particular area the chief damage was to buildings, since
most of the country is devoted to pasture and there were no crops
of any consequence to be damaged. However, when hurricanes
sweep across fields of cane, corn, or other standing crops, the
damage may be very great. For example, the hurricane of August
31 to September 2, 1933, struck the north central part of Cuba with
terrific force, the wind reaching a reported velocity of 145 miles
per hour in Isabela. In Havana the official report was 98 miles
per hour. "The damage," says an official source,[15] "was very
severe." In Cárdenas alone, it reached an estimated four million
dollars. Along the entire path of the storm, houses without number were destroyed, sugar mills demolished, sacks of sugar by the
hundreds of thousands lost, and plantations of all kinds devastated.

[15] *Censo de 1943*, p. 161.

There were some 60 lives lost and 150 persons injured. In Isabela scarcely a house was left standing.

Although all sections of Cuba are subject to hurricanes, the extreme western end experiences them with greater frequency. Of the eleven hurricanes described in the official report of the census of 1943, Pinar del Río Province was visited by five. Three other provinces—Havana, Oriente, and Las Villas—were touched by four of the storms, Matanzas by three, and Camagüey by only one.[16] Marrero, citing J. C. Millás again, provides more exact proof of the greater incidence of cyclonic storms in the western belt. According to this authority, the provinces rank as follows in the percentage of Cuban hurricanes they have suffered: Pinar del Río, 38.6; Havana, 20.0; Matanzas, 14.3; Las Villas, 11.4; Camagüey, 7.1; Oriente, 8.6. Since Pinar del Río is the main center of tobacco production, with numerous thatch-roofed houses, it is not difficult to imagine the devastating effect of these storms in that area.[17]

Floods. Although floods do not loom large as a farming hazard in Cuba, they are common and significant enough to come to the minds of farmers when they are asked about the things they do not like about farming. For example, Señor Fariñas, referred to previously, reported that the floods were one of his chief concerns. A river of some magnitude ran through his ranch, on which he pastured some 500 head of cattle. "Cattle die from the drought and the floods," he said. "At the end of the dry period, especially if the drought has been severe, the cattle are weak and are attracted to the river bottoms in search of green grass. Many of them fall off the bluffs trying to get down to the river and are killed; while a sudden downpour of rain may cause a flood which will drown many of those that were able to get down alive."

THE ECONOMIC SEASONS

The periods of activity and inactivity on the part of nature are in contrast with those of man. While the summer months are the

---

[16] *Ibid.*, pp. 155–63.

[17] It is interesting to note the hurricane shelters in Pinar del Río and Havana Provinces. These are small thatch-roofed shelters in the back yards, built in the shape of the American puptent—that is, an inverted V. An outsider would be inclined to question the security of these shelters, as they look to be almost as vulnerable as the other houses; but experience seems to indicate that they withstand most of the storms. This type of shelter is especially common in Pinar del Río.

period of rains and the awakening of life, of growth and matura-
tion, they constitute a period of relative inactivity on the part of
much of the Cuban labor force. It is called the *tiempo muerto*, the
dead season. For the sugar cane farmer there are only minor tasks
to do, such as chopping out the weeds in the cane rows, and planting vegetable gardens and caring for them. Mostly there is work
only for the year-round labor force on the *centrales* or in the
colonias (cane fields). With the advent of the rains the temporary
workers go back to the places from which they came. It is a time
of waiting for the cane to grow and mature and for the rains to
cease.

For the tobacco farmer, there is work to do in the tobacco sheds
—sorting, grading, curing, baling, and shipping to the market—
but it is not for him a rush season. For the coffee planter, it is as
much a dead season as it is for the cane farmer and more than for
the tobacco farmer. The coffee trees need little or no attention
until the berries are ripe for the harvest in October or November.
Meanwhile, he too—like the cane grower—may plant some vegetables for the family table. It is only the dairy farmer and the pro-
ducer of vegetables and field crops who must maintain a seasonal
diligence and activity during the summer months. This is especially true of the dairy farmer, to whom the changing seasons mean
little; but even to him, they do make some difference. For those
relatively few Cuban dairymen who grow cane, millet, and corn for
green feed during the dry season, the summer rains bring welcome
relief from the hard work and expense involved in cutting and
hauling feed to the dairy herd. With the rain the pastures become
green again, and the cows can harvest their own feed. The green
pastures increase the flow of milk, however, and there is more
work milking the cows and disposing of the milk. The milk "harvest" is a daily affair, regardless of season, but the dairyman's
activities in general do increase during the summer.

As October approaches and the rains fall less frequently, the
well-soaked soil begins to dry and there is a murmur of anticipation and activity in the cane fields. The *colonos*, the cane farmers,
inspect the cane and the wetness of the soil, while the mill owners
rush the final repairs on the mill. Arrangements are made to supply labor for the season's work. Up in the coffee country, red ber-

ries on some of the earlier-maturing trees tell the planter that it is time to make preparations for the harvest. The workers must be engaged, as likely as not the same ones who were hired the year before. The various supplies, picking baskets (*latas*), and other equipment must be checked and repaired where necessary. Rice and other foods have to be procured to feed the heavy-eating wagehands. The tobacco farmer during October and November transplants the seedlings which were placed in the seedbeds in August and September. The harvest season will not be long delayed, for tobacco requires only fifty-five days to mature.

The dry season, *la seca*, creeps slowly, gradually through the months of November, December, January, February, March, and April. By January 1 most of the sugar centrales are ready to fire the boilers and begin the feverish activity that will last, for some mills, until the first of June or even later. The dead season of nature is the time of the zafra, the cane harvest, the period that brings all of Cuba into its highest pitch of activity.

What connotations *la zafra* has for Cuba! For it, hundreds of thousands of black slaves were brought from Africa. After the emancipation of the slaves, free black men came from Haiti and Jamaica each year, carrying their pitiful packs of belongings including their *hamacas*, or sleeping hammocks—hordes of men to feed the huge maw that was and is the zafra. Today the work is done mostly by natives of the island. Thousands of Cubans throng the highways, the railroads, and the byways to get to the mills, to the colonias, for the zafra. Millions and tens of millions of tons of cane have to be cut. A hundred thousand machetes in the hands of a hundred thousand men will do the cutting. Millions of stalks of cane—each one held in a human hand for a few seconds while the machete in the other hand cuts it at the bottom and deftly trims the leaves before it is thrown on a pile of other stalks.

Then these millions of tons of stalks must be lifted by sweating human bodies into the large, two-wheeled carts which patient, sturdy oxen will draw to the mill or to the railroad spur. The power exerted by men and oxen in the zafra is stupendous. One wonders what the equivalent in kilowatts would be! It is hard work, often grueling for both man and beast, for Cuba has taken few steps to relegate this burden to machines.

Money flows through Cuba in great amounts and at an accelerated pace during the zafra. Workers who ate sugar cane and
bananas or other home-grown foods during the dead season now
clamor for the luxury of rice, lard, and oil, which have to come
largely from abroad. There is money now to pay the grocer who
granted credit after the money from the last zafra ran out. The
grocer in turn will pay the wholesaler and the banker. The mill
owners, the colonos, the merchants, big and little, pay back the
money they borrowed during the dead season. The railroads put
on extra helpers to handle the increased freight; they bring supplies to the centrales and to the merchants in the towns who
anticipate the expanding demand; they take the cane to the mills
from the most distant points and haul the sugar to the ports. And
the ports take on new activity, as do the ships that freight the
raw sugar to the refineries of the United States and Europe.

The zafra is like Saturday night in a frontier United States mining camp, when everybody gets his week's pay check. Cubans do
not exhibit the same intemperance that mining camp workers did,
being generally more moderate drinkers, but there is the same
free flow of money through the channels of trade. The surging
energy, the articulation of nearly half a million men with their
oxen, their carts, their railroads, their huge grinding mills; the
vast movements of men and women from their homes to the cane
fields; the squalor of the workers' barracks, the *barracones*; the
heat, the sweat, the fatigue of the long days cutting and loading
cane; the disappointments and the defeats; the joys of renewed
activity, the satisfactions of wants long felt and now fulfilled; the
meeting of old friends not seen since the previous zafra; the fiestas
of the towns—all these make the zafra the major event of the
Cuban year. It is indeed the *live* season for man, though it is the
dead period for nature.

CHAPTER IV

Locality Groups and the Settlement Pattern

There are three main patterns of occupancy of land—the farm village, the line village, and dispersed farmsteads. In the case of the farm village, farmers build their homes in a cluster rather than on their separate farms; in the line village, the farm homes are built on farms which are long and narrow in shape, so that all the houses face a highway, river, or other means of transportation and are reasonably close together without being separated from the fields. The pattern known as dispersed farmsteads is that in which the farm homes are located on the farms themselves with no attempt to group the houses along a single highway or road. This isolated farmstead pattern, common to most of the United States, Canada, and parts of South America, is also the prevailing one in Cuba.[1] This pattern is true only for the operators of farms and may not apply to the arrangement of the residences of farm laborers, among whom the pattern varies. The operators universally build their homes on the land they operate, whether they are owners or renters. On a large farm such as a tobacco *vega,* for example, the house of a renter is attached to the piece of land which the renter operates.

[1] For descriptions of locality groups in other Latin-American countries, see T. Lynn Smith, *Brazil: People and Institutions* (Baton Rouge: Louisiana State University Press, 1946), pp. 582–629; C. C. Taylor, "Rural Locality Groups in Argentina," *American Sociological Review,* IX (1944), 162–70. Also Chapter XI in Taylor's *Rural Life in Argentina* (Baton Rouge: Louisiana State University Press, 1948); and N. L. Whetten, *Rural Mexico* (Chicago: University of Chicago Press, 1948), Part II.

THE NEIGHBORHOOD

In any area where the pattern of dispersed farmsteads prevails, the first locality group beyond the family is the neighborhood, a group of families in a state of neighborly relations.[2] The neighborhood in Cuba, as elsewhere, constitutes a basis for informal visiting, exchange of food products, and mutual helpfulness in time of need. There are apparently few cases in which Cuban neighborhoods have been polarized around formal institutions, such as a church or school. In fact, it can be said categorically that the church is not a neighborhood institution in any area of Cuba. While there are schools throughout the open country, they too fail to serve as neighborhood centers.

There are several reasons for this fact. In the first place, there are very few school buildings which are owned by the government, most of them being rented or contributed by private owners. In some cases the schoolroom is merely a room in a farm residence. It therefore is not a public place where people feel free to go or a place that could be used for public gatherings. But perhaps a more important reason why the school does not serve as a neighborhood center is that the local people have little or no responsibility for maintaining it; that is a function of the Ministry of Education. In the absence of local responsibility for the upkeep of the school, interest in it is likely to be, and actually is, rather nominal. This is not to say that the farmers of Cuba lack interest in education for their children. The point is that local groups of farmers do not establish and maintain their own schools; in such matters they usually limit their activities to complaints or requests to the Ministry of Education. Thus the schools are not used as focal points of neighborhood life.

Visiting is perhaps the most important neighborhood activity. All observers are sure to note that the Cuban loves to visit, to talk, to be in the company of his friends or relatives. In a survey of Cuban communities, it was found that in reply to the question "With whom do you visit most often?" the respondents usually gave the name of a friend rather than a relative, and most often it

[2] See descriptions of neighborhoods in J. H. Kolb and E. deS. Brunner, *A Study of Rural Society* (Boston: Houghton Mifflin, 1940), Chapter III, p. 44; or Dwight Sanderson, *Rural Sociology and Rural Social Organization* (New York: Wiley, 1942), pp. 232–47.

was the person who lived next to him. Where reciprocal visiting was reported, however, relatives were usually involved. When farmers are asked whom they visit most often, they usually reply that it is their nearest neighbors. Nevertheless the friendship pattern frequently goes beyond the next-door neighbor, as is indicated by the visiting charts for Managua and Nazareno, two areas near the city of Havana (Figures 8 and 9). Moreover, a sort of chain arrangement is indicated: one person gives the name of the friend with whom he visits most frequently; yet the friend does not mention him in return, but gives the name of someone else. Among the fifty farmers of Managua, only four were reciprocal pairs, that is, each giving the name of the other; among the fifty of Nazareno, there were also only four reciprocals. In the latter case all were related, three pairs being brothers and one pair cousins. In Managua, the four pairs were unrelated.

Nevertheless kinship is an important bond in neighborhood groupings. The three coffee plantations centering on the hamlet of San Blas, which were discussed in Chapter I, are an example. One of these cafetals has recently been subdivided among the twelve children of the owner. The twelve families are very closely associated in social affairs. One daughter and son-in-law have a home in the hamlet which serves as a kind of social center for the group, while the homes of the others are dispersed over the plantation. Meetings are held in this daughter's home when the occasion

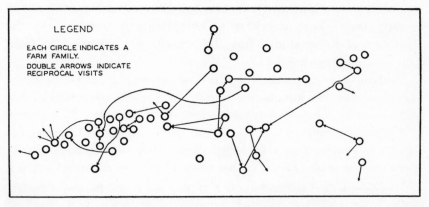

LEGEND

EACH CIRCLE INDICATES A FARM FAMILY.

DOUBLE ARROWS INDICATE RECIPROCAL VISITS

Figure 8. Family Visiting in Managua, Havana Province, Cuba, 1946

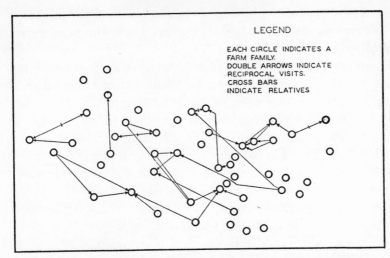

LEGEND

EACH CIRCLE INDICATES A
FARM FAMILY.
DOUBLE ARROWS INDICATE
RECIPROCAL VISITS.
CROSS BARS
INDICATE RELATIVES

Figure 9. Family Visiting in Nazareno, Havana Province,
Cuba, 1946

arises, and since the front room of the house is rather large and the
floor is cemented, it serves very well as a place to dance.

A second plantation in this area is also divided among twelve
families, all related. This kinship group is colored, although it is
not primarily color difference which segregates them but rather
the accident of their being heirs to a cafetal. It is true, however,
that they constitute a locality group distinct from the one just
mentioned and from the third cafetal of the region, which is not a
kinship group. The standard of living in the colored neighborhood
is definitely lower than that on the other two plantations, and the
moral standards of the group are likewise reported to be different
and inferior. The third cafetal has thirty-two families, all of whom
are renters. It was not learned to what extent neighborhoods exist
on this cafetal, but it is quite likely that there are at least two
groupings, based upon topography.

Kinship locality groups are not at all uncommon in Cuba. Another such group exists near Bayamo where there are five large
dairy farms owned by five brothers and brothers-in-law. They
are adjacent to each other and much visiting and neighboring
takes place among them. At one time there were nine brothers
and sisters, but two siblings died and two sold out and moved

away. These are cases which came to the notice of the author during his travels about the island, but no doubt the number could be multiplied many fold.

There is some mutual exchange of labor in certain areas, but it is not a common practice in Cuba. Some barter takes place also, but generally any exchange of goods is in terms of cash. Out of fifty farmers in Managua, only seven reported any barter with their neighbors, and in no case did the neighbors themselves report having engaged in barter; so apparently it is not an important activity. In Nazareno, however, there were thirteen families, or over one-fourth of the total, who reported barter with neighbors. Barter is more common in the coffee areas, which are somewhat isolated and less accessible to the stores.

Something akin to the house and barn raisings of the early North American frontier is found in the *cobíja*, which is a sort of "bee" for the thatching or re-thatching of a bohío with *guano* (the leaf of the palm or palmetto). The job is done in a single day by the neighbors invited to participate. The owner of the house to be thatched serves a dinner, and a bit of liquor and tobacco. As is characteristic of North American "bees," the cobíja is a combined work and pleasure activity.[3]

Mutual aid is limited quite largely to times of sickness and death. In the event of death in rural sections, neighbors carry the remains to the cemetery and, of course, help to comfort the bereaved family by keeping them company for a period before and after the interment. During the rainy season when roads are impassable in the mountainous coffee areas, the remains of the deceased have to be carried for long distances by the pallbearers. In San Blas, for example, there is no cemetery, so that a body must be carried eight kilometers to La Sierra for burial. Most of the families in the San Blas area live on the mountainsides, one or more kilometers away from the hamlet. Therefore, in addition to the eight kilometers from the hamlet to La Sierra, there is also the distance from the farm home of the deceased to San Blas. The same situation is found at El Nicho, some distance north of San Blas.

[3] A native of Yucatán informs the author that the *cobíja* is common also in that country. For evidence of still wider distribution of this folkway, see J. V. Freitas Marcondes, "Mutual Aid," *Rural Sociology*, XIII, No. 4 (December 1948), pp. 374–84.

THE BATEYES

Another locality group is the *batey*.[4] As the word is used currently in Cuba it refers to two situations: (1) the cluster of dwellings and other structures around a sugar mill, and (2) the grouped dwellings of agricultural workers on each sugar colonia.[5] There is no good reason why the term might not also be used to indicate villages of other than sugar workers, but it seems to be used only in reference to them. On a given sugar plantation, there will be a number of other bateyes in addition to the one in which the mill is located. In fact, there will probably be as many bateyes as there are colonias in the plantation.

The batey is a dwelling-place for laborers, whether they be industrial—those who live near the mill—or agricultural—those on the colonias. In the case of "administration cane"—which is grown under the direct management of the sugar company without the intermediate colono—there may likewise be bateyes located at strategic points to place the workers within easy access of their labor. The batey provides living quarters for two types of workers—those who stay the year around and those who come in only for the zafra. The migratory workers are usually accommodated in barracones, varying in quality from very rude structures to some of recent construction, modern in design and facilities.[6] The typical barracón is simply a long building, sometimes partitioned into rooms, sometimes not, in which the laborers hang their hammocks for sleeping. Usually there is another structure near the sleeping quarters which is used for a kitchen. Down the center of this building is a table about waist-high, on which there are two rails. Pots and pans rest on the rails, between which a charcoal fire is made for cooking.

In addition to the barracks, there are also residences for families. No rent is charged these families as a rule. The houses belong to the colono or to the sugar company, as the case may be, and the

[4] The word is apparently of Indian origin and refers to "a flat, clean place, like a plaza, that in the Indian villages of the Antilles, [is] used for singing and dancing, and for playing a ball game of which they were fond." From Alfredo Zayas, *Lexicografía antillana* (2d ed.; Havana: Tipos-Molina y Cia, 1931), Vol. I, p. 91.

[5] A colonia is a sugar cane farm operated by a colono. A colono may rent his colonia from the sugar company, or he may own his own farm near the plantation.

[6] The newly constructed workers' quarters on the plantation called Central Florida are an example of the better type of housing.

workers are usually provided with a plot of land on which to grow
vegetables. Sometimes this land is available near the house, while
in other cases the workers use the *guardarrayas,* the strips of idle
land which separate the cane fields and serve as firebreaks and
as roads over which to transport the cane to the loading station.
Depending upon the size of the batey, there is usually a school, a
store, and sometimes a restaurant serving the migratory workers.
In one batey containing twenty-two families on the Central
Florida plantation, there was also a club.

The batey is the nearest approach to a farm village to be found
in Cuba. It is a real village in the sense of being an aggregation of
dwellings, though they are dwellings of farm laborers rather than
farm operators. The laborers, however, are often as stable in their
occupancy as they would be if they were operators. Among fourteen families on one batey of Central Florida, one had lived there
for fourteen years, another for twelve years, and the balance of the
families for about eight years. The bateyes are usually located
along the private railroad of the central; on Central Florida there
was a telephone connection between the mill office and each of the
bateyes. The companies operate a regular passenger service over
the railway, which makes for ready contact with the central batey
and with the nearby town or towns.

In only one locality in Cuba did we see any instance of farm
operators living in a village. This was at Florencia, where a number of farmers live in town so their wives and daughters can work
in the canning factories. The farmers go back and forth between
village and farm during the busy season. The only other suggestion of village life as a possibility for farm operators was encountered in the coffee section of San Blas, where Señor Romero, in
subdividing his cafetal, had reserved several residence lots adjacent to the hamlet—one for each of his twelve heirs. Actually,
there appears to be no good reason why most of the coffee growers
should not live in a hamlet or village. Coffee trees require little
attention during the growing season, and the harvest requires only
from two to four months. In other words, during two-thirds to
three-fourths of the year the families of coffee farmers are need-
lessly isolated and might just as well be living in a village. This
fact gives rise to the speculation that there may be some tendency

toward nucleation of rural homes. The large increase in the number of inhabited places listed in 1943 as compared with 1931 might be considered as partial evidence in support of such speculation.[7] The situation in regard to numerical changes in trade centers will be discussed presently.

OTHER VILLAGE GROUPS

In the dairy section near Bayamo there are clusters of bohíos along the highway, homes of the workers on the dairy farms of the neighborhood. Some of them are year-round employees while others have only occasional work. They have a very low level of living. The income derived from work on local farms is supplemented in various ways. Some of the boys go away to work at sugar mills during the zafra. The wives of some of the laborers supplement the family income by making straw hats. One of these bohíos contained three sewing machines. The hats sell in Bayamo for fifteen cents each, ten cents of which goes to the one who does the sewing and five cents to those who gather the palm leaves from the trees. These workers have built their homes on land which they own or which is *realenga* (public domain).

Other villages of dairy workers are found throughout the dairy section near Havana. For example, the village of Lechuga near Managua, Havana Province, contains twenty-five houses, all but three of which are the homes of laborers who work on the near-by farms. The other three homes belong to farm owners who are renting their farms to tenants. There is one store in the village, a barbershop, and a school. No doubt a careful survey would reveal many such villages in this and other areas devoted to dairying. On the large tobacco vegas there are also villages of farm laborers.

TRADE CENTERS

In Cuba, as in the United States, Canada, Brazil, and other countries where farm families live on their separate farmsteads rather than in villages, the agricultural towns are the dwelling-places of the merchants, professional people, wholesalers, and other tradesmen or workers engaged largely in non-agricultural pursuits. They are the centers to which the farmers go to buy goods and services and to sell their produce. Since in Cuba there

[7] This increase was discussed in Chapter II.

is no rural free postal delivery, the towns and villages are also the places where farm people go to get their mail.[8]

Farmers come to town rather frequently, a few of them every day and many of them, one, two, or three times weekly. In more isolated regions, they come less often than once a week. Of 742 families in eleven localities representing major types of farming, 281 reported going to town less often than once a week. There were 357 who went one, two, or three times per week, and 28 who went four or more times. These figures were for the adults; young people went less often. In over half the cases (441), the visits to town were less than one a week. Frequent trips to town characterize especially the dairy section in Havana Province, the diversified farming area near Güines, and the tobacco region of Pinar del Río. Less frequent trips were reported for the coffee sections of Las Villas, the Florida sugar plantation in Camagüey, and the coffee area (Alto Songo) in Oriente.

The main object of the visits to town is to purchase supplies or to market produce, but there are many secondary objectives, chiefly having to do with pleasure. Very important to the Cuban is the opportunity which the trip to town offers him or her to meet and talk with friends and relatives. Conversation is a lively art, and every evening in the towns the cafés and restaurants are crowded with people—usually men—engaging in noisy, animated conversation. Many people congregate in the plaza where, as a rule, there is an ample supply of benches or chairs to accommodate them.

Those who are not in the coffee shops or the plaza—and obviously all of them cannot be—are walking up and down the sidewalks bordering the main highway. In spite of the large number of buses and automobiles passing through the towns on the Central Highway, for example, the promenaders in these towns on a Saturday or Sunday evening will overflow the sidewalks onto the highway itself. In some towns traffic slows to a few miles per hour as it wends its way among the pedestrians. The *paseo* (promenade) often takes precedence over vehicular traffic in the

---

[8] Owing to the fact that many farmers cannot get to town during regular post-office hours, it is customary for them to have their mail sent in care of one of the merchants with whom they trade. Thus it happens that almost every merchant acts as a sub-post office.

use of the main street. In some of the towns, the paseo is a rather formal affair in which the young people promenade around the plaza, the boys in one direction and the girls in the other. In some of the larger towns such as Santa Clara, Cienfuegos, and Sancti-Spíritus, the participants are very well dressed, and one wonders if any of them come from the farms.

Functionally, therefore, the Cuban trade center is similar to those of the United States and Canada—a place where farm people come to sell their produce, to purchase the things they need, and to find entertainment. In appearance, however, the rural towns of Cuba differ radically from those in North America. Instead of the wide streets over-arched with elms and the characteristic one- or two-story detached houses, set back from the street in spacious lawns, which characterize many towns and villages of the United States, Cuban centers have relatively narrow streets, entirely without shade trees as a rule, with the houses in solid rows abutting the narrow sidewalks of the main street. In those villages located on paved highways, the highway constitutes the main street and is often the only one that is paved.

This tendency of people to build their houses on the main highway gives the Cuban towns an elongated shape. For example, the village of Jamaica, with a reported population of 280 in 1943, has its houses strung out along the main street for half a mile; Madruga, with 4,325 people, has houses for one mile on the Central Highway. Catalina de Güines, with 2,359 people, is eight-tenths of a mile long. None of these places has more than two back streets on either side of the main highway.

As indicated above, the houses along the main street are either joined together with no space in between or, if detached, are set very close. This is true whether they are dwellings or business houses. Almost universally the latter are one story in height, except for hotels and occasional business houses. Dwellings also are typically of the one-story construction, although the high ceilings which are popular in Cuba make a single story about as high as one and a quarter stories in the United States.

The architecture of the houses is uniform. It is characterized by a high front porch supported by long pillars. In the case of houses constructed of brick or stone, the pillars are of the Grecian type;

on frame dwellings, the pillars are square timbers about four by four inches. The sidewalks are joined to the curb of the street; there is no space between street and walk for grass, as is typical of American towns. The sidewalk is narrow, usually only three or four feet wide, and on the inner side joins directly the porches of the houses. Usually the porch of a dwelling has a railing to separate it from the walk, although in the case of business houses the difference between porch and walk is marked only by the slightly lower elevation of the latter. The typical main street has the appearance of being fenced in by two rows of porch pillars; the houses may differ somewhat in height, but they never fail to have the front porch.

The dwelling houses are predominantly built of lumber with roofs of tile or metal. This is a departure from the usual design of Cuban farmhouses, in which the roof is so often of palm thatch. In our survey of 742 farmhouses, 514 were thatched. The thatched roof no doubt constitutes too much of a fire hazard in the close quarters of a town.[9] Shingled roofs, so common in the United States, are practically unknown in Cuba.

The back streets of the Cuban town are likely to be unpaved and frequently almost impassable to motor vehicles. On these streets the houses are usually detached. Rarely does one see a garden, however, which again is a point of difference between Cuba and the United States. In the small towns of North America, a vegetable or flower garden or both, represents an almost universal feature; but in Cuba gardening is not a popular activity.

In general, the plaza is the social heart of the community. Ordinarily, but not always, it is a square in or near the center of the town. Sometimes it is an oblong rather than a square and is located away from what is now the center, giving the impression that the town has grown away from the plaza. In the capitals of counties, the city hall faces on the square. The square itself is usually paved over practically the entire surface, except for a few spaces left for trees and flower beds. The latter are ordinarily not numerous. There is often a monument to Martí, the great national

[9] Towns with thatched roofs are not uncommon in the Dominican Republic. For example, Mao in the northwestern part of the Republic is almost entirely composed of thatched houses, even though the population is estimated at around 8,000 people.

hero, and to a few local persons of note. Benches and chairs are usually provided in abundance, and of an evening they are apt to be fully occupied. In the smaller centers, the benches may be of cement or concrete and may bear the imperishable and conspicuous imprint of the business firm or individual who donated them. In the larger centers, such as Matanzas, Santa Clara, and Sancti-Spíritus, there are hundreds of metal chairs, some of them rockers.[10]

In some centers there is a *prado* in addition to the plaza. The prado is a walk down the center of a main street. The most famous prado in Cuba is that in Havana, which is about half a mile long, lined on either side by ficus trees which shade it completely and paved with a synthetic marble. The prado in Cienfuegos is much less elaborate, being constructed of concrete, and somewhat narrower than the one in Havana. Along either side are benches for spectators who wish to watch the passing show of the promenaders who appear in throngs in the evening.

Increase in number of centers. If we can accept the accuracy of the enumerations of population for 1931 and 1943, it would appear that there has been a marked increase in the number of trade centers between those years. In the census of 1931, a total of 646 cities and *pueblos*, or villages, were reported, while in 1943 there were 892, an increase of 246.[11] In 1943 places of less than 1,000 inhabitants made up 68.3 per cent of all urban centers and 9 per cent of the urban population, compared with figures for 1931 of 63 per cent and 8.2 per cent, respectively.

The appearance in 1943 of 223 new pueblos of fewer than 1,000 inhabitants is so remarkable as to raise some doubts as to the comparability of the two enumerations. These doubts are accentuated

[10] In Sancti-Spíritus a fee is charged for the use of the chairs. A collector circulates around the park collecting the fees and giving a receipt similar to that given by a streetcar conductor. Obviously it would be impossible to collect from every sitter, but the city apparently gains some revenue with which to pay for the chairs and for their upkeep or replacement.

[11] *Censo de 1943*, p. 723. These figures, however, are not compatible with the actual count of population centers listed elsewhere in the same volume. In Table 6, p. 842, the centers with populations of more than 1,000 inhabitants, of which 256 are reported, are given by name of place; but on p. 723, 281 centers are indicated in this category, a discrepancy of 25. Similarly, in Table 7 the places with less than 1,000 population are reported by name. The count of these places is 608, compared with a figure of 611 reported on p. 723.

TABLE 10. NUMBER OF CENTERS REPORTED IN 1943 BUT NOT IN 1931, BY PROVINCES

Province	No. New Pueblos	Province	No. New Pueblos
Pinar del Río	14	Las Villas	22
Havana	29	Camagüey	15
Matanzas	16	Oriente	127

when the distribution of the "new" centers is shown by provinces (Table 10). The increase is extraordinary in Oriente, the province which accounts for over half of the total. The increase in Havana Province is understandable because of the growth of the city of Havana and the inevitable peripheral growth of population. The population of Havana Province increased by over 25 per cent in the twelve-year period, which gives reason to believe that the number of new centers reported for it is somewhere near reasonable expectation. Even here, however, it is not clear what criterion was used by the census in the two enumerations for including or not including an aggregation of dwellings as a pueblo.

When it comes to Oriente, the population of the province increased by 26 per cent, but the number of places enumerated as centers with 1,000 population or less rose from 92 in 1931 to 218 in 1943. This seems to be definitely, in part at least, the result of different methods in the two enumerations. However, with a number of this magnitude one can allow for discrepancies in the two enumerations and still be safe in recognizing part of the increase as valid. What is important is the general upward direction of the trend.

Centers according to size. There is no general classification of trade centers which is standard for Cuba. The terms *ciudad* (city), *villa* (town), *poblado* (small village), *pueblo* (village), and *caserío* (hamlet) are in general use, but there is much difference of opinion as to the size of each. As a matter of fact, the terms are often used interchangeably. That is, "villa" may also refer to a small city, and "pueblo" is often used in a generic sense as referring to any populated place. The categories of town, village, and hamlet in the United States ordinarily refer respectively to places from 2,500 to 5,000; from 250 to 2,500; and less than 250. These are not official definitions, but those which are coming into general use among students of rural population. The villages, that is, the group from 250 to 2,500, are sometimes subdivided into small (250 to 999), medium sized (1,000 to 1,749) and large (1,750 to 2,499).

A similar classification has been undertaken for Cuba, as indicated in Table 11, but there are a few differences. The term "poblado" has been in general use to indicate a small village and is thus preserved in this classification to include places of from 250 to 749 inhabitants. Admittedly the decision to make the upper limit of this class 749, instead of 999 as is the common practice in classifying small villages in the United States, is somewhat arbitrary, but it is believed there is some logic for this change. It is based on the conviction that for the smaller places an interval of 750 is too great, and results in a grouping of places which are markedly different from a sociological standpoint. That is to say, the social difference between a community of 250 and one of 1,000 is inevitably greater than the difference between a place with 750 inhabitants and one of 1,500. Moreover, as places increase in size, they may differ by as much as several thousand people in population without marked sociological differences. If a difference or range of 500 is preserved for the poblados, and 750 for the small and 1,000 for the large pueblos, a greater measure of social homogeneity will characterize the groupings.

On the basis of this system, the centers listed in the census of

TABLE 11. NUMBER AND POPULATION OF CUBAN TRADE CENTERS OF VARIOUS TYPES ACCORDING TO SIZE, 1943

Type of Center	Number of Centers		Population of Centers	
	Number	Per Cent	Number	Per Cent
Total 863		100.0	2,568,142	100.0
Caseríos (under 250) 234		27.1	36,848	1.4
Poblados (250–749) 300		34.8	135,928	5.3
Pueblos (750–2,499)				
Pequeño (750–1,499) 132		15.3	135,267	5.3
Grande (1,500–2,499) 60		7.0	116,886	4.6
Villas (2,500–4,999) 81		9.4	290,583	11.3
Ciudades				
Pequeña (5,000–9,999) 22		2.5	157,672	6.1
Mediano (10,000–24,999) 20		2.3	317,970	12.4
Grande (25,000 or over) 14		1.6	1,376,988	53.6
Other population (including farm residents) 2,210,347				

SOURCE: *Censo de 1943*, pp. 842–54, Tables 6 and 7.

1943 are distributed as shown in Table 11. It is quite likely that there are numerous hamlets missing from this enumeration. There are undoubtedly many more of these small clusters than are reported in the census. If all were enumerated, they should outnumber the poblados considerably instead of being actually fewer in the classification. The author, as indicated later, tried unsuccessfully to find name identifications for several small hamlets in Havana Province. Naturally if these had no names, no listing could be made of them in the census.

Distribution according to function. From the functional standpoint, Cuban centers would compare with those in the United States and could easily be fitted into the following classification developed by J. H. Kolb:

1. *The single, simple service type.* This type of center is usually an open-country neighborhood or hamlet center where single and comparatively simple or undifferentiated services are performed.

2. *The limited, simple service type.* This type of service center may range in size from about 200 to 400 or 500 people. Villages in this class fall short of providing what may be termed a "six-service standard," that is, of having agencies in all of the following groups of services: economic, educational, religious, social, communication, professional.

3. *The semi-complete, intermediate type.* This type of center averages about 800 or 1,000 people with a range from about 400 to over 1,200. . . . It is intermediate because it stands midway between the type last mentioned and the larger centers . . . It is incomplete because it is frequently lacking in fulfillment of the six-service standard . . .

4. *The complete, partially specialized type.* This type averages about 2,400 or more persons and may range from 1,200 to 5,000 or just a little over. Its agencies are numerous enough to cover all the more common needs and differentiated enough to take on specialized characteristics.

5. *The urban, highly specialized types.* These types which need further refined classifications, are, of course, represented by the larger city or even metropolitan centers . . .[12]

The geographic pattern of distribution in Cuba of these various types of centers is not known with any degree of accuracy. The

[12] J. H. Kolb and E. deS. Brunner, *A Study of Rural Society*, pp. 85–86.

census does not provide data relative to business establishments, and no local studies have been made on which we might rely. However, in logging the Central Highway by automobile between Jamaica and Matanzas, and the secondary highway between Batabanó and Havana by way of San Antonio de las Vegas, some general idea of spatial distribution was obtained. Along the Central Highway, the log was as follows:

Miles	Type of Settlement
0	Jamaica, small village of about 350 population
1.5	San José, small city of about 8,000
8.5	Open country store
10.1	Open country store, two dwellings
10.6	Open country store, two dwellings
11.3	La Gabina, small village, two general stores
14.7	Catalina, population about 2,500
23.3 to 24.3	Madruga, population about 4,500 (community was a mile in length)
24.4	A sort of suburb of Madruga consisting of a store and a group of bohíos
26.0	Open country store on highway. Back from the highway a quarter of a mile is Aguacate, population about 3,500
27.0	Open country store, one dwelling
32.6	Ceiba Mocha, a village of about 2,000 population
36.6	Open country store and dwelling
42.8	Matanzas (population 54,844)

Thus there were thirteen centers in the forty-three miles, ranging in type from a single open country store to the large city of Matanzas. The stores along the highway were not regularly spaced nor were they as numerous as expected. This may be due to two factors. One is the nature of land use and farm organization. Much of the countryside is in large farms devoted to livestock production. Another reason, and perhaps the most important one, is that the railroad parallels the highway, and since it was built at an earlier date the trade centers became established along it rather than on the highway. This factor would be important, especially over the part of the highway from Catalina to Matanzas.

If one travels from Catalina to La Gabina via Güines, instead of the direct route as shown on the log, the distribution presents some interesting contrasts. From Catalina to Güines, a distance of 6.7 miles, there is only one store and that is a mile outside Catalina. This is a region of large cane fields, and such stores as exist outside the towns are in the bateyes. From Güines to the junction with the Central Highway, a distance of about 8 miles, there are six stores and hamlets. The following is the log:

Miles	Type of Settlement
0	Güines, population about 25,000
2.0	Store, four dwellings
3.3	Store, fourteen dwellings
4.0	Store, one dwelling
5.4	Store, five dwellings
5.6	Store, two dwellings
7.7	Store, three dwellings

The almost total absence of stores along the highway between Catalina and Güines, and their frequent occurrence from Güines to the junction with the Central Highway, is largely a reflection of the difference in type of farming in the two areas. In the former, as already indicated, there are large cane colonias, where the farm workers are concentrated in bateyes located some distance back from the highway. Such stores and other services as exist in this area are located in the bateyes. In the latter area, however, farming is diversified and farms are relatively small. Under these conditions stores occur more frequently, averaging about one store, hamlet, or village to the mile.

The highway from Havana to Batabanó on the southern coast passes through the Havana "milkshed" with a succession of dairy farms, large and small. The distribution of service centers along this route is only slightly less concentrated than that in the Güines small-farm area, as the following log reveals:

Miles	Type of Settlement
0	Surgidero de Batabanó (population 6,000)
1	Batabanó (population about 3,500)
6.0	Open country store
7.0	Hamlet, two stores, several dwellings
9.0	Hamlet, Durán
12.0	San Antonio de las Vegas (population 1,500)

Miles	Type of Settlement
15.0	One store, six dwellings
18.0	One store, two dwellings
19.0	Two stores, several dwellings
19.7	One store
20.4	One store, eight dwellings
23.0	Managua, population about 1,000
26.0	Guásimas, small village
27.5	Hamlet, store, several dwellings
28.1	Village, beginning of suburban Havana

The average distance between service centers on this route is about two miles, and in no case more than three miles. This is an asphalt highway and therefore passable the year round. It is subject to heavy traffic, and until recent years little or no attention was paid to its upkeep. According to plans in 1946, several feeder roads with hard surfaces will be built in the near future. One such road has already been completed from Batabanó to Guiro Marrero. Feeder roads may be expected to stimulate further growth of the centers along this route, especially at the intersections.

In compiling these logs, the author found at least nine small hamlets without any name as far as could be determined. In four other cases local informants provided a name (in one case two names), but the hamlets were not listed among the populated places in the census nor on any of the maps in our possession.

In summary, the rural population of Cuba has a settlement pattern similar to that in the United States. Farm operators live on their farms as a rule, rather than in villages. Farm laborers on the sugar cane colonias and the large tobacco vegas live in clusters known as bateyes. Neighborhoods of open country dwellers are not well marked except in more isolated sections, notably the coffee territory. Here kinship is often an important social bond. Unlike the situation in the United States, the school and the church are not poles of neighborhood interest.

Trade centers are increasing in importance with the expansion of a more diversified type of commercial agriculture and with many small proprietors in the dairy sections specializing in the marketing of whole milk. Feeder highways being built out from the Central Highway will add to the importance of some trade

centers and may bring about changes in the pattern of distribution of the population. The "name consciousness" so noticeable in
the United States is not evident in open-country neighborhoods
in Cuba, where even hamlets of fifty people sometimes have no
name.

CHAPTER V

The Evolution of the Cuban Land System

During the four and a half centuries of occupation of Cuba by Europeans, the systems of land use, land distribution, and land division passed through several phases. These various phases were not always sharply differentiated in time. Often they overlapped and merged into or even ran parallel to each other. The dates indicated for each period are only approximate and do not in most cases represent an absolute point of beginning and ending of each land system; they do, however, include the years when each system was at its height. The following rough designation as to time periods and general characterization as to the nature of the different phases is approximately true to historical fact:

1. The *encomiendas*, 1513–1550.[1]

2. The *mercedes* and the *haciendas comuneras*, 1536–1729.

3. Breakup of *haciendas comuneras*, 1700–1820.

4. The expansion of sugar production through multiplication of the number of small mills, 1790–1870.

NOTE. This chapter appeared as an article in *Land Economics*, XXV, No. 4 (November 1949), pp. 365–81.

[1] Dating the period of the encomienda in Cuba from 1513 to 1550, the author is aware that the institution survived in the Spanish colonies for two centuries following, but in Cuba it was without important force and effect after the natives were exterminated—as they largely were by approximately 1550. For an excellent discussion of the encomienda and other aspects of land tenure in the Spanish colonies, see David Weeks, "The Agrarian System of the Spanish American Colonies," *Journal of Land and Public Utility Economics*, February 1947, pp. 153–68.

5. Rise of the large sugar estate, the sugar latifundium: increased use of railroad and other technological improvements, 1870–1895.

6. The sugar latifundium in full flower, 1900–1933.

THE ENCOMIENDAS

The encomienda was a right to the labor of a specified number of Indians granted by the Crown to a colonist. The Spaniard was made responsible for the spiritual and temporal welfare of the natives "commended" to him. In other words, the Indians were to be fed and clothed and their health looked after and, above all, converted to Christianity. Although the institution had its origin in Hispaniola (now the Dominican Republic and Haiti) under Columbus, it had its antecedents in the period of the reconquest of Spain from the Moors when the Catholic monarchs distributed lands among the Spanish chieftains.[2]

A brief exposition of the origin of the encomienda may be in order, not only because it played a role in the early history of Cuban land tenure, but also because it became so important in other parts of Spanish America. Its roots are traceable to several sources. In the first place, it is clear from the writings of Columbus that (a) the primary object of his voyages was the acquisition of gold, thought to be of fabulous quantities in Cathay, which he expected to discover (and thought he had discovered); and (b) whatever labor or toil was necessary in the new country was certainly not to be performed by Spaniards. There is apparent in his records the assumption that the people they were to meet at the journey's end would become subordinate to the will of the Spaniards. Forced labor on the part of the natives—if not actual slavery—was a foregone conclusion.

Secondly, when Pope Alexander VI divided the newly discov-

[2] See Robert S. Chamberlain, "Castilian Backgrounds of the Repartimiento-Encomienda," in *Contributions to American Anthropology and History* (Carnegie Institution of Washington, Publication No. 509), Vol. V, Article 25. In the Indies, however, the division of land (*repartimiento de tierras*) was of less significance than the "division" of the Indians. The Spanish "colonists" were by no means agriculturally inclined; they wanted gold and nothing else, except enough food to live on while securing the gold. Weeks (*op. cit.*, p. 157), while taking a different point of view from Chamberlain, agrees with the thesis that the encomienda in America had its precursors in Spain, and even in ancient Rome.

ered territories between Spain and Portugal (papal bulls of May 3 and 4, 1493), it was agreed that the first duty of the monarchs of the two countries was to convert the natives to Christianity. Hence the specification in the encomienda regarding the responsibility of the Spaniard for the spiritual welfare of the natives given him in trust. As Lesley Byrd Simpson says:

They [the monarchs] were, in fact, spiritual viceroys of the Holy See. With this assumption by the civil government of the religious mission it soon found itself between the devil of papal displeasure and the deep sea of economic necessity. On the one hand the government undertook to see that the natives were protected and made Christians; on the other, it was bound to favor the multitude of Spaniards who had gone to the Indies in the hope of some material reward, while the needs of the poverty-stricken Crown could not be lost sight of . . .[3]

The "needs of the poverty-stricken Crown" it was hoped would be met by the acquisition of the fancied gold supplies they expected to find at hand. While the islands of the Caribbean were not devoid of gold, they did not contain the precious metal in abundance. That which existed in the hands of the Tainos when Columbus arrived—a not impressive amount—represented the accumulation of generations, as S. E. Morison suggests.[4] Gold was obtained in three ways, successively. At first, the Spaniards traded the Indians trinkets for their gold ornaments. These trinkets consisted mainly of hawk's bells, bright colored caps, and other cheap merchandise, of which the sailors apparently brought abundant supplies. The hawk's bells were especially popular with the natives. In short order the ornaments on hand were obtained by this beguiling process.

After the visible supply of gold was exhausted, the only recourse was to begin mining new supplies, washing it out of the beds of rivers and smaller streams, clearing land and trenching it until by such prospecting a new productive area might be found. This involved hard labor, to which neither the Indians nor the Spaniards were accustomed. But the latter had no other thought than that the Indians should be the ones to do the hard work. In

[3] Lesley Byrd Simpson, *The Encomienda in New Spain* (Berkeley: University of California Press, 1929), p. 19.

[4] S. E. Morison, *Admiral of the Ocean Sea* (Boston: Little, Brown, 1942), p. 492.

passing, it might be in order to record the opinion of one historian
—certainly shared by many others—that the Spaniards who came
with Columbus and others in those early years were not a particularly praiseworthy lot. Simpson calls them "riff-raff," consisting of ex-soldiers, broken noblemen, adventurers, criminals, and
convicts.[5] Moreover, manual labor was looked upon as degrading
in the Spain of that period. Thus they had neither the conscience
to prevent them from enslaving others, nor the cultural condition-
ing to fit them for performing manual tasks without losing prestige.

The second stage in the quest for gold was to levy tribute upon
the Indian chiefs. This was instituted in Hispaniola in 1496. The
impossibility of this scheme of securing gold soon became apparent.
The natives, unaccustomed to the arduous toil and being poorly
fed in the meanwhile, suffered incredible mortality. During the
next trip of Columbus to Spain, matters again got out of hand in
Hispaniola. The Indians were restive under the cruel imposition
of the tribute system. Disaffection among the Spaniards, led by
Francisco Roldán, threatened the authority of Bartholomew,
brother of Columbus, who was acting governor. Roldán promised
the chiefs that no more tribute would be levied, and the Spaniards
were promised a life of ease, with plenty of Indians to dig gold for
them, free passage home, and no taxes.[6] How he might fulfill both
promises, it was not useful for him to attempt to explain at the
time.

Subsequently, however, the third system of exploitation, to
become known as the encomienda, solved the apparent paradox.
Roldán negotiated an agreement with Columbus which among
other things granted to Roldán and his followers free land grants
in Xaragua (a province on the south part of Hispaniola) for those
who chose to remain. "Moreover," says Morison, "he established
. . . a system of exploitation that became the basis of social institutions of New Spain. This was the system of *repartimientos*,
later known as *encomiendas.*"[7]

---

[5] *Ibid.*, p. 25.

[6] *Ibid.*, p. 564.

[7] *Ibid.*, p. 567. There is a great deal of confusion in the literature regarding the
repartimientos and encomiendas. In some cases the two are regarded as referring to the
same institution, implying that land grants and grants of Indians (*repartimiento de
tierras* and *repartimiento de Indios*) went together. Such was apparently the case in

This system was approved by the chiefs because it relieved them from the intolerable tribute system—fulfilling thus Roldán's promise to them—while at the same time it gave the Spaniards what Roldán had promised them—that is, Indians to do the work for them. Although some writers consider the encomienda to have originated in the administration of Ovando from 1502–1509, the essential features of the institution seem to be embodied in this arrangement between Columbus and Roldán.

The encomienda in Cuba was important for only a brief period in the beginning of settlement. It appears from the historical accounts that the colonists were more—much more—concerned with the exercise of their rights to the labor of the Indians than they were in discharging their responsibilities of feeding, clothing, and educating them. Being a rather peaceful and easygoing race, unaccustomed to hard physical labor, the natives could not endure the regime of the Spanish masters. In the space of little more than a generation they were practically extinct, killed off by overwork, malnutrition, and disease.[8]

Comparatively little land was distributed during this period, because settlers were few. The great attraction to the Spanish emigrant during the sixteenth century was the continent, where the gold and silver riches of Mexico and Peru had been discovered. Since the primary interest of the Spanish conquerors was to obtain gold rather than land, attention shifted sharply away from Cuba. It was partly due to threats of his followers to desert him that Velasquez, the conqueror of Cuba, distributed repartimientos of natives in the first instance.[9] From the very beginning of the *repartimientos de Indios* in Cuba, however, the strong voice of

Hispaniola as described by Morison. Each settler, he says, was allotted a plot of land consisting of ten thousand cassava plants, "with the Indians that were on it" (p. 567). Usually, grants of land and grants of Indians were separate acts. The encomienda strictly came to mean a grant of the right to the labor of a population of Indians. Naturally, in an agricultural country, this would involve use of the land as well. But grants of land were usually in perpetuity, while encomiendas were limited to the life of the grantee and the "life of one heir." (See quotation from a cédula of Phillip II in Simpson, *op. cit.*, frontispiece.)

[8] Ramiro Guerra y Sánchez, *Manual de historia de Cuba* (Havana: Cultural S.A., 1938), pp. 44–45, 53–54.

[9] Ramiro Guerra y Sánchez, *Historia de Cuba* (2d ed.; Havana: Libreria Cervantes de Ricardo-Veloso, 1922), Vol. I, p. 190.

Father Bartolome de Las Casas registered repeated protests with the Spanish sovereigns regarding the maltreatment of the natives. His protests, along with those of others, bore fruit in laws calling for the liberation of the natives in 1542.[10] Unfortunately this victory for the good father came after the natives had largely been exterminated. They have no known descendants today.

The period of the encomiendas, because of the cruel annihilation of the aborigines, had important consequences for subsequent Cuban history. The elimination of the native labor supply set the stage for the entrance of slavery. This meant the introduction of Negroes, who because of their physical vigor and adaptability to the subtropical climate made possible the extensive exploitation of agricultural and other resources. The demand for Negro slave labor on the part of Cuban settlers came even before the end of the encomiendas. An appeal for a license to import slaves was made in 1530, and by 1544 Negroes were said to be numerous in the island.[11]

THE MERCEDES GRANTED BY THE CABILDOS

During the two centuries from 1536 to 1729, most of the land of Cuba was alienated by means of grants, or *mercedes*,[12] made by the municipal councils (*cabildos*). Most of these grants were circular in shape with a specified radius (one, two, three, or more *leguas*, or leagues) from a given center. Under the terms of the grants, the grantee was obligated to make use of the property, to maintain an inn for travelers at the center thereof, and to supply

[10] Orders of the Crown to "grant liberty judiciously to the Indians' advantage," passed April 20, 1543, were sent to Juanes de Avila but were not put into operation. His successor, Antonio Chaves, was likewise opposed to the liberation and appealed for approval of his modification of the order to prohibit forced labor of Cubans in mining. The governor who followed him, however, Dr. Gonzalo Perez de Angulo, arrived in Santiago in November 1549 and immediately proclaimed the "entire liberty" of the Cubans. See I. A. Wright, *The Early History of Cuba* (New York: Macmillan, 1916), pp. 178–85. "From this time forward the natives cut little figure in the history of the island . . . Angulo's pronouncement seems to have had effect: in 1556 his successor, travelling through the country, said he found the Cubeños living wretchedly, abandoned to the wilderness. He estimated their number then and a little later to be not as many as two thousand, including perhaps two hundred Indians who were not native born . . ." (*Ibid.*, pp. 185–86.) The "New Laws" of 1542 nullified grants in encomienda, but were revived in 1547 with additional safeguards against mistreatment of the natives. (See Weeks, *op. cit.*, p. 158.)

[11] Guerra y Sánchez, *Historia de Cuba*, pp. 367–68.

[12] The word *merced* means gift or grant in this case and came to be applied to these cabildo grants because they were free gifts with only minor conditions attached.

meat for the municipality at a price to be fixed by the cabildo. The mercedes were devoted to the production of livestock. Those used for cattle (*genado mayor*) were called *hatos* and were usually larger than those used for sheep or goats, which were called *corrales*.[13]

How the circular form of the merced originated is not precisely known, although the place of its origin seems to be well established as Sancti-Spíritus. Here the first merced was granted by the cabildo on August 12, 1536, to one Fernando Gómez. Because of its historic significance, the application and the action of the cabildo are quoted herewith:

"I, Fernando Gómez, resident of this town of Sancti Spíritus, appear before Your Honors and state: that mindful of it having been circulated by dispatch that all residents who should so desire might request crown lands, which shall be given them in the manner of a gift, they obligating themselves to pay for development of the town and supplies for its citizens: and mindful that I have a large family and there being sufficient crown lands, I state: that around the West toward the South there is a savannah, close to a ridge of mountains, about twenty leagues more or less from this town which they call Manicaragua, or, by another name, La Sabana de la Cabeza, where a river has its source that they call Arimau, which runs to the southern sea, and from there continue other savannahs called La Sabana del Oro, La Sabana de la Yegua, Mauricio, and another, Redonda: I ask that Your Honors grant me, in the name of the king, our lord, three leagues round about,[14] in order to settle them when it be my convenience, without limitation of time, naming as principal seat La Sabana de las Cabezadas on the banks of the Arroyo Oro, and upon your making me the grant I shall give a hundred ducats for public works and a hundred

[13] If an owner of an hato wished to devote part of his hacienda to breeding sheep or goats, it was necessary for him to get permission from the cabildo. The area designated was then called *corralillo*. Similarly the owner of a corral who wished to produce cattle would have to get permission, and the area of his corral devoted to this purpose was called *hatillo* or *hatico*. See E. T. Pichardo y Jiménez, *Agrimensura legal de la isla de Cuba* (2d ed.; Havana, 1902), p. 265.

[14] The Spanish phrase is *tres leguas en contorno*, which is rather ambiguous, but which could be taken to mean a circular shape, apparently three leagues in radius. If it were meant to be a square it would undoubtedly have been so indicated, and moreover there would have been little point to specifying a center. For methods of surveying the circular form, see Chapter VI.

that a church may be raised. Wherefore I ask of Your Honors and beseech that you make me the grant I ask, since it is without harm nor hurt to anyone, and I swear that my petition is not in malice.—Fernando Gómez." The Cabildo having met, after agreeing on another matter, the following was set forth in the minutes of the session:—

"The petition of Fernando Gómez having been viewed by Their Honors, and there being no petition or grant made, nor any settlement other than the site of Asno, which does not cause any detriment to it, Their Honors stated that, in the name of the King, they do make and have made to said Fernando Gómez the grant of three leagues round about and that the principal seat be La Sabana de la Cabezada, on the bank of the Arroyo Oro, and the Procurator may place it in his possession; and first of all that he produce the two hundred ducats, so that a hundred may be given to the steward of the church and the other hundred enter the depository of the town; and having nothing else to review, this Cabildo was closed on said day, the 12th of August, 1536, as signers, &."[15]

Before this historic act on the part of the city council of Sancti-Spíritus, use was made of the circle to describe a piece of property in 1522. The situation arose in connection with the change of location of the village from its original and undesirable site, to a new one. To make this new site available, one Dª María Jiménez ceded an area of land to the village, described as being "one league in radius from the hacienda Minas."[16]

This first grant on the part of the cabildo of Sancti-Spíritus was given without specific royal authorization, and it was not until the Municipal Ordinances of 1574, approved in 1578, that the Crown recognized officially these acts on the part of the cabildos. Although other municipalities apparently had authority to make these mercedes, only those of Sancti-Spíritus and Havana did so, the former for the eastern part of the island, the latter for the western part.

[15] Pichardo, *op. cit.*, pp. 260–61.
[16] *Ibid.*, p. 260. As a footnote on page 261 this same author states: "Note that in this request [of Fernando Gómez], the most ancient of the island, already is determined the circular figure, *because it was the most natural.*" (Translation and italics are the present author's.)

In addition to the circular outline, there was another aspect of these haciendas of very great interest. This was the fact that they gradually evolved into communal properties—that is, properties held without subdivision by a number of claimants. This is one of the most interesting phases of Cuban land history. The *haciendas comuneras* arose from the fact that when the original grantee died or sold part of his merced, the new owners (his heirs, creditors, or buyers) did not subdivide the land. The reasons why the haciendas were not subdivided are not difficult to find. In the first place, technical personnel to survey the land could not be obtained. In the second place, the cost of such survey in relation to the value of the land would have been prohibitive. Finally, with livestock as the main enterprise, it was undoubtedly more economical to operate the hacienda as a large unit than it would have been to break it up into smaller and less economical areas. The latter would have placed each owner under the necessity of building his own corrals, dwellings, and so forth, an expense in those days that would have been too great to be borne. In other words, it was good sense from an economic point of view to keep the larger unit intact.

As an alternative to getting title to a specific portion of the hacienda, persons with rights in the property were given what came to be called *pesos de posesión* or *pesos de tierras*. This practice was especially common in the eastern part of the island. According to Pichardo, "this system of community that had its beginning at the end of the Sixteenth Century in the territories that today are included in the provinces of Santiago de Cuba (Oriente), Puerto Principe (Camagüey) and almost all of Santa Clara (Las Villas); was not extended to the west in the Provinces of Matanzas, Havana and Pinar del Río."[17]

In the latter provinces, the co-owners of mercedes would mark and brand their livestock so as to designate ownership. The various individuals who came to have rights in the land and used it communally, each kept his own livestock distinct from the others by means of marks and brands. New owners were allowed to establish new seats or centers for their operations which were called *hijas* (daughters) of the principal hacienda. The heirs of these

[17] *Ibid.*, p. 279.

owners could in turn establish centers which were called *nietas,* or "grandchildren" of the original ranch.[18]

Thus, during this period, property rights in land became widely distributed among the people, although the physical division of land was characterized mainly by the communal haciendas. The boundaries of these mercedes were often no more than vaguely determined. A map showing the location of the circular grants (Figure 10) reveals many cases of overlapping. The stage was set, therefore, for extensive litigation over land boundaries and titles. These disputes were not only among the circular haciendas, but within them as well.

THE SUBDIVISION OF THE CIRCULAR HACIENDAS

The increase in the number of persons with rights in a given hacienda resulted in a steady diminution of the returns per capita. Some had larger shares than others, naturally, and the larger owners were anxious to subdivide; but the small ones resisted it, being reluctant to risk the loss of even such meager returns as they were now receiving. However, it is considered likely that even before the close of the sixteenth century some subdivision was taking place.[19]

But if internal forces were fomenting the movement toward subdivision of landholdings and the breakup of the communal haciendas, there was an even more powerful force operating from without. This was the rise of the sugar and tobacco industries. Although the cultivation of cane began in Cuba during the last decade of the sixteenth century, its growth was slow for several reasons, including the scarcity of slaves, the limited market, and the tremendous cost of getting the equipment needed for the extraction of the juice. This equipment had to be purchased in Portugal; but since Cuba's trade with Spain was limited to the port of Seville, everything went through that port and many middlemen got commissions on goods before they landed in Cuba. The importation of slaves was also a monopoly which made the cost high to Cuban buyers. These impediments meant a slow growth for the sugar industry and, moreover, it meant that the

[18] *Ibid.,* p. 280.

[19] Ramiro Guerra y Sánchez, *Azúcar y población de las Antillas* (3rd ed.; Havana: Cultural S.A., 1944), p. 498.

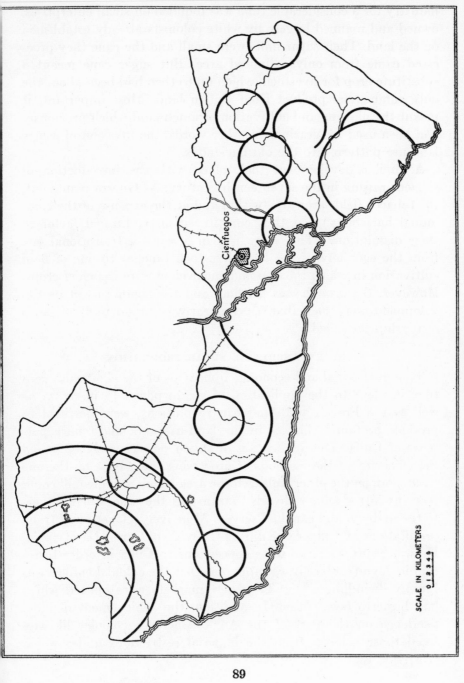

SCALE IN KILOMETERS
0 1 2 3 4 5

Figure 10. Map of the Municipality of Cienfuegos, Cuba, Showing Circular Land Division, Undated

industry for a considerable time was founded on small enterprises, owned and manned largely by white colonists already established on the land. Their sugar mills were small and the cane they processed came from only a limited area. But sugar cane meant a substitute crop for livestock, which up to then had been about the only commercial product from Cuban land. Most important, it meant the plowing and cultivation of much land which previously had been used for grazing: in other words, the invasion of a new land-use pattern into the old haciendas.

A similar development took place with the introduction of tobacco raising in the seventeenth century. As Guerra points out, the tobacco fields grew up "within and at the expense of the communal haciendas" and thus constituted an additional factor in their dissolution.[20] This stage was in a sense a transitional one from the economy of the large livestock ranches to one of field cultivation in which tobacco and sugar cane were the chief crops. However, the growth was gradual, and the conditions of its development were such that a comparatively broad basis of land-ownership prevailed.

THE EXPANSION OF SUGAR PRODUCTION

The great social and economic upheavals of the eighteenth century incident to the application of steam power to industry, as well as the French and American revolutions, were destined to produce profound changes in the land-use and land-tenure patterns of Cuba. The application of steam power vastly increased the efficiency of the methods of processing sugar cane on the one hand, and, on the other, enlarged the area which a single mill could serve by introducing railroads to transport the cane, where hitherto the ox-team and cart had served. Moreover, relaxation of trade prohibitions on Cuba came during the reign of Carlos III of Spain. He was ready to make some concessions to Cuba in order to retain its loyalty, since it was apparent that the colonial empire was rapidly dwindling away. Thus new markets were opened which had hitherto been closed. In addition, the achievement of independence on the part of the Anglo-American colonies likewise freed those colonies from the imperial restrictions under which

[20] *Ibid.*, p. 51.

they had been held and immediately opened a considerable free market at Cuba's very door.

Yet, as is perfectly clear now to students of Cuban economic history, the decisive factor in sugar expansion at that time was the successful uprising of slaves in Haiti in 1789, which was precipitated by the revolution in France. The importance to Cuba lies in the fact that Haiti had been the chief supplier for Europe of two commodities—sugar and coffee—which French capital developed there on the basis of slave labor on its large plantations. Only the force of the French military power made possible the exploitation of so many people by so few. Once that power was withdrawn, the whole structure collapsed, and the enslaved blacks took control. During this uprising, the plantations and mills were destroyed. As a consequence of this sudden wiping-out of the main source of supply for the European market, prices rose rapidly. From 1790 to 1795 the price of sugar increased from 4 *reales* per pound to 28 and 30 *reales*.[21] It was likewise a golden age for coffee production, while the new American market also absorbed many other Cuban products, especially fruits and vegetables. Thus the area of cultivated land increased at a rapid pace. Forests were cut down to make way for planting crops. The free importation of slaves, which was now permitted, resulted in a rapid increase of the human population to be fed, along with the additional work animals required by the new use of the land. Consequently, much emphasis had to be given to the production of human food and livestock feed. It was, in short, a diversified agriculture which came into being, although the cash crops were mainly cane, coffee, and tobacco.

The demand for land for these purposes knew no bounds. The breakup of the communal livestock ranches was accelerated. According to Guerra, one of the large, new-type sugar mills now required 40 caballerías (about 1,426 acres) of land. However, enterprises of this magnitude were not usually latifundia, since cane was produced largely on individually owned lands. The flowering of the latifundium in its grand form was yet to arrive. Guerra summarizes the situation thus:

While the individual interest tended energetically to the dissolution

21 See H. E. Friedlaender, *Historia económica de Cuba* (Havana, 1944), p. 112.

of the communal haciendas and the division of large rural estates, the
Spanish state did not maintain itself aloof from this intense movement;
on the contrary, it stimulated and favored it with all its efforts in
several ways. In the first place, the general and extraordinary Cortes
of 1813, by decree of January 4 of the same year, ordered the reduction to individual property of all the uncultivated land (*terrenos
baldíos*) and crown lands (*realengos*), dividing part among the servants of the nation as a patriotic reward, part among the settlers who
did not own land and who asked for it, and setting aside the remainder
for sale on easy payments to retire the national debt. In the second
place, provisions were decreed to guarantee to proprietors the free
ownership of their land in perpetuity, resolving all doubtful questions
in regard to titles in favor of the possessor in good faith, and finally,
was approved, the consultative vote of the Court of Puerto Principe
(now the Province of Camagüey) of April 1, 1819, establishing an easy
procedure, rapid and economical, for the division of the haciendas,
subject to the encumbrances of the community. Thus, promoted by
individual interest and favored and vigorously pushed by the colonial
government, the two first decades of the Nineteenth century wit-
nessed the dissolution of numerous communal haciendas and the par-
tition of numerous latifundia, creating in Cuba, in those years when
the whole continent was in rebellion against Spain, the most numerous,
strong, well-to-do and enterprising class of rural proprietors, that we
have had up to the present . . .

If the material development brought an increase in the colored population, principally of slaves, to its highest point, it had not produced
a concentration of property, but accentuated the secular process of
division and multiplication of it. The Cuban agriculturist was strongly
established, and Cuba counted thousands of families solidly organized,
rooted in land which they owned, the cultivation and use of which they
directed personally; well-to-do people on the average, desirous of
progress, of political autonomy and of playing the preponderant role
in their country to which they were entitled by their culture, their
stability and their individual and collective value . . .[22]

THE RISE OF THE SUGAR LATIFUNDIA

The fifth phase in the evolution of Cuba's land-tenure pattern
began with the termination of the Napoleonic wars. The expansion
of sugar cane was stimulated by the various factors already mentioned, but until well after mid-century, it was achieved through

[22] Guerra y Sánchez, *Azúcar y población* . . ., pp. 58–59.

the establishment of new mills, rather than by enlargement of areas tributary to existing mills. These mills were still relatively small, although operated by steam.

The immense task of transporting cane to the mills by oxen, plus the additional new job of cutting down timber for fuel and carting it to the mills—also by oxen—automatically limited the area which could be served economically by a given mill. Guerra says that a single zafra required the cutting of entire forests for fuel. While the latifundium was not yet to come in all its glory, most of the factors necessary for it already existed, including a supply of slave labor, the steam-driven mills, and an abundance of good land suitable for cane.

One factor was absent—the railroad. Invented in England in 1826, it was introduced into Cuba on a limited scale some ten years later. However, its use by the sugar mills was not on an important scale until the end of the nineteenth century, owing primarily to the high cost of rails. But when the price of steel rails in the United States declined from $106 per ton in 1870 to $44 in 1878,[23] construction of railroads was greatly stimulated, not only for use by the mills themselves, but for the public as well. Then began very active competition among the mills for larger supplies of cane, and prices paid to the independent colonos advanced rapidly. In order to secure an adequate supply of cane for efficient operation of the larger and more efficient mills, the latter resorted to the acquisition of as much land in the neighborhood as they could obtain through purchase or otherwise. However, until after the War of Independence, automatic limits were set on this expansion by the restricted market and by the difficulty of securing adequate capital.

Nevertheless, while the sugar latifundia were still to expand and undergo internal modification as regards the organization of production, and while the small landowner and worker were to be pressed to new low levels of existence, the developments subsequent to 1900 were mainly the extension and elaboration of the forms which were fashioned in the social and economic matrix of the twenty-five-year period from 1870 to 1895. During this period, many technological advances were made in the industry, includ-

[23] *Ibid.*, p. 77.

ing the introduction of the railroad on a significant scale and improvements in the milling processes and in the general organization of the industry. These changes were impelled not only by the new inventions themselves, but by a need within the industry to reduce its costs of operation. Sugar prices were at low levels, averaging only about half as much as they had been from the period from 1820 to 1870.[24] Any profits therefore had to come as a result of further rationalization of the production process.

Throughout most of this period production fluctuated around 500,000 long tons per year, but during the five years from 1890 to 1895 it increased from 632,386 to 1,004,264 long tons.[25] There was therefore a great expansion in the land devoted to cane production, although the number of mills declined from 1,190 in 1877 to 207 in 1899.[26] Thus the way was prepared for the more dramatic expansion which came after 1900.

With the conclusion of the War of Independence, new conditions appeared. There was, on the one hand, the general period of prosperity which prevailed throughout the world and in which agricultural products shared. The first two decades of the twentieth century are frequently called the golden age of American agriculture, when farm prices compared most favorably with the prices in industry. There was an expanding market for food products and Cuban sugar was destined to share in it. In addition, the Platt Amendment which governed relations between the United States and Cuba granted the former the right to interfere in internal affairs of the new republic, which had the practical effect of assuring internal political stability. This relieved American capital of any fear based on political uncertainty for its investments in Cuba. Capital thus flowed generously into the island, chiefly from the United States but also from England, Spain, Canada, and other countries. Although production of sugar increased, the number of mills declined further from 207 mills in 1899 to 170 mills in 1915, thus indicating steady concentration. Since then the number of mills has remained rather stable, varying from 184 in 1926 to 173 in 1943.

[24] See Friedlaender, *op. cit.*, p. 545.
[25] Guerra y Sánchez, *Azúcar y población* . . ., p. 262.
[26] Friedlaender, *op. cit.*, p. 431.

After the rehabilitation of the industry following World War I, production rose until a peak of 5,812,000 short tons was reached in 1925. At the same time the acreage devoted to cane increased accordingly. In 1940 it was estimated that 2,285,000 acres were devoted to this crop, constituting 57 per cent of the total cultivated area.[27]

The revolution in land tenure occurred in the distribution of ownership of land. As we have noted previously, in order to be assured of an adequate supply of cane for the mills, sugar companies acquired land on an immense scale. With adequate capital at their command, companies and individuals purchased land in great quantities until, in 1925–26, it was reported that the centrales owned about 20 per cent of the total area of Cuba. Thus the comparatively numerous small proprietors of cane farms were largely, although not entirely, eliminated. Many of them sold their land but remained as sugar colonos who rented company-owned land. Those who retained ownership of their farms in the area tributary to the mill were nevertheless dependent upon the sugar company, which owned the railroads that transported their cane to the mill. That is to say, the colono was no longer in a position to choose among several mills as a market for his product, as had been the case in the days of the numerous small mills or *trapiches*. Competition among mills was practically eliminated. Some mills operated on a basis of 100 per cent "administration cane," that is, they had no independent colonos producing for them, either as renters or owners. For their labor supply, workers at low wages were imported from Haiti, Jamaica, and other Caribbean islands.

The organization of the industry passed largely from the hands of individual entrepreneurs to those of large corporations, many of which were foreign. Thus the Cuban-American Sugar Company owned six centrales with 14,867 caballerías[28] of land; the Cuba Cane Sugar Company, twelve centrales with 10,844 caballerías; the General Sugar Company and its dependents, nine centrales with 8,972 caballerías; and the United Fruit Company, two mills with 8,578 caballerías. These four companies own about 25 per

[27] Paul G. Minneman, "The Agriculture of Cuba," *Foreign Agriculture Bulletin No. 2*, U.S. Department of Agriculture, December 1942, p. 16.
[28] A caballería equals approximately 33.16 acres.

cent of the Cuban land in the hands of centrales.[29] American-owned mills account for about one-half of the production since World War I; in 1940, for 56 per cent.[30] Mill ownership by nationality in 1940 was as follows: [31]

United States	67
Cuba	55
Spain	33
Canada	10
Britain	4
France	3
Netherlands	2
Total	174

Friedlaender[32] points out that the transition of Cuba from the status of colony to national independence coincided with the latest phase in the development of economic capitalism, the features of which were mass production, financial concentration and combination with international ramifications, and colonial imperialism. Powerful groups in the form of trusts, cartels and pools, both vertical and horizontal, national and international, dominated the scene beginning with the 1880's and influenced the policies of governments.

With the end of the War of Independence, Cuba constituted a favorable environment in which this constellation of forces might and did operate. There was the rise of the large banking institutions, the great sugar centrales, the construction of the central railway, and electrical development; and with these, the rise of a wealthy class in the cities who built elaborate homes in the suburbs of Havana.

Evidences of wealth were notably confined to the limited class of entrepreneurs of these various establishments. The other side of the shield was not so bright. Many classes suffered loss while the new class was emerging with its immense gains. Ramiro Guerra[33] has indicated that with the expansion of the sugar lati-

[29] Guerra y Sánchez, *Azúcar y población* . . ., pp. 94–95.
[30] Minneman, "The Agriculture of Cuba," *Foreign Agriculture Bulletin No. 2*, p. 25.
[31] *Ibid.*, p. 25.
[32] H. E. Friedlaender, *op. cit.*, pp. 471 ff.
[33] Guerra y Sánchez, *Azúcar y población* . . ., pp. 99 ff.

fundia, made possible by the industrial application of steam and the extension of railroads to haul the cane, the peasants lost possession of their lands. The sugar companies purchased land from the peasants where the latter could show a title, but where titles were in question—as so many of them were—recourse was had to the courts. There can be no doubt that the contest in the courts was a one-sided affair in which the companies had the overwhelming advantage. They could employ the best lawyers who knew the loopholes in Cuban land laws. They could if necessary corrupt the officials, high and low, with bribes. Many colonos sold or otherwise lost ownership of the land, and as Friedlaender says, became tied by a "triple bond" to the mill: they were dependent upon it for land to rent, for the milling of the cane, and for credit.[34]

Another class of victims of the new order was that composed of the small sugar mill operators. Before the development of the railroads for hauling the cane, the area which could be served by a particular mill was limited by the relatively short distance over which it was feasible to transport cane by ox-cart. These small mills were made obsolescent not only by the railroads but by the new technical developments in milling sugar, involving new and more efficient machinery driven by steam power. Obviously, the small trapiches could not compete with the new and vastly more efficient ingenios, the large sugar mills. Thus the drastic decline in number of mills referred to above. In the meantime, while the number of mills was declining drastically, the sugar production of the island mounted steadily, reaching a peak of nearly six million tons during 1925—nearly six times the production reported in 1902.

The expansion brought new insecurity to the owners of rights in the communal haciendas. While such rights were not always of very great value in actual gain to the individual, they were recognized as legal, and large numbers of peasants enjoyed a measure of economic security in their pesos de posesión. But the demands for additional sugar lands brought about the sale and the consequent subdivision of most of the remaining haciendas. Thus a new group of landless farm people were created.

[34] Friedlaender, op. cit., p. 471.

THE ERA OF GOVERNMENT INTERVENTION

The significance of the inauguration of government controls over agriculture, as far as our present purpose is concerned, lies in the impact of these controls on the use and ownership of land. After the "dance of the millions" of the 1920's, when sugar production and profits reached an all-time high in Cuba, the sugar market was glutted and governmental intervention toward restriction of production began.

The first step was taken in 1926. At that time it became apparent to some of the mill owners and colonos that the frenzied expansion of sugar production had reached the point where serious difficulties could be foreseen if and when prices declined. The Verdeja Act passed on May 3, 1926, called for a 10 per cent reduction in the estimated crop of sugar for that crop year and provided further that, for the 1927 crop, total production should be limited to four and a half million tons and the grinding date delayed to January 1. Each mill received a quota roughly proportional to what it had expected to realize. These measures were partly responsible for a rise in sugar prices to a point above three cents in the early part of 1927. By 1928 it was clear that the world-wide expansion in sugar production, without corresponding reductions in other competitive areas as well as in Cuba, would result in a surplus and a disastrous reduction in price.

The Sugar Defense Act of October 4, 1927, provided for: (1) A National Sugar Defense Commission to advise the president to prepare annual estimates of the amount of Cuban sugar required in foreign countries and recommend the degree and character of restrictions to be imposed over the six-year period, and to attempt to negotiate agreements with other countries. (2) A sugar-export company, to which all mill owners would belong, which would control all sugar marketed outside the United States and Cuba and which would administer a system of production quotas. Under this act Cuba reached an agreement with Germany, Czechoslovakia, and Poland as to quotas and agreed to reduce its own crop in 1928 to four million tons.

The next significant step in the direction of government intervention was the development of the so-called Chadbourne Plan adopted by the Cuban Congress and promulgated on November

15, 1930. The essential features of the plan were: (1) The segregation of one and a half million tons of sugar to be turned over to a new sugar-export corporation and marketed outside of the United States and Cuba over a five-year period. (2) The segregated sugar was to be paid for at once by the issuance of up to $42,000,000 in bonds. The bond issue was secured in the first place by the sugar bought at $4 a bag; second, by a tax of 11 cents a bag on sugar produced in Cuba during the next five years or to the end of 1935; by a further tax of 50 cents a bag for the succeeding five years, if necessary; and finally, by the unconditional guarantee of the government. (3) A third feature was the authorization of the president of Cuba to fix the quantity of any Cuban crop provided there were international agreements between producers; to fix the quantity during five years at the request of 65 per cent of the mill owners who produced 65 per cent of the preceding crop; and to fix a quota for the United States irrespective of such prerequisites. Finally, until December 31, 1935, no sugar could be exported from Cuba without a permit from the export corporation issued in conformity with the law.[35]

These measures drastically influenced Cuban land use. In the first place, the earliest act, the Verdeja Act, forbade the further cutting down of virgin forests for the expansion of the cane fields. The unrestricted competition which characterized the expansion of the sugar industry in the period following World War I took no account of the public interest in respect to conservation of natural resources, particularly timber.

In the second place, reduction of the sugar cane acreage necessarily meant unemployment for thousands of people who were dependent upon the sugar industry for what little income they enjoyed. It led the government as well as farmers themselves to attempt to find alternative ways in which to use their land. Coffee growing, which had long been in a moribund state, was given a new lease on life by a high protective tariff. The high tariff act of 1927 also greatly stimulated production of dairy products, meat, poultry and eggs, and potatoes. But one of the most dramatic changes took place in coffee production. In 1925 Cuba imported

[35] For an excellent brief discussion of this period of governmental intervention, see *Problems of the New Cuba*, pp. 240–63.

12,972,000 kilos of coffee, but by 1933, the importation amounted to only 58,600 kilos. Although Cubans drink a great deal of coffee, their wants are now mostly supplied by domestic production and frequently there is some to export.

The depression of 1930 was a major disaster to Cuba because it had geared its whole economy to the sugar industry, which was in sore straits. Voices of agrarian reform were raised with increasing force and, in 1933, culminated in the revolution which unseated President Machado and brought new elements into control of Cuban politics.

On December 23, 1933, the government of Dr. Ramón Grau San Martín issued a significant decree which said in part:

The intense world crisis of overproduction has shown the necessity of regulating production in accord with consumption and has obliged the principal nations to substitute a policy of intervention and control, for that of free trade.

It is a purpose of this revolutionary government to practice measures that will tend to make prevail the general interests of the nation regardless of the advantages that private interests may have in disposing freely of the factors of production. The measures of restriction and control promise to serve as a pattern for reaching agreements of a world character, which will give our industry more stability.

This statement heralded the beginning of a long series of governmental actions which have profoundly modified the Cuban economy. For one thing, there was a renewed emphasis on measures to protect the small farmer and the worker. Renewed animus became evident toward the foreign landowners, especially the big ones. If some of the measures could be regarded as punitive from the standpoint of the *latifundistas,* it was but a comparatively mild expression of the profound passion of peasants to possess the land on which they work—a passion common to land workers the world over which in many times and many countries has flared in much more violent form.

The *Ley de Coordinación Azucarera de 1937* and the supplementary regulations set forth in minute detail the rights and obligations of the various producers and laborers and of the sugar mills. The distribution of production quotas, the price to be paid for grinding, the amount of rental to be paid for the use of the land, the wages to be paid for labor, and procedures for administration and arbitration are minutely set forth. The distribution of the product is defined not in terms of money but in terms of the yield of sugar. The law established a minimum wage of 80 cents (subsequently revised upward) per 8-hour day for wageworkers, but specified that the daily wages during the crop period should be the value of 50 pounds of sugar, polarization 96. The minimum wage becomes effective should the value of 50 pounds of sugar fall below it. Even during the "dead season," when the workers may be engaged in off-season activities, the same regulations apply. The price of sugar used is that of the last semimonthly average. Employers and workers of course may collectively agree to wages in excess of those established in this manner.[36]

The provisions of the act with respect to wage labor were effectively supported by an article in the Constitution of 1940 which forbids the importation of contract laborers (Article 76). Previously it was the common practice to import laborers from Haiti and Jamaica for the cane harvest at wages said to be less than the Cuban worker needed to support even his meager standard of living.

The rent paid for the use of land by the colonos is geared to the price of sugar, rising and declining with price changes. The price figure used in the computation is an average of the official average semimonthly prices for the calendar year as published by the Ministry of Agriculture for the particular port from which shipment is made. In other words, rent is paid in a share of the sugar rather than in cash. The system is somewhat complicated, but essentially it is as follows:

1. Land occupied by a colono is classified three ways. Area A consists of the area actually planted to cane; Area B is additional land equal to from 50 to 30 per cent of Area A, depending on the size of Area A. The larger Area A is, the smaller is the percentage used in computing Area B. Area C includes all other land in the colonia.

2. Rent for Area A land amounts to 5 per cent of the yield of

[36] For an excellent review of recent developments in the sugar industry see José Antonio Guerra y Debén, "La evolución económica-social de la indústria azucarera en los últimos años," in Ramiro Guerra y Sánchez, *Azúcar y población* . . ., pp. 281–315.

sugar obtained by the mill. For example, if the average acre yield of sugar cane was 20 tons and extraction amounted to 12.5 per cent, there would be 5,000 pounds of sugar, 5 per cent of which, or 250 pounds, would go for rent. It would represent a value, at 3 cents per pound, of $8.75.

3. Rent on Area B land depends on the price of sugar. If sugar is worth only one-half cent a pound the rental would be $10 per caballería. It advances $10 per caballería with each one-fourth cent per pound advance in the price of sugar. Lands which are irrigated pay a rent 50 per cent higher than do those which are not irrigated.

4. Rent on Area C land is determined in the same manner as for Area B. However, these rentals apply only if no contractual arrangement exists between the landowner and the colono.[37]

One important effect of the application of the law was the establishment of protective measures against exploitation of the cane growers and the laborers. It accomplished this end in various ways—for example, in the distribution of quotas to the "small planter" at the expense of the reduction of quotas for "administration cane." It provided that returns for each factor in the productive process—mill, renter, laborers, land—should be on the basis of the physical product and the price thereof, rather than in terms of money. It established machinery for handling complaints of either party to the contracts, and for reaching collective agreements. It also provided many other protective measures, including the definition of the rights of colonos as to the occupancy and use of any lands dedicated to sugar cane production. It would be difficult to overemphasize the importance of this provision, which greatly restricts the rights of ownership. Under this provision a colono cannot be evicted so long as he continues to produce his quota of sugar cane. Thus the farmer has in effect practically all of the advantages usually associated with ownership of land and at a rental which is nominal.

While the law also grants protection to the landowner, setting forth the conditions under which a tenant may be evicted—failure to practice good husbandry or to fulfill the other conditions of

[37] See *Ley de coordinación azucarera, con las modificaciones introducidas por ley de fecha 1 de febrero de 1938* (Havana: Cultural S.A., 1938). Chapters II and IV of the law and Chapter IV of the Regulations are particularly pertinent.

the contract—it is clear from reading the Regulations that the intent of those who framed the law was first of all to protect the tenant against arbitrary action on the part of the landowner.

The Constitution of 1940 went so far as to prohibit large landholdings. Article 90 if fully implemented definitely foreshadows the end of the large latifundia when it says:

Large landholdings are proscribed, and to do away with them, the maximum amount of land that each person or entity can have, for each kind of exploitation to which land is devoted, and bearing in mind the respective peculiarities, shall be specified by law.

The acquisition and possession of land by foreign persons and companies shall be restrictively limited by law, which shall provide measures tending to restore the land to Cubans.

WHAT OF THE FUTURE?

Thus in the long course of Cuban history the land that once was distributed widely among the inhabitants, either in the form of separate holdings or in the communal ranches, became concentrated in the twentieth century in the hands of a few. The rise of the sugar latifundia was the dominant factor in this transfer of landownership. In the formation of these large holdings the small proprietors were uprooted, and at the same time the agriculture of the country was committed more thoroughly to a monoculture of such vast importance that it dominated the entire economy. Instead of a country of small proprietorships, Cuba became a land of latifundia. Instead of a country of "family farms," it became a land the rural population of which is composed predominantly of renters and wageworkers. Instead of the relative security that flows from the production of diversified crops, there is the insecurity that comes from an economy geared to a single crop and a market dependent upon foreign consumption, a market chronically unable to absorb the immense production made possible by technological progress and improved management.

Today Cuba is trying to find an alternative to the speculative economy based on sugar. It is looking with nostalgia on its past, when its peasantry possessed the land and was attached to it by a sense of property in it. There seems to be a feeling of guilt that the large sugar plantation was ever allowed to develop. The latter is regarded by many—some of whom are most vociferous—as a monster which must be slain. That part of the animus is due to foreign ownership is very apparent. Even though foreign owners are increasingly restricted, the observer is led to wonder whether any attempt will ever be successful to subdivide the estates held by Cuban landlords. The latter are an important group and, while they may lend support to any program looking toward the elimination of the large foreign owner, they naturally will be less enthusiastic about seeing their own holdings broken up. Moreover, their influence over Cuban politics is such that they may very well be able successfully to oppose any movement threatening their own position.

A final comment may be in order. One observes in the discussion of the land question very little if any attention being given to the relative efficiency of the large versus the small holding. Small proprietorships, while representing an ancient ideal, are not to be regarded as an automatic guarantee of security and welfare in the modern world. In fact, the large sugar enterprises, because of superior efficiency and management, in all probability can be made to provide greater resources for the men who grow the cane than if they were divided into small holdings. The relative efficiency of the two systems ought to be given central consideration in the development of future land policies. It has been given very little attention in the past.

This does not mean that the writer is arguing for maintenance of the *status quo* in Cuba. What seems to be in order for the Cuban people is a less impassioned appraisal of their agricultural policy, with a view to making decisions on the basis of fact rather than fanaticism. The slogans and shibboleths associated with the big landowners, and with the demands of the peasants for land, while useful in the mouths of demagogues, are scarcely adequate grounds for overturning the whole economy. Cuba wants to improve the lot of the masses of its workers, not further to impoverish them. There is no magic land-policy formula that is going to bring about this objective. Only intelligent planning based upon careful factual study will contribute toward the goal.

This question of Cuban efficiency becomes more important as the efficiency of competing areas increases. Reference has already been made to Cuba's reliance upon foreign markets, particularly the United States. Sugar production in the United States, whether from sugar beets or cane, has had to rely on a protective tariff in order to compete with Cuba and other areas. However, technological improvements are being made in both the beet and cane areas of the United States which may conceivably wipe out the previous disparity in costs of production. Meanwhile, technical changes in Cuba are made very slowly, due to the opposition of the workers whose jobs are at stake. Therefore, unless it can be shown that breaking up the sugar estates is going to increase efficiency and thus keep the industry competitive with other sugar-producing areas, such a policy would only add to the difficulty of the problem.

This brief review has revealed the close dependence of Cuba upon influences outside her borders. The changes in the world market, the political fortunes or misfortunes of various parts of the world, the crises of war, the introduction of new technologies —the railroad, steam power, the tractor, and so forth—all have had a profound effect upon and have wrought changes in the land policies of the country. This can be said of any country, more or less, but it is particularly true of Cuba.

Cuba's way out is by no means clear. Feelings of national pride lead it to want freedom from economic dependence upon other countries. Its sugar market is overwhelmingly in the United States, and it is often in a weak bargaining position because of the threat or reality of surplus production. It has to compete with growers within the United States who enjoy the protection of a tariff, yet costs of production are becoming more nearly equal. Cuban workers are demanding more of a share in the product—and getting it. Yet in terms of natural endowments, in soil and climate, Cuba can scarcely be excelled as an optimum habitat for sugar cane. Were it not for the artificial trade restrictions imposed by various nations, Cuba might well be producing double or even triple the present output of sugar. There are thousands of square miles of land suitable to the production of cane which are now used for the raising of beef cattle.

From an economic standpoint it would seem desirable that Cuba produce more sugar, since it is so eminently fitted to do so, and buy other goods abroad. However, events of the past twenty years have turned Cubans' thoughts more and more in the direction of a policy of diversification and self-sufficiency. They realize that the ups and downs of the United States economy, its booms and busts, spell only instability for Cuba and misery for its people, especially if they adhere to a policy of extreme reliance upon one crop. It is this experience which has led to demands of the peasants for agrarian reform, for driving out the foreigner, for distributing the land among smaller holders, and for a national policy of partial food autarchy. The development of greater economic stability in the United States and the lowering of barriers to international trade throughout the world would change the outlook of the Cuban people. In other words, the people of the United States, in decisions which they make on these matters, directly affect the fortunes of the people of Cuba. The two countries are mutually dependent to a marked degree. Their problems should be dealt with as mutual problems.

CHAPTER VI

Land Division, Measurement, and Registration

In Chapter V only passing reference was made to the problem of land surveys. This very interesting problem is still a cause for complaint and unrest among Cuban farmers and landowners, as it has been throughout most of the history of the country. The present situation had its origin in two historical antecedents. The first was the introduction by the Spaniards of the system of land location by metes and bounds, that is, according to topographic features, natural objects, or even less specific descriptions. This system was not peculiar to the Spanish colonizers in the New World; it was the practice followed by the settlers in the Anglo-American colonies also. The method of location by metes and bounds seems to have started in the early days when land was abundant and no serious attempt was made to establish boundaries. E. T. Pichardo y Jiménez says in this connection:

In the first petitions and grants of land, save in rare exceptions, there was no determined size or shape. For example, a *sabana* would be requested in order to stock it with cattle, so many leagues distant to leeward or windward of this capital, or of any other place, at times with an error of 20 per 100 or more in the increase of the distance; there would be indicated also sometimes, vaguely, the locality in which there had been established a seat. The grant obtained, the concessionaire occupied more or less surface, which would be sufficient or even more than necessary for his cattle.[1]

Location by metes and bounds was enough in itself to cause endless trouble over land titles, but in Cuba there was the additional complication of the circular mercedes.[2] The circular figure is defended by Pichardo as being the most "natural, elemental, and easy, because the center, the seat of the hacienda, sufficed to determine the size and shape."[3] While he recognizes that there were many difficulties in surveying and in establishing titles where the circular form was involved, this was also true in Mexico, where the rectangle was used. The fault or evil was not in the form used but in the "errors in conception, and injustice of men."[4] Granting this defense made by Pichardo—and it was not without justification, considering conditions of the time—the disadvantages of the circular form were very serious.

In the first place, dividing the island into circles leaves awkward shapes in the interstitial areas which are extremely difficult to survey and describe. In the second place, the establishment of circular boundaries is also a complicated surveying problem. This difficulty was resolved in part by creating polygons with sixty-four or seventy-two sides, but even so, describing such a shape was no easy task. Moreover, there were many cases in which the circles overlapped. Checking of applications was not practical at the time, owing to the shortage of surveyors. While this failure to examine applications was not an evil inherent in the circular form, it probably was more likely to occur in such a system than in a rectangular one. In the latter case, the circumscribing lines are at least roughly indicated, while in the circular system, the seat or center is the only point of departure. It is therefore difficult to know where the circumference will fall without costly surveys, which were not possible at the time the grants were made. The usual practice seems to have been to take the word of the

---

[1] Pichardo y Jiménez, *Agrimensura legal de la isla de Cuba*, p. 272. The circular form, according to Pichardo, occurred first in reference to Santo Domingo (*Ley 5, tit.* XVII, *Libr.* IV. *Recopilación de leyes de Indias.*) In Mexico, and apparently in other Spanish colonies, the rectangular form was used.

[2] See Chapter V.

[3] Pichardo y Jiménez, *op. cit.*, pp. 272–73.

[4] *Ibid.*, p. 273.

applicant that his merced would not encroach upon anyone else. When such overlapping does occur, however, there is another irregular shape created which is difficult to survey and describe. Thus Cuba has inherited from these early systems of land division much uncertainty in land titles, costly surveys, and endless litigation among rival claimants to the same pieces of land.

THE PROBLEMS OF SUBDIVISION AND LAND DESCRIPTION

The problem became acute when the *haciendas comuneras* were subdivided. It was hard enough to determine the boundaries as among the original mercedes, but with the breakup of the haciendas into numerous smaller parcels, there arose the additional question of determining the boundaries among the various claimants. Needless to say, this could not be done by further use of the circular design. Instead, angular forms were resorted to—rectangles, triangles, trapezoids, and so forth. There was no systematic survey by astronomically determined lines; the matter was largely one of determining boundaries by any method that would give the claimants the proportionate share of the land which was indicated by their *pesos de posesión* or other evidence of ownership rights. Most of the resulting shapes were roughly rectangular, but inevitably many were irregular.

Perhaps it was the uncertainty of titles which grew out of these experiences that gave rise to the common Cuban practice of giving each farm a name. This name is registered and becomes part of the official description of the land. Most of the farmers along the main roads also have the name inscribed on or over the entrance to the farm. The following description is a sample of the current practice in describing land:

Rural estate known as "San Juan de la Malagueta" situated in the Municipal District of Puerto Padre, Judicial section of Holguin, Province of Oriente, Republic of Cuba, composed of twenty thousand two hundred and thirty hectares and thirty ares, bordering on the North with the sea; on the South with a road from Manati to Puerto Padre, which separates it from lands of Messrs. Antonio Balbuena and Indalecio Justo; on the East with Malagueta Bay and lands of Mr. Francisco Pla; and on the West with Canyon of the Bay of Manati and road to Malagueta, which separates it from property of Mr.

Gonzalez de Mendoza; said rural estate being registered in the Property Registry of Puerto Padre, on folio one hundred and eighty-two, of volume 17th of the Municipality of Puerto Padre, farm number three hundred fifty-five of Puerto Padre, formerly number one thousand and twenty-five of Holguin.

UNITS OF LAND MEASUREMENT IN CUBA

The Spaniards seem to have been unusually ingenious in inventing different units of land measurement. No fewer than a dozen such units are in use in Cuba alone, while other units not used in Cuba are standard in Puerto Rico and Santo Domingo. In addition to the numerous units of Spanish origin, the English lineal measurements of the foot, inch, and yard are frequently employed, as well as the metric system.

The most common unit of Cuban land measurement is the caballería. This unit appears to have had its origin in medieval times when conquered lands were divided among the knights who contributed to the reconquest of Spain from the Moors.[5] In Cuba, the size of the caballería is 33.1619 acres, but it varies with the country in which it is used, including Spain, Puerto Rico, and Santo Domingo. Although the caballería is universally used throughout the island, its size is such as to make it inconvenient for reporting small areas. For this purpose other units of measurement are employed, including the *caro*—which is one-tenth of a caballería or 3.32 acres; the *cordel*, which is about one-tenth of an acre; the *besana*, which is a little over six-tenths of an acre; and the *roza*, about 1.8 acres.[6] The caro is in general use in Oriente Province, the besana in Havana, while the cordel prevails in the other four provinces.

The metric units of are and hectare are official in Cuba, and land descriptions for official documents are always expressed in these terms. The government, however, in its census of 1931 used caballerías or fractions thereof in reporting size of farms, amounts of land devoted to various crops, and so on. The agricultural

[5] Luis J. Bustamente, *Encyclopedia popular cubana* (Havana: Cultural S.A., no date), Vol. I, p. 288.

[6] Exact magnitudes of these units in terms of acres are as follows: caballería, 33.1619; caro, 3.31619; besana, 0.63969; cordel, 0.102352; are, 0.02471; hectare, 2.471; roza, 1.7769.

census taken in 1946, however, used the hectare. In the case of urban property, the most generally used measurement is the *vara española*. It is about 2.78 feet in length, and its popularity is probably due to the fact that a seller can charge as much for a *vara* as he could for a yard or even a meter.[7]

HOW LAND TITLES ARE REGISTERED

Real property titles are recorded by registrars of property located in judicial districts. In the more populous districts there are several registrars. For example, there are ten registrars in the municipio of Havana, two in Cienfuegos, Camagüey, Remedios, Marianao, and Guantánamo, but only one in the smaller districts. The registrars are appointed by the President of the Republic from a list of three names submitted by the board of examiners appointed to examine the competitive candidates. These registrars are only quasi-public officials. Although their authority derives from the national executive and they are under the general supervision of the Ministry of Justice, they receive no salary from the public treasury. They derive their compensation from fees collected from those who have their property registered and seem to be free to charge whatever the traffic will bear. It is said that there have been cases of collusion between registrars and attorneys for property owners, whereby the registrar has noted some flaw in a property title and has called it to the attention of an attorney who thereby manages to have a suit instituted against the owner, the presumption being that the registrar will share with the attorney any fees collected for legal services.

The books of registry are not kept in a public vault but in the private office of the registrar. Theoretically they are open to public inspection, but in practice, some registrars at least charge a fee for the privilege of inspecting them. The appointment of the registrar is for life, and there are cases in which sons have succeeded their fathers in the position. It is said that several fortunes of considerable magnitude have been made by registrars, particularly during the rapid expansion of the sugar plantations, when money flowed freely and the acquisition of land and the quieting

[7] It is common practice in the stores of Havana to sell cloth by the vara instead of the yard or the meter.

of doubtful titles were matters of great urgency on the part of the land buyers. The latter were quite willing to allow handsome sums to registrars to make certain of favorable action.

The function of deciding the relative merits of two or more claimants to the same property resides in the courts. Once the decision of the court is handed down, the new boundaries if any have to be located by the surveyor, and the action of the court duly registered along with the title to the land.

Property rights may be lost by a careless owner through failing to keep squatters off his land. Spanish law, still in force in Cuba, allows that property which nominally belongs to another person but which is unfenced or otherwise undeveloped may be acquired by an individual who is able to occupy it without interruption for a period of thirty years. If the squatter has a partial title, that is to say, a defective title, occupancy of the land for a period of twenty years without interruption will suffice to make his title valid. Proof of occupancy without interruption must be made before the court by means of the testimony of neighbors, evidence of payment of taxes, and so on.

Unauthorized occupancy of property may, of course, be terminated by having the squatters dislodged. East of Cienfuegos, the writer saw a number of *desalojos* who had been evicted from privately owned property and had established themselves on the public highway. They had fenced off a portion of the highway at the side of the road, built their bohíos, and were subsisting there by whatever means they could. It is easy to see that fencing of property is very important in Cuba, since failure to do so is an invitation to squatters to take possession. On the other hand, if a fence exists, it is possible to prove illegal entry onto one's property.

The pattern of land division in Cuba is one common to countries without a cadastral survey based on lines of longitude and latitude. It is a pattern characterized by irregular shapes, now rectangular but at one time mostly of circular form. Farm boundaries, now fairly well established and described, are frequently marked by line fences, and, as remarked earlier, farms are universally given names. There is still need for a cadastral survey which will facilitate description of property and forestall further litigation. Even today the influence of the circular lines of the mercedes is noticeable as one flies over the island. Many of the boundaries of local townships and counties are made up in part of segments of circles. These arcs are especially noticeable in the province of Pinar del Río, but can be seen from the air in other parts as well.

CHAPTER VII

Systems of Farming

The way in which the agricultural enterprise is organized makes a great deal of difference in the social life of rural people. Where there is a small-farm economy, one kind of community life exists; where the latifundia prevail, there is quite a different kind. Usually both large and small farms occur side by side, although there are areas devoted exclusively to one or the other. For example, large parts of the provinces of Camagüey and Oriente are utilized either as sugar plantations or as livestock ranches. In other sections of the same provinces there are areas given over exclusively to the production of field crops, with farms comparatively small.

It is difficult to find satisfactory terms to designate these different systems of farming. The word "latifundium" is coming to have general acceptance for classifying the large farm on which most, if not all, of the work is done by hired labor, including the function of management. On the other hand, the term "family farm" is often used in the United States to characterize the small unit which is operated largely on the basis of land, labor, capital, and management provided by the family itself. The latifundium, however, seems to be too limited to include all the types of farm organization which are found in Cuba. For example, a tobacco *vega*, the land of which is owned by a company or an individual but which is operated by a number of share renters, partakes of the nature of the family farm as well as of the latifundium: while

114

it is operated in small rented units, the land is owned by an individual or company on whom the operator is in many ways dependent. It is the same with many *cafetales* (coffee farms) and even with sugar plantations. For this reason, the term "large-scale enterprises" can be better used than "latifundia" to refer to the large sugar plantations, the cafetales, the tobacco vegas, and the livestock ranches—some of which could justifiably be called latifundia, while others fall somewhere between that classification and the family farm. Of the large-scale enterprises, only those related to the production of sugar, coffee, tobacco, and livestock will be considered here, although those concerned with several other crops might as logically be included. For instance, there are Cuban dairy farms, pineapple plantations, and perhaps farms of other types which may rank as large-scale enterprises. However, the four types selected for discussion are the most important, and the others would not differ significantly from them in organization.

THE SUGAR PLANTATION

Since sugar is the most important crop in Cuba, the form in which the enterprise is organized affects the largest portion of the population. It is predominantly, although not entirely, organized on a large scale. In some sections there are numbers of small farmers who grow cane as a cash crop in a diversified farming program. This is true, for example, of the area near Central Arujo near Manguito, province of Matanzas. The mill is supplied by 353 small colonos; in 1946 it produced about 98,000 sacks of sugar of 325 pounds each. By contrast, Central Florida in Camagüey Province has only 41 colonos; its 1946 production amounted to 223,500 sacks of sugar. An idea of the number of small farmers in cane production can be gained from data on quotas. Under the quotas in force before World War II, 38 per cent of the colonos were permitted 10,000 *arrobas*[1] of cane or less, which would represent the production of fewer than seven acres on the average. Over half the colonos had quotas of under 20,000 arrobas, representing about fourteen acres.[2] In 1946, according to the national agricultural census, 47,028 of the 160,000 farms grew sugar cane, on

[1] An *arroba* is 25 pounds.
[2] *Censo de 1943*, p. 265.

29,121 of which it was the principal source of income. In other words, on about 18,000 farms it was a supplementary crop, and these were very probably relatively small farms.[3]

Almost a third of Cuban land is owned or controlled by sugar interests, and these interests are highly concentrated in a few hands. The importance of large-scale producers in this industry is indicated by the estimate that in 1945, 70 per cent of the colonos produced only about 10 per cent of the cane which was milled on the island.[4] Despite the large number of relatively small colonos, production is largely under the control of the central. This is true whether the colono is a renter of company-owned lands or is independent. Even the independent colono, who owns his land, depends upon the company to transport the cane to the mill over its own railroad, to grind the cane into sugar, and usually to lend him money to make his crop.[5]

The ingenio of slavery days. The present organization of sugar production has its roots in the latifundium of slavery days, a description of which is appropriate at this point. José García de Arboleya, in about 1850, took the pains to describe various types of farming in Cuba. The following is a translation of his description of an *ingenio*:

The ingenio is the most important type of farm in the island and the largest in amount of land cultivated. It is rather like a small village with larger jurisdictional limits than a country estate, by virtue of the numerous population, extensive buildings, and costly equipment employed in the making of sugar. Of course, the same cannot be said of all, since there are some quite humble, though among those of importance because of their extent and industrial advances.

The ingenios found in this class have generally a good *casa de vivienda,* which at times deserves the name of palace, with a chapel and oratory for celebrating mass; houses of the *mayoral* and the machinist; infirmary or hospital; kitchen; *casas de purga* (houses for draining); *casas de calderas* and *casas de trapiche* (houses for boiling and grinding the cane). All these buildings, set close to each other, form an extensive plaza which bears the name "batey." The principal *guard-*

---

[3] Casto Ferragút, *Lineamientos generales para una política agraria nacional* (Havana, 1948), p. 94.

[4] *Ibid.*

[5] The Bank of Colonos which recently began operation may in time supercede the sugar company as the main source of credit for the colono.

arrayas (lanes separating cane fields), which traverse the farm in different directions, lead to it; of these [lanes], the main one is that which leads to the *talanquera* or *tranquera,* the gateway in the outer wall. Somewhat separated from the batey are the bohíos or Negro quarters, arranged along streets that intersect at right angles like a small village. The bohíos are being replaced by the barracón, a huge parallelogram with as many rooms as slaves, whose windows look out on the inner patio: when the door of this sort of structure is locked, they [the slaves] remain in complete security during the hours of sleep. The barracón and the bohíos are usually of masonry. Further on is found the *tejar,* a large building with pottery ovens for the making of objects of this kind, also the shed for the pulp, the still, the smithy, carpenter's shop, stables, cowbarn, pigsty, and lime kilns.

The buildings most notable for their good and even beautiful construction are the *casa de vivienda* and the infirmary, and for their dimensions, the barracón (where there is one) and the *casa de purga;* the latter is rectangular and has two stories; the top is a framework of wood full of circular hollows (*furos*) in which are set the ovens (conical jars of clay or tin plate) for draining the juice: through a wall at the side, purposely left open, come and go the *gavetas,* large boxes on wheels in which the sugar is put to dry. There are *casas de purga* with more than 20,000 . . . [Then follows a detailed description of a *trapiche* and the process of extracting sugar from the cane.]

The territorial extent of the ingenios is great: rarely is one found with less than 10 caballerías of land. For 1,000 boxes of sugar or, otherwise, from 16,000 to 20,000 arrobas, six caballerías of cane are calculated as necessary, but an ingenio of such production needs from twenty to thirty [caballerías] of land, since cane on depleted lands (*tierras cansadas*) is produced only two or three years in succession, and they must be left fallow or put to the alternate cultivation of other plants, the method adopted advantageously by the leading *hacendados.* Besides, one finds adjoined to these farms a *potrero* and *sitio de labor* for cattle pasture and for planting vegetables, corn, and rice to take care of the feeding of the workmen. Also a banana plot is indispensable; it is ordinarily found near the batey to guard the fruit from the gluttony of the Negroes. On some ingenios there is a vegetable garden, flower gardens, and an orchard.

Besides his bohío or his cell in the barracón, each slave is assigned a small plot of ground (*corto pano de tierra*) where he may grow vegetables and raise chickens and pigs for his own use and utility. Sober and hard-working slaves often find freedom in the *conuco,* a name given to those small garden plots and places for poultry and hogs (*plantios* and *criaderos*), for whose care they may devote only hours of leisure. The extent of the large ingenios varies from 50 to 200 caballerías of land. The personnel of an ingenio consists of a mayoral, the only chief of the Negroes and director of the farm work: a mayordomo, in charge of bookkeeping and guardian of the *casa de purga* where the produce is stored; when the mill is steam-driven, a machinist and a second machinist are needed, and if the Negroes are numerous there is a physician-surgeon: if not, they have a *practicante* in charge of the medicine chest and they pay him so much a month, just as to a physician (*facultativo*) who makes daily visits to the farm and to others near-by. On some ingenios there is also an administrator and even a chaplain, and on all it is indispensable to have, during the zafra, two *maestros del azúcar,* at least, whose skill, acquired by practice, consists in determining the time and quantity of lime and water to be added to the caldrons (*pallas*) for purification, as well as the point of sirup (*el punto del alimvar*). The ingenios also have constantly employed an ox-herd, a potter, carpenter, armorer, or blacksmith.

An ingenio of 1,000 boxes needs from 90 to 100 Negroes of both sexes, but where modern machines and methods have been adopted, this force suffices to obtain double production. The Negroes have different duties, as cooks, guards (*guardieros*) or gatekeepers (*talanqueros*) (in charge of the entrances to the farm), stokers (*fogoneros*), wagoners (*carreteros*) and *contramayorales* or overseers of work crews, and executers of the punishments imposed by the *mayoral* upon delinquents. Those assigned to hoe, plant, and cut the cane and other tasks that are performed in large groups, are referred to under the collective name of "the men" (*la gente*).

The number of ingenios and trapiches in the whole island, which in 1827 was 1,000, rose in 1846 to 1,442, and currently exceeds 2,000. Calculating them at 20 caballerías each, they occupy an expanse of 40,000 caballerías of land. The principal sugar district is the jurisdiction of Cárdenas, which numbers 280 ingenios, among them those most important, and then Matanzas, which has over 170, again many of them of the first order.

The capital represented in the sugar industry is estimated as follows:

```
40,000 cabs. of land at $1,500..............$  60,000,000
90,000 Negroes (able-bodied) at $750......   67,750,000
30,000 Negroes (very young and aged)
   at $300 ..............................    9,000,000
```

Value of buildings........................ 30,000,000
Machinery, tools, and apparatus.......... 15,000,000

Total $181,500,000
Animals   3,500,000

Grand total ....$185,500,000[6]

In another table, García de Arboleya gives the name of each ingenio and its location, amount of land, production in *cajas*, and number of slaves. Only 23 mills, all in the Matanzas and Cardenas area, are given. On the basis of these figures, he calculates production at 23 boxes and 400 arrobas of cane per man. But in less modern mills than these, production was only 11 boxes and 190 arrobas per Negro.

The contemporary central. The differences between the ingenio of 1852—when this description by García de Arboleya was first printed—and the central of today are many, although some of them are superficial. The modern central is very much larger than the ingenio, even though García was impressed by their size of that time. Instead of the 10 to 200 caballerías (332 to 6,640 acres) which characterized the old ingenios, the centrals often own or control 1,350 caballerías (44,820 acres), and some of the larger ones, 6,000 or 7,000 caballerías.[7] The status of labor, of course, is also different. The labor force of the central is free; that of the ingenio was slave. The total labor force devoted to sugar production is much greater now than it was a century ago, if we may accept his estimate for 1852 as approximately accurate. Then the number of slaves was estimated at around 90,000. Today the number of workers at the peak of employment is estimated at over 500,000.[8]

The capital structure is vastly different today from what it was in the days of slavery. In the latter period, according to the estimates of García de Arboleya, over 40 per cent of the value of the capital invested in the sugar industry was in slaves. The subtrac-

[6] José García de Arboleya, *Manual de la isla de Cuba* (2d ed.; Havana, 1859), pp. 138–40. (First edition published in 1852.)

[7] See *Anuario azucarero de Cuba, 1945* (Havana: compiled and edited by Cuba Económica y Financiera), pp. 50ff.

[8] See *Censo de 1943*, p. 265.

tion of this item leaves the total at something like 110 million dollars, including the value of land, or $45,000 without the land and slaves. This latter figure may be compared with a valuation of 364 million dollars in 1939, as estimated by Ramiro Guerra.[9] If we add to Guerra's estimate the value of the land devoted to cane production, estimated in 1945 at one million hectares, we would have a total valuation of mills and land at approximately $500,000,000. This figure, then, would be roughly comparable to the valuation of $110,000,000 in 1852. But whereas in 1852 there were upward of 2,000 ingenios, in 1939 there were only 157 operating centrals. In other words, the average value of an ingenio in 1852 was about $55,000 not counting the value of the slaves, or $92,500 if slaves are included, while in 1939 the average value of a central and supporting land was 3.2 millions of dollars.

The colono. Another important difference, which came about with the freeing of the slaves and the centralization of the industry in few rather than many mills, was the introduction of a new tenure class, the colono. In the days of the small ingenios—that is, up to approximately 1875—the production of cane and the milling of it were in the hands of a single individual, the *hacendado.*[10] "Little by little," says Guerra, "in the decade of the 1880's the *'colonias de caña,'* the name by which came to be known the fields dedicated to producing the cane for the mills, increased year by year. The farmers or cultivators dedicated to this new agricultural enterprise were designated currently by the name 'colono.' By 'colono' is understood from that time in Cuba a person dedicated to the production of sugar cane to be sold to the mills."[11]

The appearance of the colono with the exit of slavery meant the division of labor, management, and risk, as between the growing of the cane and the processing of it into sugar. It meant the rise of an important new class of agricultural operators who, in the structure of the organization, stood between the central, which not only purchased the cane but usually owned most of the land on which it was grown, and the thousands of wageworkers who did the actual work of growing and delivering the cane.

[9] Guerra y Sánchez, *La indústria azucarera de Cuba* (Havana: Cultural S.A., 1940), p. 76.

[10] *Ibid.*, p. 98.

[11] *Ibid.*, p. 99.

However, not all of the cane is produced by colonos. The companies themselves—some more than others—produce what has come to be known as "administration cane," that is, cane produced under the direct management of the mill itself. The proportion of the total production which was classified as administration cane in 1944 was 9.6 per cent. In 1940 it was 15.5 per cent. The law governing the sugar industry in Cuba (*Ley de Coordinación Azucarera de 1937*) deliberately favors the colonos rather than the mill in distributing quotas, a fact which discouraged the companies from operating very much administration cane and created an incentive to distribute more of their land among colonos. Many centrals are now on a colono basis entirely.[12]

Living quarters. What has apparently changed least of all in the past century are the living arrangements of the people who make up the working and managerial population. True, there have been some minor rearrangements. The bateyes, as described by García de Arboleya, were those connected with the ingenio itself; apparently the bateyes attached to the cane fields, so common today, did not then exist. The *casa de vivienda*—"that at times deserves the name of palace"—is no longer occupied by the hacendado as a rule, but rather by the manager of the central. There are also many more buildings in the central batey of today than there were in the comparatively smaller ones of 1850. The central is vastly larger than the small mill of that early date; there are more machine shops, warehouses, and many more barracks for the industrial workers. In fact, the central batey now is inhabited almost entirely by the men who work in the mill itself, containing agricultural laborers only on those plantations that operate administration cane. The larger population of the present-day batey involves many more services of an economic and social character. There are stores, schools, recreation centers, and the like.

But the bohíos and the barracones, today as in the time of García de Arboleya, are the living quarters of the workers. Around

[12] One interesting consequence of the new law has been the creation of "agricultural companies," corporations separate from the mills themselves but with essentially the same officers and operating officials, which assume responsibility for managing the cane lands previously classed as "administration" but, under the new operating company, capable of being classified as colonia cane and therefore eligible for assignment of quotas.

the central batey, the typical bohíos with thatched roofs are not so common, most of the houses now being constructed of lumber with roofs of tile or zinc. But on the colonias, away from the central, the bateyes are predominantly made up of the thatch-roofed bohíos, for the families of the permanent laborers, and barracones, for the migratory workers who come in for the harvest.

Summary. The sugar latifundium in Cuba, then, is a very large enterprise representing an average investment of upward of three and one-half million dollars, controlled usually by a corporation rather than by an individual, with several thousand caballerías of land either owned by the mill or under lease contract. The workers are both industrial and agricultural, the former representing the labor force for the maintenance and operation of the sugar mill itself, the latter for the cultivation and harvesting of the cane. The ratio of industrial to agricultural workers is very much greater today than formerly. Both groups live in bateyes. The industrial workers live in the central batey, with few if any agricultural workers, the presence or absence of the latter depending on whether or not the central grows administration cane. Otherwise, the agricultural workers live on the colonias or fields of cane under the direction of a colono, or his representative, the mayoral. Thus there may be several bateyes on a given plantation.

A key figure in the production of sugar cane is the colono who more often than not is a renter of company-owned land, but who may be "independent" in the sense of owning his own land. In any case he is dependent upon the sugar company for credit, transportation of cane, and the processing of it. The rent he pays is determined by the sugar law of 1937, as amended, the same law which determines the rate of wages he must pay his workers.

THE CAFETAL

Another historic type of large-scale farm organization in Cuba is the cafetal. The area included in coffee plantations (841,750 acres) is comparatively large, although the amount actually planted to coffee trees is much less (220,000 acres).[13] Most of the coffee

---

[13] *Compilación estadística sobre café, 1938* (Havana: Bureau of Industries, Cuban Ministry of Agriculture, 1938) gives the estimate of total area in plantations. The harvested acreage is from the national census of 1946.

is grown in the higher elevations of the island, between 1,000 and 1,500 feet.[14] In order to thrive, the plant must have shade, frequently provided by banana or plantain trees when the coffee trees are young, and by various other types of natural forest trees. About 88 per cent of the coffee produced in Cuba is grown in Oriente Province, 10 per cent in Las Villas, and about 1.5 per cent in Pinar del Río.[15]

The early cafetales. It is not definitely known when the coffee plant was first brought to Cuba. The first recorded introduction was in 1748 when one Don José Gelabert brought some seeds from Haiti and planted them on his farm in Havana Province. However, his main purpose was the preparation of a drink from the fermentation of the berries, and he gave little or no attention to the care of the trees or the proper processing of the fruit.[16] That coffee was being grown in Cuba in 1767 is patent from the fact that on December 9 of that year the *intendente* (subtreasurer) of Cuba had written the king that "many hacendados had applied themselves to the planting of coffee for the supply of their own households."[17] Coffee was for many years, however, considered only as a medicine and was sold in the drugstores as a cure for the effects of intoxication, for drowsiness, and for headache.[18] In 1790 some 1,850 *quintals* (a quintal is about 200 pounds) were exported from Cuba, although there were only five or six cafetales in the island. At that time Haiti, among the West Indies, was the chief source of supply of coffee and sugar for the continent of Europe. As early as 1753 the production of coffee in Haiti amounted to 70,000 quintals, and in 1789 it rose to 662,000 quintals.

The uprising of the slaves in Haiti in 1791 with the consequent destruction of the cafetales, along with the sugar plantations, provided a new impetus to coffee growing in Cuba. The impetus came in two forms: the immigration of the French *cafetaleros,* refugees from their erstwhile slaves, and the opportunity to supply the French and European market, as Haiti could no longer do. Some

---

[14] P. G. Minneman, "The Agriculture of Cuba," p. 86.
[15] National Agricultural Census, 1946.
[16] Francisco Pérez de la Riva, *El Cafe* (Havana: Jesús Montero, 1944), p. 7.
[17] *Ibid.,* pp. 7–8.
[18] *Ibid.,* pp. 8, 21.

of the immigrants were able to escape with some goods and capital to facilitate their re-establishment in Cuba,[19] but most of them were without means and had to be assisted by the Cuban government. Most of the newcomers were able shortly to find employment on farms or as renters of the new farms which were rapidly coming into existence with the partitioning of the large *haciendas comuneras*.[20] Many of these new subdivisions were planted to coffee by the immigrants. In the eastern part of the island, there was considerable public domain which was made available to the immigrants as a means of increasing the white population there. Many of these farms were small; but there were also several rather large ones, and it is the latter which concern us here.

Again, as in the discussion of the sugar plantation, it seems appropriate to reproduce the description of a cafetal in slavery days as given by García de Arboleya:

After the ingenio, the cafetal is the most important farm in rural Cuba, at times excelling the former in amenities and beauty. Its size varies from 4 to 20 caballerías of land, which is not only dedicated to the cultivation of the coffee trees, but to rice, vegetables, fruits, and garden stuff that is sown between the coffee trees. The lanes between the coffee groves are lined with palms and leafy trees which form delightful and magnificent walks.

The cafetal also has its batey formed by the home of the owner, the storehouses, the drying plots, mills, and at times an infirmary. The drying plot (*secadero*) is a square area enclosed by a low wall and paved with concrete, where the harvested coffee is put in the sun to dry, an operation necessary in order to remove the hull without crushing it. This is accomplished in a hulling mill (*molino de pilar*) which is a large wooden wheel in a vertical position rotated by oxen or mules over a circular box or canal into which fall the grain and chaff. The mill is covered by a roof on eight forked poles, called the octagon, because of the number of its sides. From there the coffee passes to the blowing fan. This is a wooden box with two screens or sieves and a rotating axle with wings which blow out the chaff and the dust leaving the clean grain whose halves (*fracciones*) fall through the screens to the ground.

The employees of a cafetal are the administrator, the mayoral, and

[19] The first cafetal in Oriente Province was established by Don Manuel Gabia in 1799. See Pérez de la Riva, *op. cit.*, p. 143.
[20] See further discussion of *haciendas communeras* in Chapter V.

at times a doctor. The maximum slave population is about 100 Negroes, and D. Tranquilinio Sandalio Noda has calculated that a cafetal of 8 caballerías cultivates 200,000 trees that produce 2,500 arrobas annually.

In 1846 there were in all the island 1,670 cafetales, of which 1,013 were in the eastern part. In 1827 there were 2,067 in all the island, with 1,239 in the eastern part . . .

The cafetales represent today [1859], without counting the value of the trees, a capital of $40,000,000 approximately.

10,000 caballerías at $1,500	$15,000,000
15,000 able-bodied slaves at $750	11,250,000
6,000 other Negroes, too old or too young, at $300	1,800,000
Buildings, machinery, and tools	12,000,000
Total	$40,050,000 [21]

Another description of a cafetal of this early period is quoted by Pérez de la Riva from Cirilo Villaverde's *Excursion a Vuelta Abajo,* published in Havana in 1891. The site of this cafetal is in Pinar del Río Province near Artemisa.

The principal house or *casa de vivienda,* as it is called in the country, a magnificent work of art, looks like a Greek temple; located at the end of a long avenue of palm trees, which resemble Doric columns of whitest marble, in eight parallel rows. The factory faces to the South; to the North of it are seen the drying floors in great number, the warehouses, mills, etc., and to the right of these the barracones, or better, the village of the slaves surrounded by a high iron fence with its door of iron in proportion, which is closed and opened at certain hours of the day and the night; to the left was another building whose use I do not recall; and between the drying floors and the barracones is one like a huge furnace that serves as a kitchen.

Still further to the North, that is, beyond the warehouses, is found the hospital, a spacious building, well ventilated and divided into two parts, one for the men and one for the women. In front are two large gardens of aromatic plants. At the right of these, in the center of an extensive batey, is seen a tower, that, we were told, serves as a prison, and to the left of it two large granaries on forked poles. Beyond the hospital, on the right hand of a field lane that runs northward, are some corrals for fattening livestock, principally hogs and sheep; and at the left is an ingenious machine, whose only power was water

[21] García de Arboleya, *op. cit.,* pp. 141–42.

brought by canal from Cayajabos, two leagues and more distant from there. All these factories are very well placed, conveniently separated, some from others, spacious, commodious, and many of them even adorned luxuriously.

At the end of them, continuing the same direction from the North, was a small cemetery, surrounded by a wall of stone, planted with some cypresses and pines; enclosing two sepulchers raised perhaps a yard and a half above the ground, made from a white hard stone from the abundant quarries in the flatlands; the one contained the mortal remains of the first owner of the farm, and the other those of a sister or relative of his.[22]

Pérez de la Riva goes on to explain that there is a great difference between the cemeteries of the cafetal and those of the ingenio. That of the ingenio was an abandoned spot in the center of some pasture, fenced with a wall of stone, a wooden cross in its center constituting the only adornment. The remains of the slaves buried there were covered only by earth, without a name, a marker, or a cross to record the place where they were interred. On the cafetal, the cemeteries were well cared for, and not only were sepulchers provided for the slaves but also at times for the owners themselves, whose simple tombs, in ruins, can be seen even now.[23] He attributes the fact that owners were sometimes buried on the cafetales, rather than in the cemeteries of the towns and cities, to the condition of the French immigrants, who often lacked the resources to buy a vault in the church and therefore buried their dead on their own cafetales. Or, he speculates, it may have been that the French coffee planters were so tied by sentiment to their farms that they desired to repose on them after death. Moreover, some of the cafetales were in the hills, rather distant from customary burial places, and it was not easy to transport a body from those isolated places to the cemetery.

It is quite clear that many of the cafetales were large, self-contained units, with populations running well up toward those of small villages. Pérez de la Riva gives a list of about 50 cafetales in Pinar del Río which apparently existed about the middle of the nineteenth century, although the date is not explicitly given. The number of slaves varied from 1 to 190, the acreage from 33 to 825,

[22] Pérez de la Riva, *op. cit.*, pp. 136–37.
[23] *Ibid.*, p. 137.

and the number of houses from 2 to 15.[24] In another list for 1807 for "the Oriental Province," he gives only the number of *peónes*— incidentally, a word rarely if ever used in Cuba today. These varied in number among the cafetales from 1 to 2 up to 121.[25]

Social life was rather well developed and comparatively rich and varied. The coffee planters as a class were people of refinement and culture, according to Pérez de la Riva. They brought over musicians, artists, architects and sculptors from Europe, especially France. They maintained libraries and encouraged the arts. They introduced the latest Parisian dress styles, held balls and fiestas, introducing such dances as the minuet, which the slaves incorporated into their own native dances. French schoolteachers came to the island and established schools, while the architects and artists brought new designs in house construction and decoration.[26]

The contemporary cafetal. The cafetal of present-day Cuba is a far cry from that of former days. It is no longer the site of palatial residences adorned with sculpture and other works of art and characterized by "gracious living." The slaves are no more, and in their places are the *partidarios* (share renters) and the *arrendatarios* (cash renters), and some proprietors. Most of the coffee land is owned by persons who do not operate it. Since coffee requires expensive processing before it is ready for the market, the cafetal usually has a processing plant which handles the product brought in from the various units under rent. The plant is operated by the landowner. In this respect, the cafetal is somewhat similar to the sugar plantation, in that the person who grows the coffee is dependent upon the owner of the processing plant to prepare the product for market. It is particularly true of the "washed coffee," which, when treated in the old traditional fashion, requires considerable equipment that would be beyond the means of the small renter.

The extent of concentration of landownership in the case of

---

[24] Pérez de la Riva, *op. cit.*, pp. 141–42. The number of houses is not proportional to the number of people. For example, on the cafetal with 190 slaves there were 5 houses, while another with 14 slaves had 15 houses. It should be borne in mind that *casas* referred not to the dwellings of the slaves, who lived in barracones, but rather to the buildings used for various purposes connected with the processing and storing of coffee. The home of the owner was called the *casa de vivienda*.

[25] *Ibid.*, pp. 143–45.

[26] *Ibid.*, pp. 117–48.

coffee is not known. It probably has changed little since the days of slavery. Of 19,721 farms reporting some coffee production in the census of 1946, there were 9,331 on which it was the major source of income. In the Cienfuegos-Trinidad area, for example, the Castaño interests own hundreds of square miles of coffee land. At San Blas in the same general area is the cafetal "El Infierno" containing 2,600 acres, rented to 32 families. At Ti-Arriba in Oriente Province, most of the land in coffee is owned by one man (some 2,200 acres). However, there are also many small proprietors in the coffee industry, and the spirit of recent discussion and legislation, including the Constitution of 1940, suggests that the number of small owners may increase, not only in coffee but in other crops as well. Also, the laws of inheritance have their influence. For example, in San Blas a cafetal of 1,650 acres has recently been divided among twelve heirs and is no longer operated as a single farm.

The picking of the coffee is done by family labor, supplemented on large farms by migratory labor at harvest time. At El Nicho in the Cienfuegos-Trinidad section, the migratory workers come in from as far away as Pinar del Río, although most of them are from Cienfuegos, Cumanayagua, and other near-by towns and cities. They work in gangs, moving from one farm to another. The same workers return to the area year after year. They bring their hammocks and hang them in a bohío which the farmer has built to serve as their barracks. They receive their meals at the family table. They are paid on a piece-rate basis, 26⅔ cents per lata (a lata holds about 28 pounds). Daily earnings will vary with the condition of the crop—that is, whether the berries are abundant or not—but will probably average about $1.75.

The coffee trees need but little attention after they have become established in suitable shade. They bloom in the winter months from December to May, depending on climatic and altitude differences. In the Cienfuegos-Trinidad area the trees bloom from January to May, and the harvest comes in September, October, November, and December. There are therefore only two or three months of great activity. During the balance of the year the people grow vegetables, maize, and rice, where land is available, and keep the weeds out from among the coffee trees. It is a time when there is little to do. In this respect coffee resembles sugar production.

The coffee farmers are the most isolated in Cuba. Their bohíos are built on the separate tracts, which they rent or own, and are scattered throughout the mountainous areas in locations which seem to an outsider almost inaccessible. Indeed, their homes are reached only by horse or mule or on foot, over trails that are almost impassable during the rainy season. One wonders how the cement for the floors of the houses (and cement floors are not infrequent in the coffee area), the furniture, and other supplies could have been transported to such out-of-the-way places.

Some of the existing plantations have been developed at little cost to the landowners by a system which enables him to exploit the labor of, and transfer much of the risk to, his tenants. The manner in which this scheme works was described by one informant as follows:

The owner of the land turns over some woodland to the coffee colono for a period of eight years; the improvements the tenant makes on the place accrue to the owner at the termination of this period. The only benefit derived by the colono consists of three harvest gatherings—two average and one good. Inasmuch as the coffee trees require from four to five years to come to bearing, the colono meanwhile leads a miserable life, and any money he may have is invested in sustenance. On expiration of the eight years, the owner, if he desires, draws up a new contract which provides that the colono, in the capacity of partidario, has to turn over 33 or 40 per cent of the crop as rental.

The same informant had this to say about the problems of the small proprietor:

The owner-operator has also been the victim of exploitation by wholesale grocers, who customarily finance the crop—true usurers, for after charging an enormous amount of interest (20 per cent) they demand as guarantee to their capital the transferance of the property to the name of the wholesale grocer or to a person of his confidence. Furthermore, the wholesale grocer obliges the farmer to buy from him the food and supplies he needs, which he sells at a high price. In all these instances, business becomes so difficult for many coffee growers that they finally lose the ranch for insignificant amounts. In the case of the partidario or arrendatario, these moneylenders remain with the harvest gatherings as they draw up documents for amounts that cover double the amount loaned.

Coffee plantations, it may be said in conclusion, while often owned in large tracts, are operated in small units by renters. The renters are dependent on the landowner not only for the use of the land, but also for processing the coffee in preparation for market, and often for transporting it by truck to the market center.

THE TOBACCO VEGA

About 160,000 acres were devoted to the growing of tobacco in Cuba in 1945.[27] In the same year, 22,750 tobacco farmers were reported. The average tobacco acreage per farm was therefore only about eight acres, which can hardly be characterized as large-scale agriculture. However, there are today, as there always have been, a number of large plantations, although the exact number is not available. The number of farms and the total area devoted to tobacco reported by the National Tobacco Commission (obviously using a different definition of "farm" from that employed by the census) for the different regions, indicated average tobacco acreage per farm for these areas as follows:[28] Vuelta Abajo, 27 acres; Semi-Vuelta, 17 acres; Partido, 6¼ acres; Remedios, 39½ acres; and Oriente, 9 acres. The first two regions mentioned are located in Pinar del Río, Partido is in Havana Province, Remedios in Las Villas, and Oriente is in Oriente Province.

In the transition from slave to free labor, the tobacco planters developed the sharecropper system, which is comparable in many respects to the system of the cotton plantations in the United States. However, the partidario system, as it is called in Cuba, involves somewhat more responsibility and capital on the part of the renter than does the sharecropper system in the United States. Usually the tobacco partidario owns his own oxen, other livestock, and farm equipment, and, of course, is responsible for doing the hand labor necessary in growing the crop. As is true in the cotton sharecropper system in the United States, the company

[27] National Agricultural Census, 1946.
[28] *Diario de la Marina*, January 27, 1946. Statistics from the *Comisión Nacional de Propaganda y Defensa del Tobaco Habano*.

furnishes the land and the dwelling-house, for which no rent is charged.

Some of the features of the organization of the tobacco-growing industry may be illustrated by a description of one of the large operating companies in Pinar del Río, the Cuban Land and Leaf Tobacco Company. It is an American-owned company with extensive holdings in the Vuelta Abajo region. Both shade and sun tobacco are grown.[29] There are a total of 81 partidarios, 19 of them growing shade tobacco and 62 sun tobacco. In addition, there are 3,300 wageworkers composed, in part, of members of the families of the partidarios. The contract between the company and the partidarios is different with respect to shade and sun tobacco. For shade tobacco, the crop is divided on a 50 per cent basis, as are also the following expenses: chemical fertilizer, cheesecloth, cost of fire curing (both labor and material), and the cost of grading the tobacco. The company provides manure free to the shade partidarios and also advances credit for the payment of wages without charging interest.

In the case of the partidarios growing sun tobacco, the company receives one-fourth of the crop but the partidarios must pay all of the costs of the chemical fertilizer, three-fourths of the manure fertilizer, and three-fourths of the cost of grading the tobacco. The company furnishes free to all of the partidarios, without additional charges, land, dwelling-house, tobacco barns, irrigation water, and medical care. A doctor is on duty every forenoon in the clinic which the company maintains, and, in addition, a male nurse is available at all times at company expense. For the wageworkers, a dwelling-house is provided, rent free, as well as a piece of land for growing vegetables, water for domestic purposes, and medical care, as with the partidarios. Contracts are written, each one being an original typewritten copy executed by a notary.

A variation in some respects is found in another large farm located near San Luis in Pinar del Río. Finca El Corojo contains 1,000 acres, about 250 of which are planted to shade tobacco. About half of the tobacco is operated by the proprietor (referred

---

[29] Shade tobacco refers to tobacco grown under artificial shade produced by means of cheesecloth spread over a supporting framework of poles. Sun tobacco is that which is grown in the open field.

to as administration tobacco) and the balance is rented to 18 partidarios. In this case, the renter pays 30 per cent of the crop, for which the owner furnishes land and dwelling (including repairs and maintenance), irrigation water, water pipes, and allows the partidarios to use the remaining 750 acres of the estate for growing vegetables, corn, or other field crops, and for grazing their oxen, milk cows, and hogs.[30] The owner also advances credit to the partidarios for current living and operating expenses, for which the interest rate is 8 per cent per annum; but in practice the partidarios pay the full 8 per cent even though the debt be liquidated after a few months. The partidario has to meet practically all the expenses of making the crop, in addition to providing his own farm implements, oxen, and so forth, paying for chemical fertilizer, the tobacco plants, cheesecloth, poles, and all the hired labor. No medical facilities are provided by the owner, though he will lend money for the purpose at the usual rate of interest. There are about 500 wageworkers on this vega, and the usual wages are $2.36 per day. They have about nine months of employment during the year.

On both the Cuban Land Company vega and El Corojo there appears to be very little mobility of the farmers. The proprietor of El Corojo said that the same families are on the place now who were there thirty-one years ago when he purchased it. When a father dies, one or more of his sons will take over the operation of the tract. The manager of the Cuban Land Company pursues a similar policy and has very few replacements, except in case of the death of a family head where there are no sons old enough to carry on. Sometimes under such circumstances the widow is able to take over active management of the farm.

In the Remedios section, in addition to partidarios, there are also *cuartarios* and *tercedarios*. The cuartario in this case rents the land from the absentee owner, and in addition to operating part of it himself, subrents to partidarios who do the hand work on their area but who have no equipment and no livestock. In this case, the partidario is practically identical with the share-

[30] The manager of the vega reported that the wageworkers, instead of growing vegetables on this land, plant tobacco and sell it to the company. Thus they derive an additional income of some $60 to $300 a year.

cropper of the cotton plantation. He receives 50 per cent of the crop and provides only the hand labor; he is essentially a farm laborer who is paid in kind. The cuartario furnishes a place for the partidario to sleep and provides board as well; which, of course, is not true of the cotton sharecropper. The partidario pays half of the cost of the seedlings. He is typically a single man from twenty to thirty years of age and lives on the farm the year round. In this same general area, there are also vegas on which the operators are cash renters.

LIVESTOCK RANCHES

Another form of large-scale operation in Cuba is the livestock ranch. There are two main classes—those that produce beef cattle only, and those that combine beef and milk production. They are located largely in the eastern provinces. An example of the first type is Finca Ceiba, located near Holguín. This ranch, consisting of about 1,000 acres, is owned by the Infante family, which is reputed to have fifty other farms in the area containing in the aggregate from 450 to 500 thousand acres on which they keep about 80,000 head of cattle. Finca Ceiba is in charge of a *mayoral* who owns a small plot of land adjacent to it on which he produces some vegetables and fruit for his own use. In addition, there is one other worker employed permanently on the ranch. During the busy seasons three or four additional workers are hired. In the dry season there are about 300 head of cattle on the place; in the spring, after the pasture improves, however, the farm will support 500 head. As the pasture begins to dry up in the fall, 200 calves are taken off the ranch and moved to another one belonging to the same company, where they are fattened for the market. This farm is used, therefore, only as a breeding place. The cattle are crossbred from *criollo* (native) and Puerto Rican stock.

The dual-purpose livestock farm—one used for both beef and milk production—may be illustrated by a finca in the neighborhood of Sancti-Spíritus. It contains about 2,200 acres and is operated by a man and his four sons. About 200 acres are subrented to tobacco partidarios. There are about 500 head of cattle on the ranch, 240 of which they were milking in the month of May. They sell about 35,000 liters of milk a month and their average monthly check from the condensed milk factory is from $1,000 to $1,500. In addition, they sell beef cattle from which they derive about as much annually as they do from the sale of milk. Besides the four sons, there are three hired laborers. Cows are milked only once a day, from 3:30 to 5:30 A.M. The average production per cow in the springtime is four liters daily and during the rest of the year only two. Characteristic of these ranches is the small amount of labor required per unit of area and the comparative isolation of the family.

FAMILY FARMS

According to the agricultural census of 1946, nearly two-fifths of the farms of Cuba were under 25 acres in size.[31] An additional 30 per cent fell in the category from 25 to 62 acres. In other words, nearly three-fourths of the operated units were in small tracts, although the total area in these farms comprised but 11 per cent of all land in farms.

A family farm is taken to mean a tract of land, used for the production of crops and livestock, on which a family resides, has responsibility for its management, and provides most of the labor requirements. It is clear from the figures cited above and those in Table 12, that the overwhelming proportion of Cuba's farms would be included under this definition. Further reference to Table 12 reveals these important facts: (1) only a little more than one-fourth of all farms employed wageworkers; (2) only after the farm size approached 200 acres did more than half of them report hiring additional labor; and (3) that nearly three-fourths of all farms—those of under 62 acres—accounted for only about 2.5 per cent of all wage labor employed.

The small farms occur in all type-of-farming areas of the country. In the areas adjacent to the cities there are dairy and truck farms supplying the city markets, along with small units producing tobacco, coffee, sugar cane, and diversified crops. About 60 per cent of the farms covered by the Special Surveys of 1946 were under 100 acres, the modal group being from 50 to 99 acres (Table 13). Even in the case of sugar cane, where large enterprises are common, small farms were an important proportion of the total.

---

[31] The definition of farm used in the census applied to any parcel or parcels of land operated as an agricultural unit, whether by the owner, renter, subrenter, manager, or others.

Size of Farm in Acres	Total Farms		Number Reporting Wage Labor		Permanent Workers		Temporary Workers		Average Number of Workers Per Farm*
	Number	Per Cent	Number	Per Cent	Number	Per Cent	Number	Per Cent	
Total	*159,958*	*100.0*	*42,893*	*26.8*	*53,693*	*100.0*	*423,690*	*100.0*	*3.0*
Under 25	62,500	39.0	6,489	10.4	1,391	2.6	18,887	4.5	0.3
25–62	48,778	30.5	11,562	23.7	4,612	8.6	41,345	9.8	0.9
63–124	23,901	14.9	9,168	38.4	5,719	10.6	44,674	10.5	2.1
125–187	8,157	5.1	4,053	49.7	3,741	7.0	29,444	6.9	4.1
188–248	3,853	2.4	2,200	57.1	3,216	6.0	20,809	4.9	6.2
249–1,235	10,433	6.5	7,450	71.4	19,322	36.0	148,274	35.0	16.1
1,236–2,470	1,442	0.9	1,222	84.7	6,539	12.2	59,334	14.0	45.7
2,471–24,700	780	0.5	659	84.5	5,766	10.7	52,356	12.4	74.5
24,701 or more	114	...†	90	78.9	3,387	6.3	8,567	2.0	104.9

SOURCE: National Agricultural Census, 1946.
*Includes both temporary and permanent.
†Less than 0.1 per cent.

TABLE 18. SIZE OF FARM UNIT BY TYPE OF FARMING IN SURVEYED AREAS, 1946

Size of Farm in Acres*	Total Farms		Tobacco		Coffee		Sugar Cane		Dairying		Diversified	
	Number	Per Cent	Number	Per Cent	Number	Per Cent	Number	Per Cent	Number	Per Cent	Number	Per Cent
Total	*724*	*100.0*	*159*	*100.0*	*111*	*100.0*	*141*	*100.0*	*165*	*100.0*	*148*	*100.0*
Under 16.5	76	10.5	25	15.7	10	9.0	22	15.6	2	1.2	17	11.5
16.5–49	174	24.0	51	32.1	27	24.3	15	10.6	13	7.9	68	45.9
50–99	199	27.5	66	41.6	39	35.2	23	16.3	34	20.6	37	25.0
100–164	96	13.3	12	7.5	22	19.8	16	11.4	29	17.6	17	11.5
165–329	77	10.6	4	2.5	8	7.2	10	7.1	50	30.3	5	3.4
330–659	41	5.7	0	0.0	4	3.6	22	15.6	14	8.5	1	0.7
660–1,655	28	3.9	1	0.6	0	0.0	6	4.3	20	12.1	1	0.7
1,656 and over	33	4.5	0	0.0	1	0.9	27	19.1	3	1.8	2	1.3

SOURCE: Special Surveys. See Appendix A for brief description of areas.
*Acres are approximate; original data were in caballerias.

135

Information is not available to give more than a general idea of the economic organization of the Cuban family farm.[32] It can be said at the outset, however, that modern equipment is scarce and that primary reliance is upon hand labor. There are very few tractors in Cuba, and those few are on the large farms. The main source of farm power is the ox. There are many horses in Cuba, but they are used almost exclusively for riding and for light transport. The most common vehicle for transport on the farm is the two-wheeled cart. Even so, this is a possession found on but a small proportion of farms. Of the 742 families—including 176 wageworkers—covered in the Special Surveys, there were 193 who reported owning small carts (*carretones*) and 119 large carts (*carretas*). Such carts, of course, are not needed on the coffee farms, and only to a minor degree in tobacco production and in the dairy sections.

Tillage implements commonly found on Cuban farms are the plow, the harrow, and occasionally cultivators. Plows of two main types predominate; one is home-made from a forked tree, the other the factory-made walking plow. These are about equally common. A few farmers possess disc plows. Among the usual hand implements are the shovel, pick, hoe, ax, and crowbar. The implement most nearly universally possessed and used is the machete. Almost every male adult in the farming sections carries a machete in a leather scabbard hung from the belt. It is not only used in such harvesting operations as cane cutting, but is even substituted for the hoe in weeding. The dexterity with which this implement is used is wonderful to see. The art of using it is learned in early youth, when the farm boy may become the possessor of a small-sized machete which he proudly dangles from his belt like the adults.

The moderate climate makes elaborate investment in barns and outbuildings unnecessary as a rule. One notable exception is in tobacco growing. Here several buildings are needed for storing and curing. Another exception is in the intensive dairy section near Havana, where it is not uncommon to find the dairy barn

[32] R. L. Tuthill has provided a detailed description of an owner-operated family farm of about 42 acres in Havana Province. See "An Independent Farm in Cuba," *Economic Geography*, XXV, No. 3 (July 1949), pp. 201–10.

equipped with stanchions, cement floors, milking machines, and other modern equipment. As a rule, however, the barn is little more than a shed, open on the sides, since there is no need to provide protection from cold.

Thus the total capital investment in the family farm may be very small by North American standards. Most of the work on a small tract is done by hand labor by members of the family. The work in the fields is done almost exclusively by men. Families are large on the average, and there are few opportunities for jobs off the farms. It is not uncommon to see several men engaged in doing a farm task—planting, harvesting, or cultivating—which with modern implements would be performed by one person, and in a fraction of the time now employed. But until and unless Cuba can develop alternate opportunities for employment of its manpower outside of agriculture, mechanization would create more problems than it would solve. Most of its family farms, therefore, will continue to be little more than subsistence farms, with seasonal unemployment and chronic underemployment.

In conclusion, it may be said that the rural life of Cuba is conditioned by the systems of farming which have prevailed in the past and which exist at the present time. From an economy that rested upon the institution of slavery, the agriculture as at present constituted has emerged in comparatively recent years.[33] Large-scale agriculture, which began under slavery conditions and centered about the production of sugar, coffee, and tobacco, exists in modified and expanded form at the present time. The most important type of farm is the sugar plantation, involving as it does over half of the cultivated land and the agricultural labor of the island. It is characterized in modern times by the large number of people dependent upon wages, who have no rights of ownership in the land and who are subject to long periods of unemployment.

This is true not only of sugar but of coffee production as well, although the number of workers involved in coffee is relatively small. In coffee and tobacco, the operating units are relatively small and as a rule many of the laborers are not wageworkers but

[33] Slavery survived in Cuba for perhaps twenty years after it was eliminated in the United States, although on a small scale.

share or cash tenants. The large livestock ranches need very little labor in proportion to the large areas operated. The small family farms, on which the work is done by the family itself with only occasional hired help, are numerically more important than the large-scale enterprises, although only a fraction of the total agricultural land is contained in them. The informal social life approximates in its characteristics and organization that of open-country neighborhood groups in the United States and other countries where family farms are dominant.

CHAPTER VIII

The Social Class Structure

Before describing the stratification of rural society in Cuba, it is desirable to examine the structure of the society as a whole. This is not an easy task, and the writer does not pretend that this analysis is conclusive. No doubt there will be objections raised by other observers that this analysis does not provide an adequate overview of Cuban classes. No student of a culture foreign to his own can feel secure in drawing conclusions based upon no more than one year of observation. Nevertheless, the presentation to follow is the author's best judgment as to the contemporary system of classes. The stratification of rural society will form the subject of the subsequent chapter.

It is a temptation for the observer of Cuban life to conclude that the class structure consists of "upper," "middle," and "lower" classes and let the statement stand. But to do so would over-simplify greatly what, in reality, is a complex situation. This observer is not at all certain that a middle class exists in Cuba, but there can be no doubt about the upper and lower classes. These appear to be well marked. Within these classes, however, there are complex variations, so complex, in fact, as to make generalization hazardous. One has the general feeling that Cuban society has not "set" or "jelled." While the island has had a history of European contact which dates back a century before permanent white settlement in North America, this contact has been complicated by various crosscurrents.

Unlike most of the other Hispano-American cultures, that of Cuba is not a result of the mixture of the Spanish and indigenous cultures, but rather that of two exotic cultures, the Spanish and African, with only slight admixtures of French, Anglo-Saxon, and Chinese. Moreover, Cuban society has been in a state of political, economic, and social turbulence and instability for approximately a century. Its political unrest did not end with the gaining of independence after practically a half-century of struggle, but has continued during the period of the Republic while the country was experiencing the birth pangs of bringing forth a national state. Its economic system, geared to the fortunes of its dominant crop, sugar, has suffered extreme fluctuations throughout its history and has not yet reached a point of stability. These conditions have inevitably affected the entire social structure. A political or governing class has emerged; wealth has been accumulated by way of speculation and expansion in the country's basic industry. Extremes of wealth and poverty are juxtaposed.

In this matrix of events there has been considerable mobility up and down the social hierarchy. People who were rich have been made poor; some who were poor became rich; some rich have become richer; and great masses of the poor have been pushed further down the scale. Cuban society, as a stable and organized structure, can properly be regarded as being in a state of emergence. It is hardly true that the Cuban state is "an almost hypothetical entity" because there is no "Cuban society," as one native writer[1] has said, for when human beings live together as long as have the Cubans, there is always a society, although its description may be difficult because its outlines are not clearly marked. Yet Miguel de Carrión expressed a feeling which any observer of Cuban life is likely to experience—a feeling of bafflement.

THE HERITAGE OF THE CONQUISTADORES

The Spanish conquerors of Cuba brought to the island the culture of their homeland. They gave the island its language, its

[1] Miguel de Carrión, "El desenvolvimiento social de Cuba en los últimos viente años," *Cuba contemporanea*, XXVII (September 1921). Quoted by C. E. Chapman, *A History of the Cuban Republic* (New York: Macmillan, 1927), p. 581.

dominant religious institutions, its pattern of family life, its political and legal institutions, and—a fact of great importance—they introduced Negro slavery. In some respects the history of Spanish institutions in Cuba differs from that in other Spanish-American countries. Especially was this true in the matter of land distribution and relations to the indigenous peoples. In other colonies, it often happened that the conquistadores during their conquests merely replaced landlords who already had dominion over a large mass of workers in a condition of complete or partial slavery. The system of encomiendas merely transferred to the Spaniards the rights to the labor of the masses which were previously enjoyed by native chiefs.

In Cuba the encomienda was also applied, but the natives of the island were not organized into a neat pattern of agricultural economy, such as existed among the Incas for example, and, moreover, were not a highly productive agricultural people at all. While they had an elementary agriculture involving chiefly the growing of cassava, sweet potatoes, and maize, they were able to provide only for their own necessities on a hand-to-mouth basis and had not developed to a more advanced economic stage.[2] Naturally, the Spanish conquerors hoped to find gold and rich treasure, but they found little of either. What food they needed was produced by Indian labor, but they used the Indians granted them under the encomiendas primarily to recover what little gold there was from the auriferous sand. Not only were the Indians overworked, but they were also badly cared for. Their food was poor; there was no concern for their health; and so great was their mortality that by the middle of the sixteenth century they were practically extinct.[3]

Traces of Indian blood undoubtedly exist among the present inhabitants of Cuba, since the conquistadores, for all their cruelty to the Indians as a group, were not averse to marrying the Indian women, and the law of the time sanctioned and encouraged such unions.[4] Nevertheless, the Indians were clearly regarded as the social inferiors of the Spaniards, expected to be servile to them

[2] See Guerra y Sánchez, *Manual de historia de Cuba*, pp. 11ff, 33.
[3] *Ibid.*, Chapter IV.
[4] *Ibid.*, p. 14.

and to perform all the manual labor. Had the Indians been able to survive and thrive under Spanish domination to the extent of providing an adequate labor supply, the present social structure would probably have been similar to that of Mexico and other continental Spanish-American countries, where there are large native populations.

Such was not the case, however, and the practical extinction of the Indians resulted in their being replaced by another ethnic group, the Negroes. The status of the Negro will be discussed later. It is first necessary to point out the importance to present-day Cuba of the inheritance of Spanish culture and its significance to the class structure. In making these observations, the writer is deeply conscious of the pitfalls of easy generalization, and hopes to avoid at least some of them.[5]

In the first place, it is clear that the cultural inheritance from Spain is largely feudal in its nature.[6] Feudalism recognized an upper class—nobles, both secular and ecclesiastical—possessed of rights of ownership of land and other forms of wealth; and a lower class, which possessed certain rights but generally did not have the right to own land. Moreover, the rights of the lower class were in general those granted by the upper. Duties were also apportioned. The duty of working the land, of doing the menial tasks, fell, of course, upon the lower class. The upper class had the duty of defending them against the depredations of competing nobles, and especially the duty of governing and dispensing justice. The

[5] Commentaries on Cuban social life are sprinkled liberally with characterizations of the Cuban "character," "temperament," and "nature." See, for example, Chapman, op. cit., at numerous places in the book, especially Chapter XXV. Many journalistic accounts abound in qualifying adjectives regarding the Cuban. These are subjective reactions of the observers, and may be more or less accurate; but after all, they are impressions and difficult to substantiate for a people as a whole.

[6] The writer has been cautioned by a well-informed friend against placing undue emphasis upon the influence of the feudal tradition upon contemporary Cuba. His attention has been called to the article by Jules Henry on "Cultural Discontinuity and the Shadow of the Past," Scientific Monthly, LXVI, No. 3 (March 1948), pp. 248–54, in which the author states there is "an exaggerated tendency to explain present social behavior in terms of past institutions," and presents the "hypothesis of discontinuous social change." The hypothesis assumes that social forms are "capable of drastic, and sometimes even swift, transformation."

This is an interesting point of view, but one with which this writer cannot agree. The Spain out of which the early Spanish colonists came was characterized by the dominance of a feudal system, and it was perfectly logical, for example, that King Ferdinand in instructions to Diego Colón, August 14, 1509, should specify that in the

upper class was not expected to do menial tasks, nor would they stoop to do them. They were waited upon by slaves and servants who attended to all their personal wants. Significantly, also, women of the two classes were especially distinct. Upper-class women had few responsibilities either for the care of their home or for the rearing of their children. These were the duties of the servants and nurses. The age of chivalry placed women—that is, upper-class women—on pedestals and rendered them practically helpless for any purpose other than to be admired. They had little or no competence in the arts of homemaking and no opportunity to learn them.

This recognition by poor and rich alike of their respective orbits in the social scheme, a recognition which characterized feudal Europe, has influenced social organization in all Western countries to the present day. However, in some countries, and perhaps most notably among the Anglo-Saxons, there has been a gradual evolution away from the feudal tradition. Certainly the ideals expressed in the Declaration of Independence by the Anglo-American colonies were opposed to it; and the literature of France, England, and the United States during the nineteenth century sought to dignify manual labor and glorify the contribution of the hand-worker to the general welfare.[7] The person or class which sought to live without working was held up to scorn and characterized as "parasitic" on the body politic. "Natural rights" of all men were emphasized as opposed to those specious "rights" granted them by their so-called superiors. This is not to say that

distribution of Indians in the encomiendas, recognition should be given to rank; that is, royal officers and *alcaldes* received 100 natives; married nobles who brought their wives with them, 80; squires, 60; and "simple farmers," 30 each. This systematic distribution based upon rank varied from place to place in numbers of natives allotted; but the essential point is the recognition of class ranks for the society of the colonies— at least as far as encomienda privileges were concerned. Perhaps the point should be made here that the existence of ranks and social classes in human society antedated feudalism, but the latter reinforced this stratification. Since it was the form in existence in Spain at the time of American colonization by that country, it seems a foregone conclusion that the structure of the Old World would be transmitted to the New. This is not to deny that modifications developed in the new environment, because culture is always undergoing change. However, it is the point of view of this work that in spite of certain modifications, there are vestigal remains of the feudal class system still subtly persisting in Cuban society.

[7] Writings of Thomas Carlyle and William Morris in England, and of R. W. Emerson and Walt Whitman in the United States especially come to mind.

there is any such thing as a classless society existing in any of the countries of the world, but it has increasingly become an ideal to be sought, and at least the way has been opened in some countries for individuals of low estate to rise more easily.

The status of women.[8] The emancipation of women has been one important aspect of the social evolution of society during the nineteenth century. An important part of this movement has been the acceptance of ever larger responsibilities on the part of the women of the upper classes especially, notably those in what may be loosely called the "middle class." Women of such status in the United States, for example, do their own housework with a minimum of domestic help. They care for their own children, do their own marketing, and generally operate their own households.

In Cuba, however, the feudal acceptance of upper- and lower-class positions still dominates women's lives. The *criada*, the maid-servant, speaks of "us poor people" and of "the rich people," while the well-to-do Cuban will not allow his wife to do any housework. Cooking, washing, or scrubbing would lower her to the status of a servant. The daughter is not allowed to soil her hands in the kitchen. She must be kept "lovely" for the husband who is to be. The children of white Cubans are cared for by a colored or lower-class white nurse. It is she who gets them ready for school, washes their clothes, takes them to the carrousel, and supervises them throughout their waking hours.

The upper-class Cuban women of the cities, therefore, have little or no household responsibility except that of general supervision.[9] Although this relief from drudgery should free them for active and effective participation in public affairs, it is only the exceptional woman who takes advantage of the opportunity thus afforded, or who feels justified in going against the ancient tradition that woman's place is in the home. Cuban women participate but little in politics. They seldom run for office nor do they appear often as members of boards, commissions, or other appointive positions at the policy-making level. They will be found in a few relatively important positions in some of the ministries, such as

[8] The position of women is further discussed in relation to the family. See Chapter X.
[9] The situation of rural women is vastly different and will be discussed later.

the Ministry of Health and Social Assistance, but they are chiefly in subordinate positions in the government service.

Nevertheless there is a growing number of women in Cuba who are exercising an increasingly important role in civic affairs, even though they are not officially in the government service. They constitute an important vanguard of the movement toward emancipation of women from the feudal tradition. They are exercising leadership and influence in programs for social betterment through the organization of clubs and societies devoted to this purpose. One of the most notable of these groups is the Lyceum and Lawn Tennis Club of Havana, which maintains one of the few free public libraries in Cuba, including a children's library under competent direction, conducts adult education classes, and is active in sponsoring programs for recreation and the establishment of playgrounds.

The entrance of Cuban women into public life and activities outside the home has been especially marked since 1933. In 1934 women were given the right to vote. They have served as members of municipal councils and have been elected to the House of Representatives and the Senate. There is in Havana a club of professional women as well as a national association of nurses.

Just as the upper-class Cuban woman does no housework, the upper-class Cuban husband assumes very few of the menial responsibilities that are almost universally accepted by his counterpart in the United States. For example, he would not expect to fix a leaky water-tap, repair light switches, mow the lawn, look after the garden, and certainly not wash his own automobile. These are tasks for the *chófer*, the gardener, and the poor boy who seeks to earn a few pennies for cleaning out the garage. They are tasks reserved for the lower class.

Charity and paternalism. This difference between rich and poor is widely recognized in Cuba in other ways. One will see, for example, a school labeled *para niños pobres* (for poor children). During the Christmas season the First Lady of the Land distributes gifts to the "poor people" in front of the Presidential Palace. The poor congregate ostentatiously before the palace in great numbers to receive their gifts. The point lies not in the fact that gifts are given to the poor—a gesture that is made in most countries—but solely in the manner of public giving, which amounts to official recognition of a class called "the poor." While this may be regarded as commendable realism, as contrasted with the practice in the United States of protecting the sensibilities of the poor by taking the gift to the home, it would seem to fortify, by public recognition, the status of being poor.

Begging is another characteristic common to the feudal system. It would be impossible to give even a rough estimate of the beggar population of the island, but it is considerable, as anyone who has visited Cuban cities can testify. Large numbers of them are women, whose favorite strategy is to carry an infant; not infrequently there is also another child of five or six years who makes the appeal to the passer-by. They are found at the gates and on the steps of the churches of a Sunday morning, begging alms of the churchgoers. Was not almsgiving a special virtue during the Middle Ages, and are not recipients indispensable for its practice?

One cannot deny that there has been and is exploitation of the poor by the rich, of the lower class by the upper, throughout all of Cuban history, particularly in some segments of the economy. But it is also true that there have been and are now examples of the not unhappy relation of benevolent "master" and faithful "slave." The attitude of benevolent paternalism finds expression today in the custom of presenting gifts to domestic servants, who may be poorly paid in terms of wages, but who expect and receive periodic gifts from their employers. In fact, generosity of the upper class has come to be regarded not only as a mere virtue to be practiced for the benefit of the giver, but almost amounts to a tax, at times simulating the "potlatch" of the Indians of the North American West Coast.

At the time of marriage, especially, an upper-class individual is particularly lavish with his bounty. In order to maintain his social standing he cannot do otherwise. Fortunate is the young man of the upper class who is able to keep the expense of his marriage ceremony under $300; frequently it amounts to $1,000 or more. Some of these are costs required by the law—for the certificates of birth, copy of the marriage license, and so on—but these official charges are but a few dollars. In practice, the lawyer

or the judge will be given a handsome gratuity, and it is un-
thinkable, too, that the witnesses should not be entertained generously. As befits their station, the bride and groom must have an
elaborate church wedding, with fees for the priest, the assistant
priest, the altar boys, the organist, the choir, not to mention the
expenditures for rings, flowers—for decorating the aisle, altar,
and car for the bride—bouquets for the bride and the bridesmaids,
photographs, and entertainment at the reception. Such expenditures are incumbent upon people of certain standing in the United
States, it is true; but the social pressure there is weak as compared
with that in Cuba, where the prestige of the *class*, and the identification of the individual with it, is involved. In Cuba, it amounts,
in practice, to a tax and is almost as unavoidable. On the other
hand, the lower class spend little or nothing at marriage. Common
law unions occur frequently, but even a legal marriage is inexpen-
sive for them.

It seems very clear that status groups marked in the local speech
of the people as "rich" and "poor" are well accepted by both
classes as little less than inevitable. This is not to say that there
are no aspirations among the lower class to rise to better conditions. Among the very lowest, however, especially the beggars,
little semblance of self-respect remains, and consequently no ambition to be other than a successful beggar. They are completely
demoralized and, unfortunately, are constantly rearing new broods
and training them in the ancient art.

Vertical mobility. From what has been said about the upper
and lower classes, it should not be inferred that the Cuban social
structure possesses marked rigidity, such as characterizes a caste
society. Vertical circulation occurs and there appear to be forces
at work tending to accelerate it. One such force is the labor movement. A brief account of the history of organized labor in Cuba
will indicate its influence.

Although wage laborers constitute the overwhelming majority
of the Cuban working population, as a group they had not exer-
cised any significant influence on national policies before 1933. In
August 1933, however, it was a general strike of workers throughout the island which brought about the overthrow of the Machado
dictatorship. The strike was especially important in the capital

city of Havana, where industrial paralysis was practically complete. It later spread to the sugar mills, with workers taking over control of a number of them.

Machado had suppressed and driven underground the real labor unions, although the right-wing Cuban Federation of Labor was given his blessing. He had shown little or no consideration for the welfare of the workers. While the sugar companies were making the profits that financed the spending orgy known as the "dance of the millions," cane cutters were being paid at the rate of twenty-five to sixty cents a day. The spectacular boom that brought unprecedented wealth to the few, who lavished it on luxurious and unseemly high living in the cities, left the masses in a more miserable condition than ever.

It was to be expected that the revolution that overthrew Machado would represent a reaction against everything that melancholy regime stood for. The revolution would have been in vain had not the new government set about to alleviate the plight of the workers. Although the uprising coincided with the very depth of the depression, steps were taken by the new government to introduce such regulations as the eight-hour day and to establish minimum wages and improved working conditions. The government's pro-labor attitude was abetted by the rise of the Communist movement. Communism was introduced into Cuba in the early 1920's, and, as might be predicted in a country with such a large mass of disadvantaged people, it soon achieved a relatively large following. Party organizers furnished much of the leadership in establishing labor unions, both industrial and agricultural, and the National Confederation of Labor since its organization in 1934 has been under Communist control.

After the fall of Machado, a wave of strikes during August and September of 1933 spread through the sugar industry. It has been estimated that thirty-six mills were occupied by the striking workers.[10] In 1932 the National Confederation of Labor had organized the National Syndicate of Workers in the sugar industry, and at a conference in December of that year, delegates from thirty-two mills attended. The strikes of 1933 were therefore largely under the control of Communist leaders, and had for

[10] *Problems of the New Cuba*, p. 183.

their aims the seizure of the mills, establishment of soviets, and the arming of the proletariat. These extremely radical aspects of the revolution were dissipated by stern action of the new government, but no post-Machado regime has failed to manifest interest in and concern for the working classes.

Minimum wages were placed at eighty cents a day. During World War II the minimum was increased as living costs went up. Sugar cane workers were paid on the basis of a share of the sugar, so that their cash income varied according to the sugar content of the cane and the price of sugar.

The Constitution of 1940 gives signal recognition to the needs of labor. It forbids discriminatory practices of any kind on the part of employers. It provides for a minimum salary or wage, a maximum eight-hour day, and a work week of forty-four hours with pay for forty-eight; equal pay for equal work regardless of person; a month's paid vacation each calendar year; and the right to organize and to strike is guaranteed. Children under fourteen years of age may not be employed for wages. There are a number of other provisions concerning labor, but these are sufficient to indicate the favorable tone of the document.

The government of President Ramón Grau San Martín had the support of the Communist party (called the Partido Socialista Popular), although the party had opposed his election in 1944. The fact that the Confederation of Labor was given practical control of the Ministry of Labor, and was in a position to bring about serious embarrassment if not the downfall of the Grau government by withdrawing support, meant that the government labor policies would definitely be left of center. There was continuous agitation for the expulsion of foreigners from Cuban economic life, and against foreign landholders and "American imperialism."

Besides the Communist-led labor groups, however, there is a large labor movement somewhat more conservative, which probably has greater potential vitality than does the extreme left. Although Cuba has a large number of people who live at or below the margin of subsistence, and is by that fact vulnerable to the Communist appeals, it would be a serious error to assume a permanent trend toward the extreme left. The middle-of-the-road or left-of-center unions would readily increase their comparative strength if some of the agrarian reforms called for in the Constitution of 1940 were implemented by legislation and put into force.

The rural strength of the labor movement is among the sugar mill workers, although many of the workers on the sugar colonias are also organized. The fact that they are poor, and thus unable to pay dues, makes the organization of agricultural workers in any country a difficult undertaking. Nevertheless, the conclusion is warranted that the Cuban workers have had their wants and needs made articulate through the organized groups which have been established, and nobody can deny that their voices have been heard in Havana. The labor legislation and decrees over the years since 1933 testify to that.

Grass-roots leadership among Cuban farm workers has not been developed because there has been so little opportunity for local people to get experience in organized group life. But if the unions and other organizations in rural areas can have freedom to grow, indigenous rural leaders may be expected to develop. In any case, the social, political, and economic position of the agricultural worker is vastly better in mid-century than it was at the beginning, or during the first three decades, of the century. There are exceedingly complex economic problems confronting the Cuban people, but there can be little question that the voice of labor will have much more to do with their solution than has been true in the past. This prospect makes it all the more important that statesmanlike leaders be forthcoming from the ranks of labor—and, one might add, from the ranks of other segments of Cuban society as well—if the problems are to be successfully met.

Another factor operating to promote vertical mobility in the Cuban class structure is the slow but gradual expansion of small industries. This has not assumed large proportions but is nevertheless significant. Condensed milk factories, canning factories, and numerous small industrial plants, of which the rubber tire manufacturing plant near Havana is an example, are introducing new occupations into the culture, providing release from agriculture and domestic and personal service for some of the excess workers. Such industries also represent an increase in the small- and medium-scale enterpreneurs. Nevertheless, the ancient tradition of a privileged and a working class is a tenacious one. Under its sway, the "common" man tends to remain common and the born "gentleman" a gentleman.

The ethnic groups in Cuba are predominantly immigrants from Spain, the Chinese, and the Negroes. Natives of Spain form the main-stream of white blood in the population, coming chiefly from Asturia, Catalonia, Galicia, the Basque provinces, and the Canary Islands. In the early days of settlement, the Spanish immigrants were mainly from Castille and Andalusia and were composed largely of military and bureaucratic elements. The former groups were largely from agricultural, commercial, and artisan classes.

Like all immigrants from Europe to the New World, there were those who came to Cuba for the purpose of making a fortune and retiring to the homeland, and those who came with the idea of making a permanent home. This difference in motivation became a distinction between the "Spanish" on the one hand—those who hoped to return to the mother-country—and the "Cubans" on the other—those who planned to make permanent homes in Cuba. The difference was marked by special privileges conferred by the Spanish government on "Spaniards" over "Cubans."[11] Under the Constitution of 1901, children born of foreign parents in Cuba were not regarded as Cubans unless they declared their Cuban citizenship on becoming twenty-one. The constitutional law of 1934, however, reverses the situation. Offspring born in Cuba automatically become Cuban citizens unless they request registration as Spaniards at the age of twenty-one.

The distinction between Cubans and Spaniards amounts to class consciousness on the part of the two groups in present-day Cuba. This separation is noted in the numerous clubs maintained by both, but especially by the Spanish.[12] The various *centros*, or

[11] *Problems of the New Cuba*, pp. 36f. Raimundo Menocal y Cueto in his work, *Origen y desarrollo del pensamiento Cubano* (Havana: Editorial Lex, 1945), considers three classes in Cuba after 1820—the Spaniards, the Negroes, and the white Cubans; the Spanish dominating commerce, the Cubans agriculture, while the Negroes formed the proletariat. (See pp. 489–95 in the work mentioned above.) This probably roughly characterized the society before Cuban independence, but would be untrue today. However, it is recognized that these criteria are influences in the social stratification of Cuba.

[12] For example, at the beach in Cienfuegos one of the yacht clubs is referred to as the "Spanish club."

clubs, are chiefly of Spanish origin. Centro Asturiano and Centro Gallego are perhaps the most notable. They maintain palatial buildings which they constructed and occupy on the Parque Central in Havana. Within the population, there is general recognition of Spanish or Cuban identity. One frequently hears the distinction made in familiar conversation with neighbors—"That is a Spanish family living over there," or "My husband is Spanish, but I am a Cuban."

Acculturation between these two groups should not be difficult, inasmuch as their cultural roots are the same. They have the same language and customs derived from the mother-country. It seems unlikely that such differences as there now are will be of long duration. The decline of the "Spanish" population in relation to the total, which was marked during the 1930's, will no doubt continue. More and more the membership in clubs is coming to be a mixture of both Cuban and Spanish elements. As the Spanish population declines numerically and the ordinary processes of social assimilation continue, the distinctions between the two groups will become less and less.

Foreigners in various industries. The number of persons and various nationalities engaged in specific occupations is not reported in the census, although such data are available for the major industries. The breakdown on specific occupations gives only citizenship (Cuban or foreign) and color. Table 14 shows that in 1943 foreigners made up 8.4 per cent of the labor force. They constituted exactly the same proportion of those engaged in agriculture, livestock, and fisheries, but were under-represented in the industries of mining, construction, manufacturing and mechanical industry, transportation, banking and finance, recreational services, and government service. On the other hand, they were relatively over-represented in commerce, domestic and personal services, and professional service, and in a general category called "diverse services" which included primarily garage and repair services for automobiles, services on motors, bicycles, refrigerators, business machines, and the like.

Foreigners engaged in commerce made up a disproportionate share of both wholesalers and retailers, but the great preponderance was in the latter class. It is highly probable that these foreign-

TABLE 14. PROPORTION OF FOREIGN CITIZENS IN THE CUBAN LABOR FORCE IN 1943,
BY INDUSTRIAL GROUPS

Industry	Total Labor Force	Foreign Citizens	
		Number	Per Cent
Agriculture, livestock, and fisheries	630,556	53,217	8.4
Mining	5,057	343	6.8
Construction	25,878	1,682	6.5
Manufacturing and mechanical industries ...	187,645	11,215	6.0
Transportation and communication	33,922	1,965	5.8
Commerce	146,572	24,190	16.5
Banking and finance	2,312	157	6.8
Domestic and personal service	73,963	8,861	12.0
Domestic service	49,051	5,159	10.5
Laundry	6,400	2,614	37.9
Services of recreation	5,315	372	7.0
Professional services	31,739	2,787	8.8
Government	60,763	380	0.6
Diverse services, rent, repairs, etc.	2,582	227	8.8
Unclassified	314,297	22,361	7.1
Total	1,520,851	127,757	8.4

SOURCE: *Censo de 1943*, pp. 142f, Table 1.

ers are largely from Spain, with Chinese also heavily represented
in relation to their total in the population. It is commonly said
in Havana that the Spaniards are the small shopkeepers, and
casual observation by any visitor will also indicate the large number of Chinese who sell vegetables, especially on the streets.

Many Spaniards also fall in the group of domestic servants.
When one inquires about employment of a domestic in Havana,
one is immediately asked to specify a choice between Spanish and
colored. Within the domestic service category, the laundry workers are reported separately, and in this group 37.9 per cent are
foreign. Here again, it is well known that the Chinese practically
have a monopoly on the laundry business, although Spanish people
are represented also.

The over-representation of foreigners in the professional group
is accounted for by the large number of foreign clergymen and
charitable workers, who make up 31.4 per cent of the total foreign
group in the island. Foreigners show a lesser predominance in the
fields of education and engineering, where they constitute 9.7 per
cent and 8.5 per cent, respectively. Civil and electrical engineers
account for the excess in the field of engineering. These engineers
are no doubt predominantly from the United States, as are many

of the foreign clergymen. The Protestant church leadership constitutes a small number in the total, coming largely from the States, while the Catholic church leadership contains a large proportion of Spanish clerics. Although no precise data are available on this point, it is well known that a number of priests and other functionaries of the Catholic church are Spanish in origin. An additional contingent comes from France.

The factor of color. From statistics on the color of those engaged in various industries and occupations, it is possible to see the relation of this factor to social stratification.[13] The reader is again reminded that color in this connection includes black, yellow, and mixed. The first point of importance to note is that there are no occupations listed in the census from which colored workers are entirely barred (Tables 15 and 17). However, they occur in certain groups only in small numbers, but make up vastly greater proportions of others. The colored people constitute about the same proportion of the labor force (25.9 per cent) as they do of the general population (25.6 per cent).

Something of the disparity of representation in the broad industrial classifications can be seen from Table 15. The colored group exceeds the national average which they constitute of the labor force in four of the categories—namely, skilled workers, unskilled workers, "other" agricultural workers, and personal serv-

TABLE 15. PROPORTIONS OF COLORED AND WHITE WORKERS IN THE CUBAN LABOR FORCE BY MAJOR OCCUPATIONAL GROUPS

Occupational Group	Percentages		
	Total	White	Colored
Professional and semiprofessional	100	84.7	15.3
Administration of farms	100	91.3	8.7
Farmers and farm laborers	100	77.2	22.8
Proprietors, managers, and high officials	100	85.0	15.0
Office workers, salesmen, etc.	100	84.1	15.9
Skilled workers	100	58.5	41.5
Unskilled workers	100	63.8	36.2
Services of protection	100	80.1	19.9
Personal services (excluding domestics)	100	66.1	33.9
Other agricultural workers	100	73.2	26.8
Total	100	74.1	25.9

[13] In the undifferentiated group listed as *agricultores* (agriculturists), colored workers fall below the national average.

ices other than domestic. But in managerial positions, proprietorships, in office and sales forces, and in the "protective" occupations (firemen, police, etc.), they fall considerably short. However, it is significant that in none of the broad groups do they fall markedly low, a fact which must be accepted as evidence that there is no rigid color line so far as the major occupations are concerned.

Naturally, when individual occupations are considered, larger differences can be observed. These occupational figures only reflect in greater detail the picture given by the generalized industrial groups. Colored persons are most notably under-represented in the professional groups other than teachers, actors, and artists. Among the doctors, lawyers, engineers, pharmacists, chemists, architects, dentists, clergymen, editors and reporters, professors, and so forth, they fall short of the average figure. Also, there are few colored bank cashiers, proprietors of business establishments, office employees, or telegraph and radio operators.

An interesting fact, however, which can be noted from Table 15 is the extent to which the colored group is represented in the skilled occupations. These include bookkeepers, typists and stenographers, radio mechanics, boilermakers, jewelers and watch repairmen, and mechanics, all of which contain colored people to an extent approximating the national average. Among the following groups they constitute one-third or more of all workers: artists, musicians, bricklayers, dressmakers, carpenters, decorators, tinsmiths, linotypists, automobile mechanics, bakers, plumbers, tailors, cigar-makers, shoemakers, servants (over 50 per cent), stevedores, painters, barbers and manicurists, cooks, and shoeshiners.

Both occupational and color differences are manifest in the income data as reported in 1943.[14] Reference to Table 16 will reveal at once the somewhat higher proportion of colored people in the income group under $30 per month, and a smaller percentage in the succeeding, higher income groups. This color differential occurs

[14] It is difficult to appraise the value of these data, since only two-thirds of the labor force answered the income question. (See *Censo de 1943*, p. 1098.) They probably have some value for Negro-white comparisons and for comparisons of occupations. In the latter instance, however, it is probable that fewer of the upper income group reported than the lower. Moreover, the question called for monthly cash income and would therefore not include the value of rent and other perquisites which individuals received.

TABLE 16. DISTRIBUTION BY PERCENTAGES OF CUBAN LABOR FORCE
ACCORDING TO MONTHLY CASH INCOME, BY COLOR, 1943

Monthly Income in Dollars	Percentages		
	Total	White	Colored
Total	*100.0*	*100.0*	*100.0*
Under 30	39.6	37.4	46.6
30–59	42.5	42.8	41.4
60–69	12.4	13.4	9.4
100–199	14.0	4.7	1.7
200–299	0.8	0.9	0.4
300 or more	0.7	0.8	0.5

SOURCE: *Censo de 1943,* Table V.

TABLE 17. PERCENTAGES OF CUBAN LABOR FORCE IN SELECTED MAJOR
INDUSTRIES REPORTING MONTHLY CASH INCOMES OF $100 OR MORE,
BY COLOR, 1943

Major Industry	Percentages	
	White	Colored
All industries	7.1	2.6
Banking and finance	36.0	23.4
Professional	23.4	14.2
Transportation and communication	14.2	9.3
Mining	12.7	3.7
Recreation and entertainment	10.8	3.1
Commerce	10.6	5.4
Government	10.3	3.8
Construction	10.1	4.7
Manufacturing and mechanical industries	7.1	3.0
Domestic and personal service	2.3	1.2
Agriculture and fishing	1.5	1.0

SOURCE: *Censo de 1943,* Table V.

throughout the major industrial groups. The occupation in which
the largest proportion of colored workers was receiving $100 or
more is banking and finance (Table 17), followed by the professional group, transport and communication, commerce (wholesale
and retail establishments), construction, government service, mining, recreation and entertainment, manufacturing and mechanical
industries, domestic and personal services, and agriculture, livestock, and fishing. There was less color difference in the amount of
income in the agricultural group than in any other.

Nevertheless, while there is a distribution of colored workers among all the occupations, it is clear that they are predominantly the "hewers of wood and drawers of water." They have benefited from the absence of strict caste lines among the occupations, but their inheritance of a low estate deriving from slavery and the persistence of their poverty have left them either without aspiration to rise to the higher occupations or without the means to obtain the training necessary to achieve higher goals. It is likely that both factors have been important, but one is inclined to give slightly greater weight to the latter.

There are no formal segregation regulations between the colored and white populations—no "Jim Crow" laws. Intermarriage among the races is common, as is indicated by the mulatto population of nearly three-quarters of a million in 1943. During the twelve-year period between the censuses of 1931 and 1943, the Negroes increased by only 25,000 while the mulattoes increased by over 100,000. The proportion which the latter constitute of all colored groups has been steadily rising since 1907, while the corresponding figure for the Negroes has been steadily declining.

This is not to say that there is no "color line" in Cuba. The figures presented earlier in this section point to the conclusion that in subtle ways the upper class—composed mainly of whites—keeps the door closed as far as possible against the Negro. High government positions are not for him, for example. While orators on Memorial Day (December 7) pay glowing tribute to one of the greatest national heroes of the War of Independence, the colored General Antonio Maceo, no man of color seems to have been appointed in recent years to the council of ministers, and only rarely to immediately subordinate positions. Some colored politicians get elected to the national Congress, although not in the ratio which the colored population bears to the total. The governing class, in other words, is predominantly white and appears to regard affairs of state as a white preserve. In the Cuban Senate, as of 1945, there were 5 colored senators out of a total of 54; in the House of Representatives, composed of 127 members, 12 were colored. This is less than half what would be considered as proportional representation.

Cuban Negroes have been conscious of discrimination against them not only in government positions but in private employment as well. In 1911 Negro political leaders waged a campaign for the purpose of obtaining more recognition for members of their race in the distribution of political positions. It became an open revolt which was soon suppressed, but only after 3,000 Negroes lost their lives. Meanwhile the United States felt it necessary to land a detachment of marines at Guantánamo to afford protection to Americans in that area if it should prove necessary.[15]

In 1934 the *Comite por los Derechos del Negro* made a report in which it declared: "There are industries where they cannot work; in commerce, in the great foreign enterprises, above all, Negroes are not employed. In certain industries they work where the pay is least: for example, in the graphic arts they may be compositors, but seldom linotypists; in the tobacco industry they are cigar-makers and strippers, but not sorters or trimmers, who are the employees that earn the best wages."[16]

But if the colored people are denied top positions in government, they find an outlet for leadership in other ways. They are active in the leadership of labor organizations, both agricultural and industrial. The secretary-general of the Cuban Federation of Labor is a Negro, as is also the president of the sugar workers' union (*Federación Nacional Obrera Azucarera*), which claims to be spokesman for 450,000 workers. The president of the *Confederación Campesina de Cuba*, a nation-wide organization of farmers and farm workers, is a mulatto. In the political parties, also, the colored people are active and occupy positions of leadership, particularly in the Socialist or Communist party, which is making a special appeal to the people in the lower income levels.

Cuban tourist guides like to tell visitors from the United States that in Cuba if a man has any white blood in him, he is a "white man," while in the United States, they like to point out, if a man has any Negro blood in him, he is a Negro. Like so many pat observations, this one probably contains a little but not all the truth. It cannot be denied that there is a consciousness of color in Cuba, although it is true that color plays a less conspicuous role in social stratification than it does in the United States. While the man of

---

[15] Chapman, *op. cit.*, p. 312.

[16] Quoted in *Problems of the New Cuba*, p. 32, from *Informe de la comision investigadora de los sucesos de Trinidad y otros trabajos del comite por los derechos del Negro* (Havana, 1934).

color pervades practically all of the occupations, he is predominantly in those which are further down the social hierarchy. The clubs which are so important in urban social life of Cuba are strictly on a color basis. The various yacht clubs are exclusively white. If the colored people want club life they must provide their own, also on an exclusive basis. There are at least two clinics offering medical care exclusively to colored people, although there is no discrimination practiced in the other clinics except in those maintained by white clubs.

IS THERE A MIDDLE CLASS IN CUBA?

If the "upper" and "lower" classes are clearly recognized in Cuba, the same is not true of the middle class. An arbitrary classification on the basis of income and occupation might be made which would reveal a range of classes with a pattern not unlike that of the United States. However, on the more subtle sociopsychological basis, there is a more difficult task of identification. Cuban society, as we have said, can more easily be classified into two groups only, upper and lower—or perhaps it would not be too inaccurate to say those who hire servants and those who do not; or, if one wishes, those who work with their hands and those who work with their heads, or do not work at all. The latter are the heirs of the old aristocracy, the former, the heirs of their serfs and slaves. The one group scorned work with their hands, the others were "to the manor born." This simple dichotomy of "upper" and "lower" is based primarily on a tradition, on socio-psychological factors, rather than on differences in income and wealth, which are secondary criteria. It is very likely that on the basis of occupation, there would be included in the upper group not only the wealthy and well-to-do, but also the professional workers of all kinds and the "white-collar" workers, even though among the latter there may be many with lower incomes than would be found among the skilled manual workers.

Considering the weight that must be given to this element of tradition in analyzing the class structure, and at the same time recognizing the wide range of differences in both the upper and the lower classes, it seems reasonable to make a classification somewhat as follows:

A. *Upper class,* consisting of all those who do the managerial tasks, clerical work, and who are descended from upper-class families regardless of their present state of wealth and income.

1. *Upper upper,* consisting of the very wealthy, the top governmental officials, and some professional men who combine with their professional prestige considerable wealth and family tradition.

2. *Middle upper,* containing the majority of the professional group (doctors, lawyers, university staff, engineers), a number of the sugar colonos, managers of sugar mills, medium to large landowners, and medium-sized business proprietors.

3. *Lower upper,* consisting of the smaller proprietors, elementary and high school teachers, bank employees at the clerical level, small colonos who own their land, government workers at the lower professional level (but exclusive of those holding *botellas,* offices held which do not involve any actual labor), bookkeepers, accountants, and small landowners.

B. *Lower class,* consisting in general of those who do manual work, and who are descended from families of this class.

1. *Upper lower,* consisting of many smaller shopkeepers, government employees of the non-civil service type, garage and other mechanics, bus and streetcar conductors and motormen, barbers and beauty parlor operatives, etc., small farmers, and cash and share renters.

2. *Middle lower,* consisting in general of common labor, domestic servants, and agricultural wageworkers.

3. *Lower lower,* consisting of street venders and beggars.[17]

In attempting to devise a classification based mainly on occupation, many difficulties are encountered. It is possible that a given occupational group—for example, the elementary and high school teachers—may have representatives in several of the classes indicated, from lower lower to middle upper. Similarly, some groups that are placed in the upper classes may have representatives throughout some of the lower ones. However, this tentative classification, arrived at after numerous interviews and analysis of existing statistical data, may be useful as a hypothesis for further study and possible modification as more adequate data become available. It may well be that further investigation will

[17] This sixfold system of classes is similar to that developed by W. Lloyd Warner and associates, except that no middle class is recognized. See W. Lloyd Warner and Leo Srole, *The Status System of a Modern Community* (New Haven: Yale University Press, 1942).

provide more convincing evidence than now exists of a true middle
class in Cuba, a class which most American observers usually
assume to exist. C. E. Chapman, for example, divides Cuban
society into the three standard classes of upper, middle, and lower:
he calls the lower the "laborers, many of them negro or negroid,"
the upper he calls the "land-holding class made up of people of
white blood," and "in between are the professions and the politicians."[18] This scheme greatly oversimplifies the facts in the opinion of the present writer. It is clear without much familiarity with
Cuban life that no account is taken of the great heterogeneity
existing among "the land-holding class," the "laborers," and the
"professions and the politicians."

It might be argued that the classes proposed earlier as "lower
upper" and "upper lower" might be combined into a middle class.
There is serious objection to this, however, as long as the psychological barriers exist between those who work with their hands
and those who work with their heads. I think this barrier will fade
eventually, as it has in the United States, but it will take a longer
time in Cuba. In a strictly economic and political sense one might
be justified in postulating a middle class in Cuba, but in the more
subtle psychological sense it is very doubtful that the classification
would be valid.

[18] Chapman, *op. cit.*, p. 587.

CHAPTER IX

Social Stratification in Rural Cuba

Farmers and farm workers in 1943 constituted about 41 per cent of the labor force in Cuba (Table 18). The next most important occupation group from the standpoint of numbers is that composed of unskilled workers, followed by the clerical and sales group, the skilled workers, the proprietors, managers, and high employees, and the professional and semiprofessional groups. The distinctively rural character of Cuba's population makes it important to analyze further the status structure of this segment of Cuban society.

While most of the rural population would fall into the lower class, as indicated in Chapter VIII, there are some who are properly placed in the upper categories. Some of the colonos, for example, are wealthy and come well up into the middle upper if not the upper upper class. However, it may be debatable whether these individuals are in reality rural, or whether they do not more properly belong in the urban group. Since they reside in the city and spend little time in the country, the latter classification seems most logical. Even leaving them out of consideration, however, there is a considerable range in classes within the rural population.

The criteria of social status of greatest importance in the rural areas are: (a) tenure, or property relationship to the land; (b) size of farm; (c) color; (d) mobility; and (e) level of living.[1]

[1] The factor of level of living is treated separately in Chapter XI.

TABLE 18. NUMBER OF PERSONS 13 YEARS OLD AND OVER "REPORTED WITH OCCUPATION"
IN VARIOUS OCCUPATIONAL GROUPS IN THE CUBAN CENSUS OF 1943

Occupational Groups	Number	Per Cent
Total	1,520,850	100.0
Professional and semiprofessional	56,598	3.7
Farmers, farm managers, and farm laborers	621,798	40.9
Proprietors, managers, and high employees	130,716	8.6
Clerical, salesmen, and similar	209,445	13.8
Skilled workers	192,861	12.7
Unskilled workers	260,279	17.1
Protective services	28,525	1.9
Personal service	20,628	1.4

SOURCE: *Censo de 1943*, p. 1112, Table 1.

LAND TENURE

The most important criterion of rural class position is property relationship to the land. The major tenure classes are owners, managers, cash renters, share renters, wage laborers, and squatters. Their relative social status is about in that order of listing. Census data relating to these tenure groups is available from the preliminary reports on the Agricultural Census of 1946. The census gives the following definitions of the various groups:

1. Owner-operator (*proprietario*), who owns the land he farms.

2. Manager (*administrador*), hired by the landowner to operate the farm.

3. Renter (*arrendatario*), usually paying cash.

4. Subrenter (*sub-arrendatario*), who subrents from a tenant.

5. Share renter or sharecropper (*partidario*), who pays a share of the crop for rent. Included in this group are workers who are paid for their labor in a share of the crop, corresponding to the sharecropper in the United States. Like the sharecropper in the States, he has no equipment. However, some of the operators included in this category are true share renters in the American sense.

6. Squatters (*precaristas*), unauthorized settlers on land, the title to which is held by others. They occupy unused land on ranches or sugar plantations, construct bohíos, plant some banana trees, and live a meager existence. Under Spanish law, title can be acquired if they can prove they have lived there for 30 years.

7. "Others" includes some who have been given right of usufruct on land which belongs to another (*tienen en usufructo*), and those whose tenure was not reported by the enumerator.

TABLE 19. NUMBER AND PER CENT OF CUBAN FARMERS IN
EACH TENURE CLASS, 1946

Tenure Classes	Number	Per Cent
Total	159,958	100.0
Managers	9,342	5.8
Owners	48,792	30.5
Renters	46,048	28.8
Subrenters	6,987	4.4
Sharecroppers	33,064	20.6
Squatters	13,718	8.6
Others	2,007	1.3

SOURCE: National Agricultural Census, 1946, preliminary release.

Landowners make up only slightly more than 30 per cent of all operators (Table 19). Renters, including sharecroppers, constitute about 54 per cent of the operators, with managed farms accounting for nearly 6 per cent and squatters and "others" around 10 per cent. Thus nearly 70 per cent of the enumerated farms are operated by people who have no ownership rights in them.

It would be a mistake to assume that these tenure classes are homogeneous within themselves. On the contrary, there is great variation. Owners range from the proprietor of a small farm of a few acres to one whose land is measured in thousands of acres. The social status of owners within the class depends quite largely on the amount and value of the land owned. A large operator, whether tenant or owner, is far higher in social status than the small. In fact, the large operator of rented land may approximate in rank the owner-operator. There are many wealthy sugar colonos who operate rented land.

Renters in their turn also differ within their respective classes. The cash renter rates above the share renter because he has greater freedom of action. He assumes most if not all the risks of production and has more prerogatives as to what he shall plant and the operation of the farm in general. Here again, as in the case of the owners, the size of the farm is a factor in determining status. If the unit is large enough to justify the hiring of workers in addition to the family members, status is higher than otherwise.

About the same can be said of the partidarios (also called *aparceros*), or share tenants. They vary widely in status within the general class. In some areas—for example, the tobacco region near Cabaiguán—the share renters are of three kinds: cuartarios, who pay one-fourth of the crop as rent; tercedarios, who pay one-third; and partidarios, who pay one-half. The social class in which one is placed depends partly upon the amount of capital one possesses, in the form of oxen and farm equipment, and the opportunity one has to acquire a piece of land on appropriate terms. For example, a cuartario is in the favorable position of having to pay no more than one-fourth of the crop, because he has the equipment and capital necessary for what might be called complete operation and has been able to drive a good bargain with the landowner. In the case of the tercedario, it is sometimes necessary for the landlord to furnish part of the capital necessary to make the crop. At other times, the tercedario may have sufficient equipment for complete operation, but in order to get land has been willing to bid as high as one-third of the crop. The partidario is at the bottom of the social hierarchy in this case, with no capital or equipment at all and able to furnish only the work of his hands, for which he receives one-half the crop. In fact, he is the farm laborer of this area, paid in kind. Board and room are furnished by his employer, who may be a cuartario, tercedario, or arrendatario. One cuartario told us that his chief aim now was to become an arrendatario, and perhaps later, to be an owner.

In the Special Surveys of 1946, the distribution by tenure groups was as follows: owners, 24.8 per cent; cash renters, 29.0 per cent; share renters and croppers, 22.5 per cent; and wageworkers, 23.7 per cent. These categories and percentages are not comparable with those of the 1946 census, as will be readily seen. Among other differences, the census included managers and did not include wageworkers.

The Special Surveys also revealed differences in the incidence of tenure groups by type-of-farming areas. Share renting is most common in tobacco farming. In the coffee areas, cash and share renting are equally common, but in dairying and sugar cane growing, cash renting is practically universal. In cane production, wageworkers were dominant. Ownership is most common in dairying and mixed farming and least in tobacco, with sugar cane next lowest, followed by coffee. It is in these three farm types—tobacco, sugar, and coffee—that the latifundium prevails and social stratification is greatest.

In the tenant group, some differences probably exist according to the form of the lease, whether written or oral. In the Special Surveys of 1946, of 397 renters and croppers, 201 were covered by written and 186 by oral agreements. Written agreements are more common where cash rent is involved. Nearly two-thirds of the cash renters, compared with only one-third of the share renters, had written contracts. Written contracts were more common also in tobacco, sugar cane, and coffee farming than in the diversified and dairy areas. In mixed farming, share renters were scarcely ever covered by written contracts, although some of the cash renters had them. The absence of written agreements may have little effect upon status in some areas, but since they generally provide additional security to the individual, they must be considered as a supplementary factor in stratification.

There can be no doubt about the generally low status of the true sharecroppers and the *precaristas*. The lives of the latter group are what the word implies, precarious. About 60 per cent of them are on farms of less than one acre.

Farm laborers. Those who work for wages make up the bulk of the rural population of Cuba. The Agricultural Census of 1946 reported 423,690 farm laborers, employed on 37,715 farms. The average period of employment was 4.1 months, but the most frequent time reported was 3 months. This reflects the influence of the sugar and coffee harvests, which usually complete most of the work in 3 months. An interesting fact revealed in the census is the large number of workers employed on rented farms (Table 20). The fact that even squatters may be "employers" of labor seems strange, but some were reported in the census. The explanation would seem to be that there are some persons nominally classified as squatters—meaning that they are occupying land which does not belong to them and have no rental agreement covering its use—who are operating acreages sufficiently large to warrant the hiring of help.

Wage laborers are of various types. There are those who are employed the year round and those who are migratory and seasonal. Among the seasonal laborers are sons of farmers in the area near

TABLE 20. NUMBER OF WAGEWORKERS IN CUBAN AGRICULTURE
BY TENURE OF EMPLOYER

Tenure of Employer	Number	Per Cent
Total	423,690	100.0
Owners	96,630	22.8
Managers	76,561	18.0
Cash renters	176,653	41.7
Subrenters	15,873	3.7
Share renters	49,076	11.6
Squatters	3,644	0.9
Others	5,253	1.2

SOURCE: National Agricultural Census, 1946, preliminary release.

the place of employment, who return to their parental homes during the time they are unemployed. Wage laborers' social status varies somewhat with their classification. If they are permanent employees, they are able to live generation after generation on the same colonia or finca and enjoy such community life as exists in the area. Of course, their rank in the scale of prestige is low— beneath the renter and the landowner. If the laborer happens to be a part-time farmer—that is, one who owns a small tract of land and works off his farm for additional income—his status is advanced by the fact of his ownership of land and the additional security which he would have as a result. Those without any such stable residence as the permanent employee or the part-time farm- er—the precaristas and the migratory seasonal workers—occupy the bottom of the status ladder. The precaristas, although they occupy a tract of land, have uncertainty of residence and depend for supplementary income on such work as may be available on the near-by farms in the busy season.

SIZE OF FARM

Reference has already been made to the importance of size of farm in determining status. This factor cuts across the tenure rela- tions to a large extent. The distribution of the number and total area of farms by size is shown in Table 21. The wide disparity in land distribution is readily apparent. Less than 0.1 per cent of Cuban farms contain one-fifth of all agricultural land, and 8 per cent of the farms embrace 70 per cent of the land. These large land-

TABLE 21. NUMBER AND TOTAL AREA OF FARMS BY SIZE IN CUBA, 1946

Size of Farm in Hectares	Number of Farms		Total Area in Farms	
	Number	Per Cent	Hectares	Per Cent
Total 159,958		100.0	9,077,086	100.0
Less than 0.4	1,148	0.7	280	...*
0.5 to 0.9	1,877	1.2	1,399	...*
1.0–4.9	29,170	18.2	84,354	0.9
5.0–9.9	30,305	18.9	210,701	2.3
10.0–24.9	48,778	30.5	725,071	8.0
25.0–49.9	23,901	14.9	789,714	8.7
50.0–74.9	8,157	5.1	488,648	5.4
75.0–99.9	3,853	2.4	329,681	3.6
100.0–499.9	10,433	6.5	2,193,600	24.1
500.0–999.9	1,422	0.9	992,531	10.9
1,000–4,999.9	780	0.5	1,443,500	16.0
5,000 or more	114	...*	1,817,602	20.1

SOURCE: National Agricultural Census, 1946, preliminary release.
* Less than 0.1 per cent.

holdings are typically devoted to sugar cane, tobacco, livestock, and coffee. Small farmers, although numerous, have a pitifully small share of the land. Those with farms under 25 hectares in size (about 63 acres) constitute 70 per cent of all operators and have only 11 per cent of the land—about 9 hectares (22 acres) each, on the average, but most of them much less. This is a matter of grave concern in Cuba, where thousands of small operators and landless workers are clamoring for possession of land. The political implications are such that no government can long ignore them.

COLOR

The data available do not permit an adequate analysis of the incidence of colored people in agriculture. The Census of 1943, as previously noted, placed all nonwhites in one category and failed to differentiate agricultural people according to tenure. The classification *agricultores,* or agriculturists, includes practically the entire working force in agriculture. Three agricultural categories—managers, farmers and farm workers (agricultores), and "other" agricultural workers—were reported in 1943. The managers are unquestionably under-represented: over 9,000 were reported in the 1946 agricultural census, but only 161 in the population census of 1943.

However, the classification by color in the census of occupations permits the general statement that in agriculture the whites and nonwhites are represented roughly in proportion to their numbers in the total labor force. If anything, the colored group is slightly under the average for all occupations. This may be due to their excessive migration to urban centers.

Negroid persons constitute the vast majority of those reported as "colored," with Chinese constituting a small minority. The Negroes and mulattoes are, of course, descended from the slave labor brought to the Caribbean in early times. Most of them are native-born Cubans, but some have drifted in from Haiti, Jamaica, and other islands.

TABLE 22. DISTRIBUTION BY COLOR AND TENURE OF 734 CUBAN FARMERS, 1946

Type of Tenure	Total		White		Mulatto		Negro	
	Number	Per Cent	Number	Per Cent	Number	Per Cent	Number	Per Cent
All groups	734	100.0	642	100.0	47	100.0	45	100.0
Owners	182	24.8	166	25.9	13	27.7	3	6.7
Cash renters ...	212	28.9	199	31.0	9	19.1	4	8.9
Share renters ..	167	22.8	134	20.9	18	38.3	15	33.3
Wageworkers ...	173	23.6	143	22.2	7	14.9	23	51.1

SOURCE: Special Surveys.

The Special Surveys of 1946 reveal some differences in tenure on the basis of color (Table 22). The sample must not be regarded as representative of the entire agricultural group, however, and should be considered only as indicative of the general situation. The numbers of persons of color are too small to be relied upon for generalization, and the areas were chosen primarily with type of farming as the criterion. These data suggest, however, that among mulattoes, especially, ownership is about as common as among whites. There were fewer cash renters proportionally and more sharecroppers in the mulatto group as compared with the white. The Negro group was quite significantly concentrated in the share renter and laborer categories. This distribution is in accordance with general observation. The Negro undoubtedly occupies a position below the mulatto in the social scale.

Income data from the 1943 census, while subject to question as to its reliability, also indicates color differences when the labor

TABLE 23. PER CENT OF CUBANS ENGAGED IN AGRICULTURE IN VARIOUS
INCOME GROUPS BY COLOR, 1943

Monthly Income in Dollars	White		Colored	
	Number	Per Cent	Number	Per Cent
Total	331,515	100.0	95,514	100.0
Under 30	190,950	57.6	58,449	61.2
30–59	126,167	38.1	34,412	36.0
60–99	9,926	3.0	1,713	1.8
100–199	2,578	0.8	366	0.4
200–299	764	0.2	195	0.2
300 or over	1,130	0.3	379	0.4

SOURCE: *Censo de 1943*, p. 1098.

force in agriculture is considered (Table 23). Although these differences are not marked, it is clear that larger proportions of colored persons fall in the lowest bracket. In the groups receiving more than $200 monthly there is practically no difference between the two classes.

But the most important manifestation of the color factor in social stratification is in community social life. The Negro and white mingle to only a limited extent. Usually the visiting pattern and such other social activities as exist are exclusively white or Negro. The mulatto, as one farmer at El Nicho expressed it, functions as a go-between for the two races, being free to marry either white or black. In the El Nicho area, incidentally, all social activities are on a separate color basis except cockfights where the races mix freely. Intermarriage of blacks and whites is not common. "Such marriages are very difficult," said one informant.

MOBILITY

The extent to which people move from place to place is related to their social status. While a certain amount of movement may be beneficial to society and to the individual, it is well recognized that excessive mobility is a disadvantage to both. Those who find it necessary to move often are in a position of relative insecurity, economically and socially. The most migratory persons are often the most impoverished, and because of their mobility are unable to enjoy a normal family and community life.

The fact that differences in geographic mobility are associated

TABLE 24. YEARS OF RESIDENCE ON THE SAME FARM BY TENURE CLASS, CUBA, 1946

Years on Same Farm	Owners	Managers	Cash Renters	Sub-renters	Share Renters	Squatters
Total	100.0	100.0	100.0	100.0	100.0	100.0
Less than 5 ...	17.9	29.4	21.1	21.0	37.5	44.3
5–9	13.3	18.3	19.8	21.9	22.1	22.5
10–14	12.2	14.7	21.5	22.1	15.2	16.7
15–25	19.0	15.1	18.4	17.9	11.5	14.1
Over 25	36.1	20.8	17.8	16.2	9.5	1.2
Not reported ..	1.5	1.7	1.4	0.9	4.2	1.2

SOURCE: National Agricultural Census, 1946, preliminary release.

TABLE 25. LENGTH OF RESIDENCE ON PRESENT FARM OF 742 CUBAN
FAMILIES BY TENURE CLASS

Years on Present Farm	Total		Owner or Part-Owner		Renter		Share-cropper		Wage-worker	
	Number	Per Cent	Number	Per Cent	Number	Per Cent	Number	Per Cent	Number	Per Cent
Total	742	100.0	184	100.0	215	100.0	167	100.0	176	100.0
Under 1 year .	28	3.7	2	1.0	9	4.2	2	1.2	15	8.5
1–4.9	121	16.3	15	8.2	23	10.7	39	23.3	44	25.0
5–9.9	125	16.8	15	8.2	29	13.5	34	20.4	47	26.7
10–14.9	122	16.4	22	12.0	45	20.9	25	15.0	30	17.0
15–19.9	80	10.8	12	6.5	42	19.5	20	12.0	6	3.4
20–29.9	128	17.3	44	23.9	45	20.9	25	15.0	14	8.0
30 or over, and not reported.	138	18.6	74	40.2	22	10.2	22	13.2	20	11.4

SOURCE: Special Surveys.

with tenure is shown in Table 24 from the Agricultural Census of 1946. While all rural Cubans seem to be less mobile than farm people in the United States, the differences among the tenure classes are similar to the pattern in the States. The owners are most stable, renters next, then sharecroppers and squatters. No data were reported in the census on the mobility of wageworkers, but information was secured in 1946 in the Special Surveys (Table 25). These figures reveal a pattern similar to that shown in the 1946 census, and in addition show the great mobility of the wage-worker, who in general occupies a rather low status in Cuba as he also does in the United States. The wageworkers migrate into the sugar, coffee, and tobacco areas for the harvest, moving in rather well-defined patterns. For example, the assistant manager

TABLE 26. PLACE OF PREVIOUS RESIDENCE OF 742 CUBAN FAMILIES BY TENURE CLASS

Previous Residence	Total		Owner or Part-Owner		Renter		Share-cropper		Wage-worker	
	Num-ber	Per Cent	Num-ber	Per Cent	Num-ber	Per Cent	Num-ber	Per Cent	Num-ber	Per Cent
Total 742		100.0	184	100.0	215	100.0	167	100.0	176	100.0
Always on this farm ..272		36.7	98	53.3	76	35.3	50	29.9	48	27.3
Other farm, same town-ship 119		16.0	25	13.6	35	16.3	26	15.7	33	18.7
Other township, same county.190		25.6	35	19.1	59	27.4	54	32.3	42	23.9
Other county, this prov-ince 107		14.4	23	12.5	36	16.7	21	12.6	27	15.3
Adjacent province ... 29		3.9	1	0.5	1	0.5	11	6.6	16	9.1
Nonadjacent province ... 16		2.2	1	0.5	4	1.9	4	2.4	7	4.0
Foreign country 6		0.8	1	0.5	4	1.9	1	0.6	0	0.0
Not reported . 3		0.4	0	0.0	0	0.0	0	0.0	3	1.7

SOURCE: Special Surveys.

of Central Florida, in western Camagüey, reported that their workers who come in for the zafra originate mainly in the small farm areas of Las Villas, the next province to the west. Similarly, the coffee pickers of El Nicho come largely from the county in which the community is located, and the same workers return year after year.

The permanent group of laborers who live in the bateyes of the colonias are relatively stable; many of them were reported in the Special Surveys as having lived on the same farm for long periods of time. The number of years of residence on the present farm as reported in the census is only a partial measure of differences between the tenure classes, but it is at least indicative. It would be necessary to have data on the ages of the groups before any conclusion could be drawn. For example, it is highly probable that the partidarios, taken as a group, are younger than the arrendatarios, and that the latter are younger than the owners.

Not only does the laborer move more often, according to information from the Special Surveys, but he is likely to move greater distances as well (Table 26). While most of the moves of all groups were for comparatively short distances, sharecroppers and wageworkers made up most of those who moved greater distances—that is, from other provinces.

Thus social stratification in rural Cuba is related to tenure, size of farm, color, and mobility. The four factors are to a large extent interrelated. As pointed out elsewhere in this report, rural social organization in a formal sense is not elaborate, so that it is difficult to say how color differences, tenure, and other factors affect community participation. The dichotomy of large and small operators is important everywhere, however, whether the operators are owners or cash and share renters. In Bayamo there were two different livestock associations, one for the small and one for the large operators. In Cabaiguán, a cuartario who was a member of the board of directors of the county association of tobacco planters complained that the large planters dominated the organization. He thought the small operators should have an organization of their own to protect their interests.

In general, rural social stratification is less marked in the diversified farming and dairy regions and greatest in the sugar cane, tobacco, and coffee areas. It is in these farming areas that the latifundium exists, with its sharp cleavages between the managerial and working classes.

CHAPTER X

The Cuban Family

The family occupies a basic position in practically all societies throughout the world, but it is particularly important in some because of the weakness or absence of other institutions. Cuba is such a society. In most of the other Latin-American countries, for example, the family shares with the church much authority over its members. In North America, there is not only a wide distribution of church organizations, but the schools, farm organizations, and clubs and societies of every kind also compete for the attention of family members. In Cuba the church plays only a minor role among farm people.[1] In rural areas not only is

---

[1] Although there are several active congregations of Protestants in Cuba, well over 90 per cent of the population is nominally Roman Catholic. The chapels of both Protestants and Roman Catholics are located, without exception as far as the writer could ascertain or observe, in the cities and towns. Yet Cuban farmers live generally in the open country. Their contact with churches is therefore minimized. Their attitudes suggest general indifference, a condition which is widely recognized.

Church inactivity has its roots in the history of the island. Historians are generally agreed that the quality of the clergy sent to the island in colonial times left much to be desired. There were exceptions but they were few. They were often "ecclesiastical exiles from the peninsula because of offenses which forbade their exercising their sacred offices among people who knew their offenses." As church and state were one in the colonial days, the clergy shared with the political authorities the criticisms of the local inhabitants. Finally, in the War for Independence, the church hierarchy was inevitably on the side of Spain and thus completely divorced from the people of their parishes.

Church and state were made separate institutions in the new Republic, with the result that the church could no longer depend upon the public treasury for its financial support. There is no evidence that the church showed any concern for the social and

the church usually nonexistent as a regularly functioning institution, but often there is no school and usually no other formal group or association. The family and the neighborhood provide most of the social contacts for the people.

HISTORICAL BACKGROUND

In contemporary Cuba family characteristics vary with the social classes, with rural and urban groups, and with ethnic differences. The upper-class family is quite different from the lower-class and the urban from the rural, while cutting across all these factors are color differences. Nevertheless, no matter what group or class is involved, there is a basic pattern of family life which is part of the heritage of Spanish culture. The respective positions and roles of the father-husband, the wife-mother, and the children are essentially those of the Roman Catholic family of feudal Spain, with such modifications as have come about through experience in the New World. Included in that experience was the influence of the now extinct native peoples with whom the conquistadores came in contact, and especially that of the African Negro who formed, and still forms, such an important part of the population of the island.

The founders of Cuban civilization were the Spanish conquistadores of the sixteenth century. They gave to the Spanish white people the dominant position in the colonial society, and established Spanish law and institutions as the bases of social organization. For the family, this meant an essentially patriarchal structure, with the father the dominant authority over mother and children. The wife-mother's position was subordinate, but at the same time she was expected to be a model of virtue and modest behavior, characteristics which in turn inspired reverence and respect on the part of the man. Divorce, of course, was forbidden by the Roman Catholic church and by Spanish law which held sway during colonial times. The double standard of morality condoned disloyalty of the husband while imposing the strictest moral

economic welfare of the population. The pastoral visits of the priests occur about once a year, and then only to baptize the infants—for a fee. The reader will find a review of the situation of the Roman church in the colonial period in Charles M. Pepper, *Tomorrow in Cuba*, pp. 240–51. The Protestant churches are discussed in J. Merle Davis, *The Cuban Church in a Sugar Economy* (New York: International Missionary Council, 1942).

standards for the wife. Even premarital unchastity was not regarded as an especially serious infraction of the moral code as far as young men were concerned, but for young girls it was a calamity of the first order. The girls were protected by most extraordinary zeal, involving a careful system of chaperonage. The middle- or upper-class wife-mother was enthroned as a sort of queen with servants to do the manual work and to care for the children. Neither she nor her daughters were allowed to do any work, but she was expected to live a rather cloistered life, seldom to be seen in public except at church. She was a bird in a cage, a sheltered creature—a victim of the extreme romanticism of the age of chivalry.

The position of Cuban women in the cities at about the middle of the nineteenth century is suggested in the following extract from García de Arboleya:

The fair sex is distinguished in our cities from the others in that it is not allowed to go out by day unless in a carriage, except to go to mass on festival days if the church is near. Even to go to the chapel it is always necessary that the woman have a page who carries her floor rug which he spreads out in the selected place in order that his mistress may be able to kneel upon it.

At the evening promenades, our women are not able to attend except in a carriage and all attempts that have been made to attend on foot have been unfruitful. Only at night are they permitted to do so. At night also they are seen in the clothing stores, flower and fashion shops, in the silver shops, and even more in the glass and ice shops; but not in other kinds of establishments. Also they make and receive visits at night. She who has no carriage lives, therefore, from the time the sun rises until it sets, in perpetual seclusion; from which she is diverted in the afternoon in the windows, then opened wide. A little later arrives the hour of the visits, of the diversions and amusements, the talk-fests (*tertulianos*), the evening military parade, the theatre, and the ball . . .[2]

Male dominance. The Spanish Civil Code, which is the basis of Cuban law, regarded the husband as the protector of his wife, whom she was obliged to obey.[3] He is the administrator of the

[2] García de Arboleya, *op. cit.*, pp. 261–62.

[3] Angel C. Betancourt, *Codigo civil* (3rd ed.; Havana: Imprenta y Papeleria de Rambla, Bouza y Cia, 1934), Art. 57, p. 68.

conjugal or joint property. If he is less than eighteen years of age, however, he cannot administer it without the permission of his own father, or if he has none, of his mother; or lacking both, of his tutor.[4] The husband is the representative of his wife and she is not able to appear in court without his permission.[5] The wife is not allowed to engage in financial transactions without the permission of her husband, except when she is purchasing consumer goods for the household.[6] The husband and his heirs can claim nullification of acts which a wife has undertaken without permission of her husband.

Moreover, says Article 58: "The wife is obligated to follow her husband where he wishes to fix his residence. The courts, however, are empowered with just cause, to exempt this obligation when the husband transfers his residence to a foreign country."[7] "The wife shall enjoy the honors of her husband, except those which were strictly and exclusively personal, and will conserve them so long as she does not contract a new marriage."[8] This is an especially significant characteristic of the patriarchal family. The wife shines by reflected glory. While a strict interpretation of this code could scarcely be called typical of the contemporary Cuban family, it is part of the heritage and is manifest in many, though attentuated, ways.

The favored position of the male is demonstrated in the laws governing divorce as they existed in the old Spanish Code and were incorporated into Cuban law. Under the Code which prevailed in Cuba before the passage of the law of 1918, which specifically gave it legal sanction, a divorce was very difficult to obtain, especially by a woman. Adultery was the main cause, but especially adultery of the wife. Article 105 of the Code puts it this way: "The adultery of the wife in any case, and of the husband when it results in a public scandal, or the neglect (*menosprecio*)

[4] *Ibid.*, Art. 59, p. 69.
[5] *Ibid.*, Art. 60, p. 69. This provision is no longer in force, but was part of the early code.
[6] *Ibid.*, Art. 61 and 62.
[7] *Ibid.*, pp. 68–69.
[8] *Ibid.*, Art. 64, p. 72. A footnote points out that this no longer has practical application in view of the "constitution and the democratic ideas that inspired it," but since the article has not specifically been abrogated, the author keeps it in the text as if in force.

of the wife."[9] What the article does is to recognize the double standard of virtue. For the woman the punishment is harsh and unequivocal. For the man—well, it is all right for him to have a mistress as long as he does not neglect his legal wife or stir up a public scandal. If he is careful about it, there is no danger that his standing in the community or his nominal relation to his legal family will be affected.[10]

Position of children. According to this ancient pattern of family life, children were entirely subject to the disposition of the parents, with little or no protection guaranteed by the state. Article 154 of the Civil Code says:

The father, or in lieu thereof, the mother, has dominion over their legitimate children; and the children have the obligation to obey them while they remain in their control and to pay them respect and reverence always.

The natural children which have been acknowledged and those adopted minors are under the dominion of the father or of the mother who recognize or adopt them, and have the same obligation of those spoken of in the preceding paragraph.[11]

Parental duties toward children were also set forth in the Code as follows:

The father, and in lieu thereof, the mother, have in respect to their minor children:

1. The duty to feed them, have them in their company, educate them and instruct them with regard to their fortunes, and represent them in the exercise of all the actions that can redound to their benefit.

2. The power to correct them and punish them moderately.[12]

The obligation of parents to support, educate, and care, for their children is thus clearly specified in the law. Only in "complete

[9] *Ibid.,* p. 93.

[10] According to Edward Westermarck, "In Spain separation . . . may be obtained if the adultery of the husband has given rise to public scandal and he has completely abandoned his wife, or if he keeps the other woman in the house." *The History of Human Marriage* (5th ed.; London: Macmillan, 1921), Vol. III, pp. 357–58.

[11] Betancourt, *op. cit.,* p. 106. In a footnote the author explains that in earlier legislation the mother did not have parental dominion over her legitimate children. This authority was given for the first time in the Law of Civil Matrimony of June 18, 1870, and made applicable to Cuba in 1883. This is another revelation of the inferior status of women in the early family system.

[12] *Ibid.,* Art. 155, p. 106.

state of indigency," says an explanatory footnote of the author, would the public authority provide for the needs of the child. Under such an arrangement, ordinary cases of neglect or exploitation or failure to educate and care for the children would not come to the attention of the legal authorities. However, Article 156 provides that parents may seek the support of government authority if need be, in order to enforce their own authority over an unruly child.[13]

The decline of the aristocratic family. By 1946 the broad pattern of family structure indicated above as part of the Spanish heritage prevailed in any substantial form in only a small minority of Cuban families. Indeed, it is doubtful if it can be said to exist in its purity at all, since modifications of the legal code underlying family relations have been made periodically and always in the direction of a more democratic type of organization.

There were, as previously implied, certain elements in the new environment which made the persistence of a strictly feudal, Catholic family quite impossible. One of these influences was the fact that the feudal estate was not established in Cuba as it was in so many other countries in the early period. The large plantation is a comparatively recent phenomenon in Cuba. According to the historical records, there was originally a rather wide distribution of land.[14] This stands to reason, for there was plenty of unappropriated land up until the War of Independence for whoever wanted to acquire it. While most of the island was at one time included within the large circular haciendas, these were often communally owned and property rights were therefore widely distributed. The relative unimportance of the latifundium meant a less favorable environment for the perpetuation of the feudal family. There was a considerable number of sugar and coffee plantations and tobacco vegas which permitted the old aristocratic type of family to survive for a time; but plainly the general picture was one of a small farm society, which promoted the development of the egalitarian type of family so far as the rural areas were concerned.

The Negro. Another factor of importance in Cuban family history is that of the Negro. Obviously, the transplantation of the

---

[13] *Ibid.*, Art. 156, p. 107.
[14] See discussion of the Cuban land system in Chapter V.

Negro from his native home and established institutions in Africa to the New World with its strange new life of slavery meant severe disruption of his family life along with all other aspects of Negro culture. In short, the Negro was so completely subjugated to Spanish culture that within a few generations he lost almost completely all but minor traces of his own. Conditions of slavery were, of course, very unfavorable to the maintenance of family life. The fact that a slave was property and therefore subject to sale and purchase meant that the normal ties of affection which bind husband and wife and parents and children were frequently broken. Such an existence was not conducive to the establishment of moral standards of responsibility in parents. Even though the Negro was converted to the Christian faith and no doubt was taught the Christian mores governing family life and the relation of the sexes, during slavery days it was not an easy matter for him to practice these precepts, no matter how much he may have wanted to do so. It is not to be inferred that the Cuban Negro family is of one type and the Cuban white family quite another; but there is some evidence to indicate that the contemporary Negro family in Cuba has inherited a certain instability from its slavery background, just as it has in the United States.

In particular, there appears to be a greater casualness about the relations of the sexes. The proportion of colored[15] couples in 1931 who were living together without legal sanction was more than double that for the whites. The illegitimacy rate is likewise about double that for the whites. On the other hand, it must not be overlooked that although the rate of common-law unions is very high, more than half of the colored unions in 1931 were legally sanctioned. This should be taken as evidence of the large measure of assimilation which has been achieved by what has been historically a greatly disadvantaged group and one which has had to adapt to a completely alien culture.

One factor which no doubt has accounted for the progress of the Negro toward acceptance of the mores derived from the Spanish heritage has been the freedom with which intermarriage has taken place between the white and colored groups. Evidence

[15] The census statistics are reported only for the white and colored population, the latter including mulattoes and Chinese as well as Negroes.

of this is the fact that mulattoes outnumber Negroes two to one. The Spanish immigrants were overwhelmingly men, if they married at all it was with Indian or Negro women. At the same time, there was an apparent tendency to import Negro slave women in numbers approximately equal to Negro men.[16] This meant that after the Indian population was eliminated, the women available to the white Spaniards were largely Negroes. José García de Arboleya, writing in 1869, said that among the Spanish immigrants scarcely 8 per cent were women, and of immigrants from the Canary Islands, 20 per cent. In the total population, he said, only 44 per cent were women.[17] This means that there were 127 males per 100 females.

An excess of females apparently existed among the mulatto group. The general shortage of white women meant that there was a relatively large number of interracial unions. These unions were facilitated not only by the unequal sex ratio of the white immigrants, but also by the fact that among the Spanish there were not the psychological impediments to intermarriage such as characterized the relations of the two races in the United States. In the latter country, miscegenation is prohibited by law in many of the states. No such strictures exist in Cuba. The country is by no means free of racial prejudices, but at least there is no legal objection to intermarriage.

It is impossible to say what influence the native Indian women may have had upon the Cuban family. The period of contact between the Spanish and the indigenous culture was brief—scarcely more than a generation—before the latter was exterminated, so that the number of Spanish immigrants who had experience with Indian culture was relatively small. Perhaps the most important aspect of Indian culture which has come down to the present day and affects the family is the type of dwelling which is most common in rural Cuba, the bohío. But aside from this material trait and a few others, including the primitive Indian agricultural practices, there is no evidence of influence from this source.

[16] For example, in the monopoly to import slaves granted by Charles V to Governor de Bresa in 1523, permission was given to bring in 750 men and 750 women slaves to the West Indies. (See *Report of the Census of Cuba, 1899*, p. 67.)

[17] José García de Arboleya, *Tres questiones sobre la isla de Cuba* (Havana, 1869).

Although many Negro women were brought to Cuba along with Negro men, numerical equality was probably never achieved in practice. According to Pezuela, *Diccionario de la Isla de Cuba*, in 1792 there were 41,955 slave Negro males to 10,500 slave Negro females. However, there were only 15,845 free mulatto males to 18,040 free mulatto females. Among the slave mulattoes there were 5,769 males to 6,366 females.[18] In 1827, however, the ratio of men to women among slaves was very much reduced to about 1.8 to 1, a ratio which also held in 1847.[19]

PRESENT-DAY CLASS AND RURAL-URBAN DIFFERENCES

The most important differentiating factors among Cuban families are probably those of class and rural or urban location. It is necessary to discuss the two together because in some respects the categories are the same. That is to say, the rural family is most often a lower-class family; or to put it another way, the upper-class people all, or practically all, live in the cities. The cities, of course, also contain lower-class families.

The terms "upper class" and "lower class" are used almost exclusively because it is doubtful if there is a middle class in the true sense in Cuba.[20] Yet, as we have previously noted, there is a great range in the incomes of people in the upper and the lower classes. Some of the upper lower-class incomes exceed those of the lower upper-class group, but the difference between the two major classes is nevertheless distinguishable. The difference is not entirely or even primarily economic, but is socio-psychological and traditional.

The upper-class family. In general, the upper-class family approximates most closely the traditional type briefly characterized at the beginning of this chapter. The father is dominant, the mother submissive and secluded. The husband is usually in one of the professional occupations or a government office of the higher rank, or he may be one of the well-to-do farmers, a sugar colono, a coffee or tobacco planter, or livestock raiser. His home in the city will be rather commodious, with separate quarters for one, two, or more servants and perhaps for a *chófer*. The household is

[18] See reference to Pezuela in *Report of the Census of Cuba, 1899*, p. 704.
[19] See *Censo de 1943*, p. 713.
[20] See discussion of this point in Chapter VIII.

operated completely by the servants. The cook does the shopping for groceries as well as the cooking. The maid will clean the marble or tiled floors and porches daily, or at least twice a week; she may or may not do the family washing and ironing, depending on particular arrangements in force; and she makes the beds and generally keeps the house. If there is not a special nurse for the children, she may also take care of them in addition to her other duties. The chófer drives the husband to his work, returns and takes the children to school. After that he may drive the cook to the market to do the shopping, or the señora to a downtown store or to the beauty parlor. He repairs leaky toilets, water-taps, and light switches, serves as a kind of general handy man about the house.

The wife-mother has few duties and few cares, as far as general appearances go, although there may be many worries and anxieties beneath the surface. These might arise from financial stringency, from neglect of her by her husband, and the like. She is seldom seen outside the home except to go to church or to get into the car to go shopping. In the evening she may be seen with other members of the family sitting on the front porch in a rocking chair engaging in that favorite Cuban diversion, conversation. She is sheltered, respected, and waited upon. She even has little to do with the upbringing of her children, as far as their daily wants and needs are concerned.

The children likewise live sheltered lives. They are guided about by a nursemaid during their childhood and accompanied by adults practically everywhere they go. When they become of school age they are taken to school by the chófer in the family car or in a school bus.[21] In all probability it will be a private rather than a public school which they attend. The children in this social class have practically no responsibilities in the home. They are given no chores to do and no errands to run as children would be in a home in the United States with a comparable income and status. Daughters are not expected to help with dishwashing, making the beds, or other household tasks considered by North American families as part of a girl's responsibilities as a family member as well as necessary training and experience.

[21] In Havana each of the various private schools operates a bus.

In the lower half of the upper-class group, living is on a more modest scale. There may be only one servant, a maid-of-all-work; there would be no automobile and hence no chófer. There are more stresses due to financial limitations, since such a family has all the wants and desires of the upper group and feels frustrated that they lack the income to satisfy them. Yet they will make great sacrifices in some ways to keep up appearances in others. A new hat to a woman in this group is much more important than a savings account, because its visibility is greater. Emphasis is placed on the purchase of objects which are within the budgetary limits and at the same time will contribute most to the achievement and maintenance of identification with the upper class. The children in this group receive more attention from the mother since hiring a nursemaid is not possible for financial reasons. As they get old enough, they may also be expected to perform more duties in the home and may even go out on errands unaccompanied by adults.

In most of the homes of the upper class there are one or two grandparents or other relatives. Family ties are strong, there is much sharing of resources, and general assumption of responsibility one for another. When a member of a family loses a job or money, the other members—father, brothers, or sister—will be expected to come to the rescue. The family definitely would lose caste if a member were to go hungry or be compelled to ask for charity. Similarly, if a member of a family obtains wealth or high position, he is expected to spread the benefits among his relatives. If one achieves a high government office, for example, it is expected that he will use his authority to have his relatives appointed to good positions. Nepotism is not condemned; it is the general practice. During the political campaign of the summer of 1946, a member of the House of Representatives of the Cuban Congress and former president of the Senate ran a full-page advertisement in a Santiago newspaper in support of the candidacy of his son, also running for election to the House of Representatives. The main point of the advertisement was that the father was willing to wager $25,000 against $20,000 that his son would be elected, and pointed out the advantages of having a father-and-son combination which would be "difficult to improve upon. Thus has been demonstrated in five consecutive campaigns our triumph in defending our own interests and aspirations of friends." There apparently is no basic objection in Cuba to having father and son as representatives from the same province.

The close in-group feeling of the Cuban family has been observed by a number of outside commentators. W. F. Johnson says that love of children, to the extent of being willing to make any sacrifice for their happiness,

. . . [is] perhaps an exaggerated development of the motherly instinct. A Cuban mother will yield to any caprice of her children, even though she may realize that in so doing she endangers their future. As a result, Cuban children, although lovable and affectionate, are not always well behaved or gentle mannered . . .

The love which parents, rich or poor, educated or ignorant, bestow on their children, no matter how many little ones may compose the family, or how small the purse which feeds them is proverbial . . .[22]

However, Johnson's further observation that "no child, even of a far removed relative, is ever permitted to enter an institution of charity if it can be avoided, but will find instead an immediate and hearty welcome in the family of a man who may not know at times where to look for money for the next day's meal"[23] may be open to question so far as contemporary lower-class families are concerned. It is no doubt quite true of the class-conscious upper-class group that even though a family should fall on evil days financially, it would be able to depend on relatives rather than upon public charity. In fact, it is likely that relatives would not permit public charity because of the reflection upon the family name.

The lower-class urban family. It is a different story with the Cuban family of poorer class. Here there is a greater readiness to accept charity and few inhibitions caused by considerations of pride. Also there is less hesitancy about committing a child to an institution that is willing to care for it. In fact some mothers, hard-pressed by poverty and their own inability to care properly for a child, will seek by whatever means are available to get a child

[22] W. F. Johnson, *The History of Cuba* (New York: B. F. Buck and Co., Inc., 1920), Vol. V, pp. 2–3.
[23] *Ibid.*, p. 3.

committed.[24] Even so, however, there can be no doubt of the strength of the affectional bond between parents and children, regardless of social status. It is only the severe pressure of poverty which drives mothers to the dire necessity of giving up custody of their children.

Life presses hard upon many of those who do manual work, and it is such people who compose the lower class. Their living conditions in the cities are characterized by extraordinarily bad housing with much overcrowding. Many of them live in *solares* in the upper-class sections, where they are accessible as domestic servants. The solares consist of alleys lined on either side by one-room quarters, each of which may be the abode of several unmarried persons or of one or more families.[25] Children are left to fend for themselves while mothers and fathers work. Women in this class not only do their own housework, but also earn their living by doing housework for the upper-class families. While their own children run in the streets and generally care for themselves, they may be acting as nursemaids for upper-class children.

There are compulsory school-attendance laws but they are not enforced. Since upper-class families would send their children to school whether laws to compel them existed or not, the violators of the laws are usually the lower-class parents. Their children may go to school for a few grades and then drop out and try to earn money shining shoes, running errands, carrying market baskets, and doing whatever incidental tasks they may be able to find. They solicit coins of passers-by and collect paper scraps and all sorts of things they might possibly be able to sell as salvage. Pilfering is common. In short, almost the entire childhood population in the lower-class urban families might be classified as "neglected" in a better regulated society. In the last analysis, how-

[24] A case in point came to our immediate attention in Havana. Our maid, a mother of six, tried for months before she succeeded in getting her boy into an institution.

[25] Juan M. Chailloux Cardona, *Sintesis historica de la vivienda popular: los horrores del solar Habanero* (Havana: Jesús Montero, 1945). In his survey of 50 solares, he found 1,434 rooms, in each of which at least one family lived. The overcrowding shown in this survey is almost incredible. In one case 16 persons, 12 adults and 4 children, occupied one room about 10 by 16 feet. Other cases involved 15, 14, 13, 12, and 10 occupants per room. Sanitary facilities are unbelievably bad. In one solar in Vedado — an elite residential area — there lived 187 persons, for whom two toilets were provided. Rents are high and such housing provides profitable investment. Average rent was $12 per month, which was 37.5 per cent of the minimum wage of $45.

ever, this whole, underprivileged urban group is necessary to the upper class. What the latter would do without them is hard to imagine. They would have difficulty surviving! Therefore, the upper class might well pay some attention to the welfare of the less fortunate groups.

The farm family. The farm family in Cuba is not much different in composition, organization, and general pattern of life from that found in North America. As a rule, perhaps, the rural Cuban father-husband occupies a more dominant position than does his counterpart in the United States, but generalization must be made with caution. Farm women do their own housework although they practically never work in the fields.[26] Their inferior position vis-à-vis the male is probably symbolized by the custom of men eating without the company of the women. The latter serve the meal but seldom sit and eat with the men of the household. This practice is by no means universal, but it is common.

Obedience to and respect for parents is developed in the child. This, it appears, is accomplished without harsh punishment. Although the use of tobacco is very common among men in Cuba, it is customary for grown sons not to smoke in the presence of the father until after the son is married. This is apparently a gesture of respect, as there seem to be no moral taboos against smoking. Children are generally considered to be subject to the will of the parents—notably the father—until they are married, whatever their ages may be.

OTHER CHARACTERISTICS OF CUBAN FAMILIES

Age at marriage. The legal age of marriage is 14 for boys and 12 for girls. However, the consent of parents is necessary for marriages between these ages and 21 years. While accurate records of age at marriage are not available, the census gives the ages of the married population. For 1931 the data indicate that 7.6 per cent of all couples living together, whether with or without legal sanc-

---

[26] This fact seemed to impress one of our informants, an immigrant from Spain, who related this story: A Spaniard came to Cuba many years ago hoping to make his fortune and return to the old country. He did well, and in course of time he returned to Spain. As he set sail from Cuban shores he said, "Farewell, paradise for horses and women; hell for men and oxen." (Horses are the pampered darlings of the Cuban animal world.)

tion, were under 21 years of age. Of the legally married, only .7 per cent of the males were under 21, compared with 6.2 per cent for the females. Of the common-law unions, the males who were under 21 represented but 1.1 per cent of all males in this class, while of the females in the group 12.1 per cent were under 21.

The data for 1943 seem to indicate that the age at marriage is advancing in Cuba, since at that date only .3 per cent of the married males and 2.3 per cent of the married females were under 20.[27] Early marriages are apparently not very common among the Cuban population, particularly among the males. There is a marked difference between the median ages of married men and married women. Among the Cuban native white population in 1943, the median age of the married man was 41.6 years, compared with 36.1 years for the married women. Among the colored group the differential was slightly greater, the median for the men being 44.9 and for the women 37.5, both being greater than for the white group.[28] In the census of 1919, the average age of the married men was 41 and of married women 34, a difference of seven years.[29] The large age differential between husbands and wives is also revealed in the data secured in the Special Surveys of 1946. In the case of 44 couples in Managua, near Havana, the average age of husbands was 47.4 years and that of the wives 42.7. Among 11 couples at San Blas, the average age of the husbands was 50 and of the wives 44. At Managua there were three couples in which the wife was older than the husband, and one case in which the ages were identical. As a general rule, the Cuban male chooses a wife four or more years younger than himself. The median ages of husbands and wives in the 742 households covered by the Special Surveys show a difference of 4.7 years (Table 27).[30]

[27] Unfortunately the age groups for the two census periods are not comparable. In 1931 the group included those of 20 years of age, while in 1943 the upper limit was 19. While certainly a good many more would have been reported as married in 1943 if the 20-year-olds had been included, it is doubtful if this would account for all the difference shown between the two figures.

[28] Medians were computed from data in Table 19, p. 949, *Censo de 1943*.

[29] *Census of the Republic of Cuba, 1919*, p. 346.

[30] The 44 Managua couples reported above are included in these totals. However, in the tabulation offered here, no attempt was made to get the age difference for each couple, as was done for the Managua sample. The latter is a more accurate method. However, the calculation of median ages for large numbers of husbands and wives gives further support to the conclusion regarding age differences.

TABLE 27. DIFFERENCE IN MEDIAN AGES OF HUSBANDS AND WIVES AMONG
742 CUBAN FAMILIES, BY TENURE CLASS

Tenure	Median Ages		
	Husbands	Wives	Difference
All	45.2	40.5	4.7
Owners	56.7	49.2	7.5
Renters	46.8	41.8	5.0
Sharecroppers	39.5	38.1	1.4
Laborers	38.5	34.6	3.9

SOURCE: Special Surveys.

The difference was greatest for owners and least for sharecroppers. Why this difference should exist is not clear.

Family composition and size. According to evidence from the Special Surveys, the typical Cuban family is composed of husband, wife, and their children. The situation may be illustrated by the data from Managua regarding 50 families. The number of normal families—that is, those with husband, wife, and children present —was 33; those with husband and wife only, 4; those with mother and children only, 2; with father and children only, 2; and those containing other persons than the husband, wife, and their children, 9.

These last nine families are listed below to show the typical variations that occur:

1. Husband, wife, 5 single children, 2 married sons and their wives, 1 grandchild.

2. Mother, 2 daughters, 3 stepdaughters.

3. Mother, 2 sons, 1 boy unrelated.

4. Husband, wife, 2 children, husband's brother and father.

5. Husband, wife, 1 son, wife's sister.

6. Husband, wife, 9 children, wife's sister.

7. Husband, wife, 4 children, husband's father.

8. Husband, wife, 2 single children, wife's sister, a divorced daughter and her son.

9. Husband, wife, 2 married sons and their wives, and their 4 children.

Thus in fewer than 20 per cent of the 50 Managua families were there persons outside the normal family group, and these were other relatives in all cases except one. Grandfathers were present in only 2 cases, or 4 per cent of the families.

TABLE 28. PERCENTAGES OF CUBAN FAMILIES (HOUSEHOLDS) IN EACH SIZE GROUP,
AND AVERAGE FAMILY SIZES, BY PROVINCE, 1943

	All Provinces	Pinar del Río	Havana	Matanzas	Las Villas	Camagüey	Oriente
			Percentage Distribution				
Family size in persons:							
1 ....14.2		11.0	18.0	15.0	11.0	16.4	11.7
2 ....11.1		8.5	15.0	11.2	9.0	11.1	8.1
3 ....12.7		10.9	16.0	12.8	11.8	12.3	10.0
4 ....12.7		12.2	14.0	12.6	12.7	12.7	11.5
5 ....11.4		12.0	11.0	11.4	12.2	11.4	11.3
6 .... 9.7		11.3	7.9	10.0	10.8	9.6	10.5
7 .... 7.9		9.6	5.7	8.0	9.1	7.6	9.0
8 .... 6.1		7.6	4.0	6.1	7.1	5.8	7.6
9 .... 4.6		5.7	2.7	4.5	5.3	4.4	6.0
10 .... 3.3		4.1	1.8	3.0	3.7	3.1	4.5
11–15 .... 5.4		6.3	3.0	4.7	6.2	4.5	8.0
16–20 .... 0.7		0.6	0.4	0.5	0.7	0.6	1.1
21 or more .. 0.3		0.2	0.2	0.2	0.2	0.3	0.3
			Average Number of Persons per Family				
Total population. 5.18		5.57	4.43	5.00	5.47	5.03	5.85
Urban 4.50		4.73	4.22	4.53	4.83	4.67	5.35
Rural 5.70		5.74	5.21	5.29	5.78	5.20	6.04

SOURCE: *Censo de 1943*, pp. 996f, Table 23.

The Cuban family on the average is about one-fourth larger
than that of the United States. In 1943 the average number of
persons per family was 5.18[31] (see Table 28). The corresponding
figure for the United States in 1940 was 3.8.[32] For Cuba the average family in 1931 was 5.24 persons, indicating only a very slight
decline by 1943. Table 28 shows differences among the provinces
in the average size of families, a reflection largely of the different
proportions of rural and urban people. Havana Province, with its
large (88 per cent) urban population ranks lowest in family size,
while Matanzas ranks next. In the latter province also a large
proportion (53.4 per cent) of the population lives in cities. Camagüey also ranks low, even though only about 46 per cent of its
population is urban. The reason for this low rank is not clear.
Oriente, with over 60 per cent, and Pinar del Río, with nearly 70

[31] This figure was obtained by dividing the total population by the number of
families.

[32] *Statistical Abstract of the United States, 1943* (Washington: United States Bureau
of the Census, 1944), p. 46.

per cent of the population rural, rank highest in average size of family.

Variation in the size of household by region and farm type is very great, although not consistent. That is, it can scarcely be said that there is a close association between type of farming and the size of household. The two dairy areas, Sancti-Spíritus and Bayamo, differ significantly on this item, as do the two diversified-farming areas (Güines and Florencia) and the tobacco regions (Pinar del Río and Cabaiguán). The sugar regions (Manguito and Florida) and the coffee areas (Trinidad and Alto Songo) compare more closely with each other. The coffee areas are both extremely isolated geographically, and this factor, more than the type of farming, appears to be the significant one.

The size of the farm households included in the Special Surveys varied not only by regions but also by tenure. Larger average households were found among the upper tenure groups (Table 29). That is, owners ranked highest, renters next, sharecroppers next, and laborers last. The large number of single person households in the laborer group tends to reduce the average. In all other categories, the modal group—the one which occurs most frequently— is that of "10 or more."

Marital status of the population. Data are available in the various censuses of Cuba since 1899 to show the number of single, married, and widowed persons in the population. For 1931 and 1943 the number of divorced persons is also reported. The figures for 1943, shown in Table 30, reveal a rather small proportion of the population as married—for males, 33.9 per cent and for females, 35.5 per cent. Comparable figures for the United States as of 1940 are 61.2 and 61 per cent respectively. The data are not comparable, however, since percentages for the United States are based upon the population 15 years of age and over, while those for Cuba include girls of 12 or more and boys of 14 or more in the base population. In addition, the Cuban census does not classify a couple as married unless the bond has been legally sanctioned. Common-law marriages are not regarded by the census as marriages, and those so united were included in the category marked "single." It is not known how many such unions there were in 1943. When the number of girls and boys under 15 was subtracted from the Cuban population and marital condition computed on the balance, the result was a percentage married of 41 for the males and 47.4 for the females. This figure is somewhat closer to that of the United States, although it is still much smaller.

TABLE 29. PERSONS PER HOUSEHOLD AMONG 742 CUBAN FAMILIES IN THE SPECIAL SURVEYS, BY TENURE, 1946

Tenure Class	Total	Persons per Household										
		1	2	3	4	5	6	7	8	9	10 or More	Median
All classes	742	14	39	75	92	81	86	88	70	40	157	6.8
Owners	184	1	8	15	21	18	17	24	21	7	52	7.5
Renters	215	3	8	24	26	23	19	22	27	20	43	7.2
Sharecroppers ...	167	1	6	16	21	19	23	23	14	6	38	6.9
Laborers	176	9	17	20	24	21	27	19	8	7	24	6.7

TABLE 30. MARITAL STATUS OF THE CUBAN POPULATION OF MARRIAGEABLE AGE BY PROVINCES, RURAL AND URBAN, 1943*

Province	Percentages							
	Single		Married		Widowed		Divorced	
	Males	Females	Males	Females	Males	Females	Males	Females
All provinces	62.7	56.6	33.9	35.5	2.9	7.0	0.5	0.9
Urban	59.3	52.2	36.8	27.2	2.9	9.0	0.9	1.5
Rural	65.2	60.4	31.7	34.0	2.9	5.3	0.3	0.3
Pinar del Río ...	65.7	61.0	30.9	32.9	3.1	5.7	0.3	0.4
Urban	58.7	55.4	37.2	35.1	3.5	8.7	0.6	0.8
Rural	66.9	62.2	29.8	32.4	3.0	5.1	0.2	0.3
Havana	55.1	47.7	40.7	41.5	3.3	9.0	0.9	1.8
Urban	54.9	47.8	41.0	40.8	3.1	9.5	1.1	2.0
Rural	55.8	47.9	39.8	44.3	3.8	7.0	0.5	0.8
Matanzas	59.6	54.1	36.4	38.1	3.5	7.3	0.5	0.6
Urban	58.3	54.6	37.4	35.4	3.6	9.0	0.7	1.0
Rural	60.3	55.2	35.9	39.8	3.4	6.2	0.3	0.3
Las Villas	60.6	56.8	35.7	37.1	3.3	7.3	0.4	0.5
Urban	69.7	54.1	37.1	34.8	2.6	9.4	0.5	1.0
Rural	54.9	58.3	41.1	38.3	3.7	6.2	0.3	0.3
Camagüey	66.4	67.7	30.7	36.3	2.5	6.2	0.4	0.7
Urban	59.2	61.0	36.6	36.4	2.9	8.3	1.2	1.2
Rural	69.1	70.9	28.4	36.3	2.2	5.0	0.4	0.3
Oriente	71.4	67.3	26.1	26.8	2.1	4.9	0.4	0.6
Urban	62.6	61.0	33.9	30.5	2.7	7.3	0.8	1.2
Rural	74.4	70.9	23.4	25.0	1.9	3.8	0.3	0.3

SOURCE: *Censo de 1943*, p. 939, Table 17.

*Percentages were computed on the basis of the sum of those reported in the four categories of marital status. Those reported as unknown were left out of consideration, as were those below marriageable age—that is, girls under 12 and boys under 14. The urban figures represent population in cities and municipios of 5,000 inhabitants or more.

Table 30, which is designed as a general presentation of the census data, shows the following significant facts:

1. Proportionately more women than men are married, considering the population as a whole. This is true for all of the provinces, although there is a good deal of variation in the differences. For example, in Camagüey almost 6 per cent more women than men are married, while in Oriente and Havana Provinces the difference is less than 1 per cent.

2. When rural and urban populations are compared, there are important differences to be noted. In the urban population of all provinces, the proportion of men married exceeds that of women, a result primarily of the excess of women in the cities.

3. In the rural population the situation is reversed, with the proportions of women married exceeding those of men. The province of Las Villas is the only exception.

4. Generally, the proportions of the population married are greater in the cities than in the rural areas, according to these figures, a fact undoubtedly due in large part to the definition of "married" which was followed by the census. In the city the proportion of couples living together and married legally is undoubtedly much greater than it is in the country, where there is not such easy access to legally designated officials and where there is often not enough money to pay the necessary costs. The small percentage of those married in Oriente can by no means be regarded as representative of the total couples who are living together.

5. The proportions of widowed in the population are much higher for women than for men, a fact found to be true in population groups elsewhere. This seems to be due to three factors: (a) the widowed male is more likely to remarry than is the widowed female, so that at the time of any enumeration the remarried widower is classified as married rather than widowed; (b) women have a longer life expectancy than men and are therefore more likely to survive their husbands; and (c) Cuban husbands are on the average several years older than their wives.

The proportions of widowed in Cuba compare with 4.2 per cent for males and 11 per cent for females in the United States. Thus the Cuban rates are considerably lower. Even when Cubans under

15 years of age are subtracted, for comparability, the rates are still less than those for the United States, being 3.5 for males and 9.3 for females. The total numbers of widowed Cubans enumerated in 1943 was 46,760 for males and 107,002 for females. The rural-urban distribution of the widowed follows a pattern familiar to students of the United States population. Larger proportions of widowed women are found in the urban centers, to which they tend to migrate. However, the difference between rural and urban in the Cuba data is not great; it would no doubt be more marked if analysis could be made for centers smaller than 5,000 population. The proportions of widowed men are the same for rural and urban.

6. The proportions of divorced people in the population are not large, amounting to only .5 per cent for men and .9 per cent for women. The fact that the proportion increased from 1931 over three times (.2 per cent of the total population in 1931, as compared with .7 per cent in 1943) was the occasion for rather extended comment by the writer of the text to the population census.[33] The increase is attributed to changes in the laws, which have facilitated the securing of divorces, and to the "great economical and spiritual instability." Divorced males in the United States constituted 1.3 per cent of those 15 years of age or over, and divorced females 1.7 per cent.

Marriage rates and sex ratios. The variation in percentages of males and females married in the various provinces is definitely related to the differing proportions of the sexes in the populations (see Table 31). In general, it will be noted that the greater the excess of males in the population, the lower the proportion of men and the higher the proportion of women who are married. The relationship would be more clearly evident if the census reported all marital unions, not merely those which were legally consummated.

Distribution of excess males. While discussing the relationship to the marriage rate of the proportions of the sexes in the population, it is of some interest to note the great excess of men in the group classified as single, particularly in certain of the provinces (Table 32). Generally, an excess of males is to be found in the rural population, although for some strange reason there seems

[33] *Censo de 1943,* p. 769.

TABLE 31. NUMBER OF MALES PER 100 FEMALES IN THE POPULATION OF THE VARIOUS PROVINCES AND PERCENTAGES OF THE TWO SEXES WHO WERE MARRIED, 1943

Province	Sex Ratio	Percentage Married		
		Men	Women	Difference
Havana 104.0		40.7	41.5	0.8
Oriente 108.9		26.1	26.8	0.7
Las Villas 110.4		35.7	37.1	1.4
Matanzas 111.1		36.4	38.1	1.7
Pinar del Río 112.0		30.9	32.9	2.0
Camagüey 122.4		30.7	36.3	5.6

TABLE 32. NUMBER OF EXCESS MALES IN THE GROUP REPORTED AS "SINGLE" AND SEX RATIOS, BY PROVINCES, RURAL AND URBAN (— INDICATES DEFICIT)

Province	Total		Urban		Rural	
	Excess Males	Sex Ratio	Excess Males	Sex Ratio	Excess Males	Sex Ratio
All provinces 139,862		116	32,824	109	107,038	122
Pinar del Río 11,431		116	—784	93	12,215	121
Havana 32,168		114	15,540	109	16,688	134
Matanzas 11,263		118	—482	98	11,745	131
Las Villas 26,535		116	29,316	153	—2,781	97
Camagüey 35,881		143	1,516	105	34,365	162
Oriente 22,584		109	—12,222	84	34,806	119

SOURCE: *Censo de 1943*, p. 939, Table 17.

to be a deficit of men in rural Las Villas. This may be due to faulty or incomplete enumeration. Also worthy of note is the surprising excess of men in the urban Las Villas population. Camagüey presents an extraordinary picture of numerical disparity between the sexes in the rural population, with 162 men for every 100 women. These differences between rural and urban are the result of migration. In Cuba, as in the United States, women leave the rural areas in greater proportions than do men, tending to depress the female marriage rate in the city, where there is an excess of women, and the male rate in the country, where there is an excess of men.

Marriage as a civil act. All officially recognized marriages in Cuba must be performed by civil officials—notaries or judges usually—who are granted authority by the state to perform them. The Constitution of 1940 provides, among other things, that "marriage shall be valid only when performed by officers with legal capacity to do so." Nevertheless, practicing members of the

Roman Catholic church do not regard themselves as really married until they have had a church ceremony and received the sanction of the church. The church ceremony cannot take the place of the civil one, however, which has also to be consummated. For the orthodox, in other words, two ceremonies are necessary.

TABLE 33. PROPORTIONS OF PERSONS LIVING TOGETHER WITH AND
WITHOUT CIVIL MARRIAGE, BY SEX AND COLOR, 1931

Color and Sex	Total	Legally Married	Mutual Consent
Both classes	100.0	73.8	26.2
Males	100.0	77.0	23.0
Females	100.0	70.7	29.3
White	100.0	78.3	21.7
Males	100.0	80.8	19.2
Females	100.0	75.8	24.2
Colored	100.0	55.2	44.8
Males	100.0	60.9	39.1
Females	100.0	50.1	49.9

In view of the new constitution, common-law unions are not officially recognized until the court has ratified them. For this reason no special category listing them was included in the 1943 census. In all previous censuses since 1899 common-law marriages were listed in a special column labeled *sin sanción legal* (without legal sanction). The incidence of common-law marriages is indicated by the data from the 1931 census reported in Table 33. It will be noted that about one-fourth of all couples living together at the time of the census were common-law unions, that such unions were more common among women than among men, and about twice as frequent among the colored population as among the white. Although the table does not indicate it, the incidence was also greater among the rural areas than the urban.[34]

It is not to be assumed that common-law marriages are any less stable as social entities than those which have the blessing of the state. Previous to the recent constitution and related legislation, there was a certain amount of insecurity in these unions when it came to economic matters, however, involving a larger responsibility for the mother than is now true. The Constitution of 1940 states, "The courts shall determine those cases in which,

[34] For confirmation see the Census of 1931, Table 16 (unpaged).

for reasons of equity, a union between persons with legal capacity to marry shall, because of their stability and exceptional nature, be given the same status as civil marriage."[35]

Divorce. Under Spanish law, divorce was prohibited except for reasons of adultery and a few other extreme types of cases. This situation prevailed in Cuba for a considerable period after its independence. The census of 1899, for example, made no enumeration of divorced persons, explaining that their status was not recognized by Spanish and Cuban law. The same is true of the censuses of 1907 and 1919. The census of 1931 and that of 1943, however, both enumerated divorced persons. The first Cuban law which authorized divorce was instituted in 1918. In 1934 the law was revised and somewhat liberalized. The changes made undoubtedly account for the rather marked increase in the proportions of divorced persons in the population between 1931 and 1943. The Roman Catholic church, naturally, opposed both the 1918 and the 1934 laws, since the church itself disapproves of divorce.

The Constitution of 1940 states, "Marriage can be dissolved by agreement of the spouses or on petition of either of the two for the reasons and in the manner established by law." In addition:

Living allowances for the woman and the children shall enjoy preference over every other obligation, and against that preference no plea can be made of non-attachability of any property, salary, pension or economic income, regardless of its kind.

Unless the woman has proven means of subsistence, or is declared guilty, an allowance shall be fixed for her in proportion to the financial position of the husband and also taking into account the needs of social life. This allowance shall be paid and guaranteed by the divorced husband and shall continue until his ex-spouse marries again, without detriment to the allowance that will be fixed for each child, which must also be guaranteed.

Adequate penalties shall be imposed by law on those who, in case of divorce, of separation or for any other reason, seek to escape or elude that responsibility.[36]

While the rise in the proportion of divorced persons—from 0.7 to 2.1 per cent, an increase of 200 per cent over a twelve-year

[35] *Constitution of 1940*, Article 43.
[36] *Ibid.*

period—can only be characterized as remarkable, it should be borne in mind that since the legalization of divorce is a comparatively recent development in Cuba, many of the recent divorce cases represent only formal recognition of a situation which previously existed in fact although it was not legally condoned.

Illegitimacy. Approximately one-fourth of the population of Cuba in 1943 was reported as illegitimate (Table 34). While the proportion seems to be very high, it does not mean necessarily that all children thus classified are denied a normal family life. Much depends on definition. Unless the parents were legally married, their children were considered nominally illegitimate. The instructions to census enumerators read as follows:

An "extra-matrimonial" child who has been registered is one whose parents are not legally married, but who has been registered in the Civil Register, or in the register of the church if born before 1885, by the father, the mother, or both. An unregistered "extra-matrimonial" child is one whose parents are not legally married, and who has not been recognized by the father or the mother, and who as a consequence does not appear on the Civil or Church Register.[37]

Of the total number of 1,207,451 illegitimate persons in 1943, the births of some 452,053, or 37.4 per cent, had not been registered. Of those of legitimate birth, only 6 per cent were unregistered. Undoubtedly the failure to register births, as well as the failure of many couples to marry legally, is in part due to the fact that in Cuba such acts usually require money, and many people are too poor to afford them. While civil marriages are performed by designated civil officials ostensibly without charge, as is the registration of children, in practice the public officials involved expect a fee. If none appears to be forthcoming, it is said, the official will cause delays or other annoyances until exasperated individuals resort to small bribes to secure the desired official response.

Illegitimacy rates have changed very little since the census of 1919. It is of interest to observe, however, that the proportion of illegitimacy contributed by the colored group has steadily declined since that time. They still contribute about half of the illegitimate persons in the population, although they make up only one-fourth of the total.

[37] *Censo de 1943*, p. 1248.

TABLE 34. ILLEGITIMATE OFFSPRING BY COLOR, AS REPORTED IN VARIOUS CENSUS
ENUMERATIONS IN CUBA

		Total Percent- age Illegit- imate	Illegitimate					
	Total Population Number		All Classes		White		Colored	
Year			Num- ber	Per Cent	Num- ber	Per Cent	Num- ber	Per Cent
1943	4,778,583	25.3	1,207,451	100.0	606,951	50.3	600,500	49.7
1931	3,962,344	24.9	985,952	100.0	360,519	36.6	625,433	63.4
1919	2,889,004	24.0	693,455	100.0	256,553	37.0	436,902	63.0
1899	1,572,797	11.8	185,030	100.0	58,940	31.9	126,090	68.1

SOURCE: Censuses for 1899, 1919, 1931, and 1943.

Under the new constitution the illegitimate child is destined
to enjoy the same rights as those born in wedlock. Although the
laws to implement fully the constitutional guarantees in this as in
many other respects remain to be passed by the Congress, the
theory and intent of those who drafted the constitution is very
clear in the matter, as witness the following:

Children born out of wedlock to a person who at the time of conception was competent to marry have the same rights and duties as
specified in the preceding paragraph, except as to what the law pre-
scribes with respect to inheritance. To this end, the same rights shall
pertain to those born out of wedlock to a married person, when such
person acknowledges them, or the relationship is declared by a court
decision. Investigation of paternity shall be regulated by law.

All qualifications as to the nature of the relationship are abolished.
No statement whatever shall be entered, differentiating births, nor as
to the marital status of the parents, in the birth records, or in any
certification record of christening, or certificate referring to the relationship.[38]

Family life in Cuba, as elsewhere, is undergoing changes in response to the influences which are affecting society in general. One
of the more important factors involved in these changes is the
"emancipation" of women. As Cuban women more and more seek
equality of opportunity and expression, finding their way into the
professional and business world, their situation with reference to
the family is greatly modified. In this process, women come increasingly to make independent decisions or to influence decisions
favorable to them. Economic independence for those who find

[38] *Constitution of 1940*, Article 44.

employment outside the home gives rise to independent thought and action in political and social affairs. One outcome of this process now evident in the cities is the demand for more and better services on behalf of their children. Better schools, parks, playgrounds, libraries, and health services are being called for. In short, the familistic society is being modified in the direction of a society in which the community is the essential basis of organization.

The increasing importance of labor unions in providing better wages and working conditions will in time bring about a higher level of living for the lower classes, and the provision of education and other community services which have previously not been available. Much social legislation, protecting workers from the caprice of employers and providing minimum wages and other benefits, has already been achieved, and more is being demanded— and promised.

In Western nations, social changes usually originate in the urban centers and spread to the countryside. Thus in Cuba it can be anticipated that changes in the pattern of family life will spread from the cities to the rural areas. Improved means of travel and communication help to accelerate this process, and Cuba is undergoing rapid improvements in these phases of its life. Urbanization, as we have already seen, means smaller families. It also means greater freedom for the individual, a weakening of parental authority over children, and increasing transfer of responsibility for many aspects of life from the family to the community. For better or for worse, depending on the point of view, these trends are coming to Cuba, not only to its cities but to its rural areas as well.

In concluding this brief and inadequate survey of the Cuban family, it is appropriate to point out the need for further study. More data should be collected in future censuses of the population to enable scholars to analyze more fully the changes that are taking place, and to interpret their findings for the use of policy-making bodies in planning to meet changed conditions and bring about the improvements needed to make life better and more satisfying for all the Cuban people.

CHAPTER XI

The Level of Living

The level of living of the Cuban farm population in 1946 was probably higher than it had ever been before; at least it was higher than at any time since the early 1920's. This situation rested on the fact that more widespread employment opportunities were available as a result of the war and postwar demands for sugar and other agricultural commodities. The statement is made with full knowledge that there were thousands of families in rural Cuba who could not afford to purchase at inflated prices the clothing and food articles in the stores. It does not mean that the level of living had reached a plane that could be characterized as high. It simply means that there was more money in circulation, and that farmers generally were getting more of it than they had in the recent past. Some of them, in fact, were doing very well by any standard.

For a long time after slavery was abolished, Cuba was a land of very low incomes. Cheap labor was one of the major assets of the sugar latifundia, the cafetales, the tobacco vegas, and of Cuban business enterprise in general. However, with the overthrow of the Machado regime, the revolutionary movement sought to better the lot of the workers and the peasants. The workers particularly were successful in getting protective legislation, including the eight-hour workday, minimum wages, and vacations with pay. The result has been an increase in the rate of pay of both agricultural and industrial workers. Even so, however, the median weekly cash income of the agricultural class, workers and farm operators alike, was less than one dollar a day when the census was taken in 1943.

Farm incomes in 1946 were undoubtedly above those of 1943, and farm wages had also increased. Although it is not possible to say by what percentage wages and incomes rose, the wage rates were increased by official decree in August 1944 by 10, 15, and 20 per cent, depending upon the wage being paid. The higher increases were applied to the lower wages and vice versa. In addition, other increases have come about through collective bargaining agreements in various industries. In April 1944 the general minimum wage was set at $2.00 per day for urban and $1.60 per day for rural workers. As of 1946, the minimum wage for sugar cane workers was $1.92 per day.[1] The survey of Florida Central made in May 1946, showed 99 laborers, cane cutters, cane haulers, and other miscellaneous agricultural workers in 56 households. The average reported income from all sources during 1945 was $448 per worker. The average income per household was $793. There were on the average 1.77 workers per household. Some of the workers were boys 14, 15, 16, and 17 years of age, but they were undoubtedly able to contribute a fair amount to the family income.

HOUSING

The prevailing type of house in rural Cuba is the bohío, which may be built almost completely from material furnished by the royal palm tree. The roof is thatched—preferably with the fan-shaped leaf of the *caña* palm, although royal palm leaves are sometimes used. The walls are made from the bark of the royal palm, called *yagua*, or from boards cut from the trunk of the palm, known as *tabla de palma*. The floor is most often the ground itself. The framework is of poles securely fastened by nails or tied with strips of palm leaf fiber. There may or may not be interior partitions, although there usually is at least one. The kitchen is usually a small room separated from the remainder of the house by a few feet, with an alleyway covered with thatch so that one

---

[1] The Cuban Federation of Labor as of September 1946 was asking for a general increase of 30 per cent in wages actually being paid, and also in the minimum wage.

may pass from the house to the kitchen in rainy weather without getting wet.

Construction materials. The Special Surveys of eleven communities made in 1946[2] give some figures regarding the material from which farmhouses are constructed. In 377 or about half the houses in the areas surveyed, the floors were earthen; in 223, cement; 48 were tile; 81 were lumber; and 13 unspecified. There was much variation among the areas in this as in other respects. In San Antonio de las Vegas, a dairy section, only 15 per cent of the houses had dirt floors, compared with 80 per cent in Florencia, a diversified farming area. San Antonio is near Havana, a comparatively high proportion of the farmers are owners, and urban influences are more noticeable than in other sections. Florencia is, by contrast, much more isolated; farms are small and incomes much lower. In between these extremes are the other areas, where the percentages of houses with dirt floors are as follows:

	Per Cent
Cabaiguán	70
Alto Songo	about 65
Pinar del Río	about 65
Bayamo	about 65
Florida	60
Cienfuegos-Trinidad	60
Sancti-Spíritus	50
Manguito	30
Güines	25

Boards made from palm trunks are used for the walls of farmhouses more often than any other material. Lumber comes next and is almost as popular as tabla de palma. Palm bark or yagua, which is the historic wall material for bohíos ranks third, followed by brick, adobe, and miscellaneous types. Yagua appears to be going out of use as a major material in house construction. In fact, the main difference among the 11 areas is in the relative use of lumber and palm boards. For example, in the Pinar del Río sample, composed to a large extent of families on the Cuban Land and Leaf Tobacco Company, 88 per cent of the houses had lumber walls. On the other hand, in Alto Songo two-thirds of the

---

[2] See Appendix A for a brief description of the areas included.

houses were made of palm boards, while another 24 per cent used
yagua for the walls. Palm boards ranked first in all other areas
except Güines, where lumber was more frequently used.

A thatch of palm leaves, called *guano*, was the most important
type of roof in all areas except San Antonio de las Vegas, where
tile holds first place. Of the 742 houses surveyed, 514 had roofs
of guano, 143 of tile, 74 of zinc or galvanized iron, and 11 of tar
paper, concrete, or unspecified material. The favorite material for
thatching is the fan-shaped leaf of the *caña* palm. When this is
not readily available the leaf of the royal palm is used.

Cost of bohíos. A small bohío built with lumber walls, thatched
roof, and dirt floor could be built in 1946 for about $200 worth of
materials. Such a house in course of construction near Melena del
Sur in Havana Province in August 1946 cost $221 for materials:
$161 for lumber for the sides, $48 for poles to make the frame for
the roof, and $12 for guano for thatching. The labor on this house
was contributed by neighbors in the same manner as the house-
raisings of the American frontier.

The newer type of cottages, which is supplanting the bohíos as
fast as the economic position of the farmers permits, is of much
more substantial construction. The roof is usually of tile, the floor
of cement, and the walls are of a good quality of lumber. The cost
of such houses comes much higher, probably around $2,000 for a
rather modest one.

General condition. The Special Surveys interviewers were asked
to appraise the general condition of the houses according to their
individual judgments. The classification into three groups—good,
medium, and bad—is shown by area in Table 35. According to
this classification, the highest percentage of bad houses was found
in Alto Songo, followed by Bayamo, Florida, and Cabaiguán, all
with 45 per cent or more listed as "bad." The best housing was in
San Antonio de las Vegas, with Pinar del Río next. A large part
of the tobacco-farming sample was from the vega of the Cuban
Land and Leaf Tobacco Company, which constructs better-than-
average houses for its workers and tenants and maintains them in
better condition. Less than 7 per cent of the houses in Alto Songo
were considered "good." Bayamo, Cienfuegos-Trinidad, Florencia,
and Cabaiguán also had small proportions of good houses.

TABLE 35. GENERAL CONDITION OF DWELLINGS IN DIFFERENT AREAS
AS JUDGED BY FIELD INTERVIEWERS

Area	Total Number	Percentages		
		Good	Medium	Bad
Total 740		29.7	37.2	33.1
Pinar del Río 98		54.1	26.5	19.4
Cabaiguán 74		17.6	36.5	45.9
Cienfuegos-Trinidad 82		13.4	58.5	28.0
Alto Songo 30		6.7	30.0	63.3
Florida 63		28.6	23.8	47.6
Manguito 78		21.8	42.3	35.9
Sancti-Spíritus 36		33.3	36.1	30.6
Bayamo 31		12.9	38.7	48.4
San Antonio 100		57.0	27.0	16.0
Florencia 69		10.1	43.5	46.4
Güines 79		32.9	44.3	22.8

The families were also asked whether or not they were content with their houses, on the assumption that if a large proportion declared themselves dissatisfied with poor housing, it would be reasonable to expect that some improvement would be made as soon as economic conditions permitted. As long as people are content to live in poor houses, however, it is unlikely that improvements would be made. The results, for what they may be worth, reveal a remarkable degree of contentment with things as they are. Only in Alto Songo was any notable dissatisfaction expressed, and in that case it was almost unanimous. As we have seen, housing in Alto Songo was about the poorest of all areas surveyed. On the other hand, in Bayamo, where the general status of housing was but little better than in Alto Songo, there was an almost unanimous expression of satisfaction, only 3 out of 31 expressing any discontent. Paradoxically, it was in the areas where the best housing exists, Pinar del Río and San Antonio, that more frequent expressions of discontent occurred. Perhaps this is because the standards of better housing are familiar to the dwellers in these areas, and they are discontented with any house that falls below those standards.

HOUSEHOLD UTILITIES

According to the Special Surveys, the drinking water of three-fourths of the families studied is secured predominantly from wells. The next most important sources were rivers (8.6 per cent), small streams (7.4 per cent), and cisterns and springs (3.1 per cent each). This does not mean that each family had a well. Although no question was asked on this specific point, it is known that some families carry water from a neighbor's well, storing it in a barrel or other container. There was little variation among the areas in the sources of water, except that in the mountain regions of Alto Songo and Trinidad the small streams (*arroyos*) and springs were most important. The most common receptacle for storing water in the house is a jar, with barrels ranking next, followed by what was called a tank. The latter was reported particularly in those cases where there was running water. Of the 742 families, 463 said they used a special dipper to dip the water from the container.

Kerosene provides the main source of light, being reported by 596 or 80.3 per cent of all the families. Of the remainder, 71 had electric lights (9.5 per cent) and 68 had gas (9.1 per cent). At least one family from each of the eleven areas except Florida reported having electric lights. They were most numerous, however, in Pinar del Río, Cabaiguán, Sancti-Spíritus, and San Antonio de las Vegas, the two former places being devoted to tobacco growing and the other two to dairying. The fuel most often used for cooking was wood (543 families), while 148 reported using charcoal. The latter is the almost universal fuel in urban Cuba.

Refrigeration was practically nonexistent in the survey areas. Only 8 families reported mechanical refrigerators, while 34 said they used ice. The other 699 families had no refrigeration at all. This point should be kept in mind in connection with food consumption figures. There is no doubt that much food is wasted. It is a common practice not to attempt to carry over any "leavings" from a meal. Whatever is not consumed of the food prepared for a meal is thrown in the garbage, which in rural areas means it is given to the hogs and chickens.

In Table 36 are presented the number of common household items possessed by families in various areas. The prevalence of the sewing machine in these bohíos is an interesting point and reveals something of the extent to which rural Cubans are dependent upon household manufacture and renovation of clothing. Ready-made garments are of course available and widely used, especially in some of the less isolated sections, but a large part of the family

Locality	Total Families	Domestic Mill	Sewing Machine	Radio	Wind-mill	Stone Grinder	Corn Grinder	Musical Instrument	Mosquito Bar
Total *742*		*463*	*524*	*109*	*39*	*218*	*378*	*134*	*244*
Pinar del Río 100		25	53	12	1	28	24	16	53
Cabaiguán . 74		69	69	11	4	8	61	17	13
Cienfuegos-Trinidad . 82		74	64	7	3	35	67	11	12
Alto Songo . 30		3	9	0	0	1	22	4	2
Florida 63		34	25	1	53*	3	8	9	44
Manguito .. 78		66	67	11	9	49	23	16	29
Sancti-Spíritus . 36		34	26	8	10	0	29	16	8
Bayamo ... 31		27	19	2	7	2	16	4	8
San Antonio de las Vegas ...100		38	83	39	7	47	61	13	29
Florencia .. 69		63	47	5	5	7	40	9	16
Güines 79		30	62	13	3	38	27	19	30

*Obviously an error, since the Florida sample was composed entirely of laborers. Some apparently reported existence of a windmill on the colonia on which they worked. This figure is omitted in the total.

TABLE 37. TOILET FACILITIES IN SELECTED RURAL AREAS OF CUBA, 1946

Locality	Total	Type of Facility			
		None	Sanitary Latrine	Unsanitary Latrine	Indoor Toilet
Total *740*		*448*	*43*	*204*	*45*
Pinar del Río 99		21	13	59	6
Cabaiguán 74		59	5	9	1
Cienfuegos-Trinidad 81		64	3	13	1
Alto Songo 30		22	1	7	0
Sancti-Spíritus 36		12	3	17	4
Bayamo 31		6	2	23	0
San Antonio 100		59	5	10	26
Florencia 69		59	0	10	0
Güines 79		56	3	16	4
Florida 63		27	4	30	2
Manguito 78		63	4	10	1

clothing is made in the home. The small number of radios is in marked contrast with the situation in the United States, where from 80 to 90 per cent of the homes have them.

It is an astounding fact that 448, or about 60 per cent, of the families reported no special toilet facilities (Table 37). An additional 204 said they had unsanitary privies (*latrina no sanitaria*), while only 43 reported sanitary privies and 45, indoor toilets. All but 19 of the latter were in the San Antonio area.

FOOD

The Cuban diet runs heavily to starchy foods. Corn meal, rice, wheatbread, starchy vegetables, plantain, and sugar constitute the most important foods. Rice is in great demand, but since most of it is imported, the cost during World War II and the immediate postwar years was too high for many to obtain it. However, in the prewar years 1935 to 1940, the annual rice consumption amounted to 500 million pounds, or about 110 pounds per capita.[3] Estimates of the consumption of the 742 households interviewed in the Special Surveys ran much higher than this figure, however, exceeding 200 pounds per capita. Rice is more important than corn and wheat combined as a food in Cuba.[4] Before the war rice was imported from the Orient, but when this source was cut off, it had to come largely from the United States. Corn meal is consumed in large quantities, the annual per capita consumption reported in the Special Surveys being 93 pounds.

Looming largest of all in the diets of rural Cubans are plantain and vegetables. Plantain, a form of banana, is used as a vegetable both in the green (*plátano verde*) and ripe (*plátano madura*) stages. The green ones are sliced into thin chips and cooked in hot grease. They resemble potato chips and are very palatable. Sometimes they are boiled and in this form resemble mashed potatoes. The ripe plátano is sliced longitudinally and fried. Most of the farmers have a few plantain trees, and those who do not grow their own can obtain them from neighbors at small cost or by barter. Other vegetables, grown locally, which form a large part of the Cuban diet are *boniatos* (sweet potatoes), *malangas, yuca*

[3] *Censo de 1943*, p. 403.
[4] *Ibid.*, p. 403.

(cassava), *ñame* (yams), and potatoes. All are essentially carbohydrates.

The consumption of beans is very great even though a large
part has to be imported. In 1940 the per capita consumption was
estimated at 35 pounds.[5] Black beans constitute about half the
total consumption, and these are produced on the island. Most of
the other varieties are imported from Chile, Mexico, and the
United States.

Eggs are not commonly eaten in the farm home, but are sold
instead. Cooking oil made from peanuts is used to a large extent,
but lard is preferred. The "green and yellow" vegetables which
are important sources of vitamins are almost totally absent from
the rural diet. Lettuce and other salad greens, cabbage, carrots,
cauliflower, radishes, parsnips, spinach, and the like are almost
unknown.[6] Tomatoes, especially the very small variety, are rel-
ished by the Cuban people, but they are seen mainly in the urban
markets. The varieties popular in the American market are grown
in Cuba, but almost entirely for export to the United States. The
fresh fruits most commonly grown in Cuba are *guayaba*, *fruta
bomba* (papaya), oranges, lemons, limes, grapefruit, mangoes,
and pineapple.

Coffee is widely used, and reports from various regions show
estimates of annual consumption varying from 20 to 41 pounds per
capita, the average being about 30 pounds. Sugar consumption is
of course very high, but estimates as to amounts are not available.
Those obtained in the Special Surveys were so erratic as to be
unusable. Sugar, as a rule, is used in the "raw" stage—that is,
before the final refining—and contains a considerable amount of
moisture. Many rural families also eat large quantities of sugar
cane during the dead season when they do not have money to buy
other foods. Milk is used rather widely, according to the reports
of families in the Surveys, but again the estimates were not considered sufficiently reliable to justify using them.

Some sections reported the consumption of large quantities of
fresh meat other than pork, while others reported none at all. One

[5] *Ibid.*, p. 406.
[6] The only garden containing some of these vegetables which we saw in the island
was in the tobacco region of Cabaiguán. One of the most enterprising farmers had obtained the seed from the Ministry of Agriculture.

area estimated meat consumption at 300 pounds a year per capita! This estimate is excessive, but it is true that Cubans are very fond of meat and when they can obtain it, consume it in large amounts. The supply is not steady even in the cities, since cold-storage facilities are not available. The meat supply for the city of Havana, for example, is slaughtered daily and distributed each morning to the meat shops. A fondness for chicken meat leads most Cuban farmers to keep poultry flocks. Chicken with rice (*arroz con pollo*) is about the most universally favored dish. Needless to say, it is not within the reach of large numbers of the rural population —or the urban, for that matter.

In the Special Surveys, a long schedule of questions was used covering a wide range of topics, of which food was only one. The interviewers were not trained in home economics and for the most part were lacking in the experience necessary to secure exact information regarding the dietary habits of the population. However, the information obtained may be of some value in showing the relative importance of certain foods, even though the actual amounts reported by the families may upon more careful investigation be shown to be inaccurate. A summary of information on various foods is presented in Table 38. The weights in pounds represent gross estimates. For example, a family asked to estimate the number of pounds of plantain consumed in a year would give the answer in terms of *racimos,* or bunches. The standard weight used in estimating pounds from racimos is 25, but since this weight includes stem and peel, the actual edible portion would naturally weigh much less than 25 pounds.

Missing from this list of foods are eggs, milk and milk products, fruits, sugar, green and yellow vegetables, fresh meat other than pork and chicken, and cooking oil. Of these only milk, sugar, and fresh meat would be used in any significant amounts. What the table shows chiefly is the heavy reliance of Cuban people on carbohydrate foods, a fact that is widely recognized. Plantain, vegetables, corn meal, and rice account for 75 per cent of the reported food consumption.

Cubans eat only two meals a day, at noon and evening. Coffee and a piece of wheat bread are usually taken in the early morning, but this is not regarded as a meal. Coffee with hot milk (*café con*

TABLE 38. AMOUNTS OF VARIOUS FOODS CONSUMED ANNUALLY PER CAPITA
BY CUBAN FARM FAMILIES*

Food	Pounds	Per Cent
Total 1,460		100.0
Bananas (plantain) 456		31.2
Vegetables† 355		24.3
Rice 194		13.3
Corn meal 93		6.4
Beans 92		6.3
Pork 86		5.9
Bread 86		5.9
Lard 78		5.3
Chicken 20		1.4

SOURCE: Special Surveys.

* Based on reports of 539 households containing 3,817 persons.

† Chiefly sweet potatoes, yuca, yams, and malangas, with lesser amounts of Irish potatoes.

leche) is preferred in the morning, but a demi-tasse (café solo) is frequently drunk throughout the day.

Casto Ferragút of the Cuban Ministry of Agriculture calculated the amounts of various foods which would be necessary to provide the island's population with an optimum diet. With his metric weight figures translated into pounds, the amounts and percentage distribution are shown in Table 39. Clearly, as Ferragút points out, the provision of an optimum diet would require radical changes in the agriculture of Cuba and much larger imports of foods which could not be economically grown in Cuba. More important still, perhaps, it would require revolutionary changes in the food habits of the people. The net result would be to reduce drastically the intake of carbohydrates and to increase consumption of eggs, meat, milk, and the "protective" foods. It is a notable commentary on Cuban dietary habits that while 70,000 of the 220,000 metric tons of green and yellow vegetables required for an optimum diet are produced in the country, 27,000 tons are exported. Similarly in the case of fruits, although total production falls short of meeting the requirements for the optimum diet, over a fourth of what is grown is exported.[7]

Improvements in the diet are clearly needed if the nutritional level is to be raised. Leaders in agriculture, health, and education

[7] C. Ferragút, op. cit., p. 93.

TABLE 39. AMOUNTS AND PERCENTAGE DISTRIBUTION OF VARIOUS FOODS
REQUIRED FOR AN OPTIMUM DIET*

Food	Pounds	Per Cent
Total†	*1,027*	*100.0*
Eggs	20	1.9
Meat	121	11.8
Fats and oils	48	4.7
Vegetables (green and yellow)	97	9.4
Fruits rich in vitamin C	97	9.4
Other fruits	79	7.7
Sugar	59	5.7
Vegetables	242	23.6
Corn, rice, beans	161	15.7
Bread	103	10.1

* Casto Ferragút, *op. cit.*, p. 92.
† Also included in the diet would be 200 liters of milk.

are well aware of the dietary deficiencies, but they also recognize the magnitude of the problem involved in bringing about changes. Over all is the force of tradition, with which is associated the problem of poverty that rests like a cloud over a large section of the population. Yet the fact remains that the soil and climate are capable of producing a wide range of foods, including many not now being utilized to any extent. If, through effective programs of education on the part of the relevant government agencies, people can be taught the essentials of an adequate diet, it would be possible for them to meet many of their needs through their own efforts. In other words, if desires can be created for a better diet, the people could satisfy those desires in large measure even within the present limitations as to income.

RECREATION

No matter how dismal life may be in some of its aspects, people always find ways of satisfying their basic desire for play and relaxation. Cubans are no exception. To some observers from the outside, the pattern of life for many is such that it is difficult to see how any portion of joy could be wrung from their stark existence. Nevertheless, one who remains long enough to penetrate beyond superficial appearances will discover that fundamentally, Cubans are a happy people. They find relaxation in a multitude of ways, most of which are informal and spontaneous. There is little of what is commonly referred to as "organized recreation." But the latter phrase is in itself something of a paradox, for the essential in recreation is spontaneity.

Cubans delight in family and neighborhood visiting and conversation. In rural areas where radios, newspapers, books, and magazines are few or lacking, "much talk" is substituted. Folk music and dancing also provide pleasant diversions from hard work. The favorite musical instrument is the guitar, often supplemented by *claves*, two hardwood sticks which accentuate the rhythm with a clacking sound. *Maracas* are also used, two gourds containing seed or metal shot which are shaken in tempo with the guitar. These musical instruments are widely distributed, and many people are able to play them. No rural neighborhood is without a guitar or someone to play it.

Besides the entertainment which families and neighbors provide for themselves, rural people participate in recreational activities in the trade centers. While trips to town are not frequent by American standards, they are motivated by similar desires.

In the hope that the Special Surveys might reveal more clearly the patterns of leisure-time occupation, the surveyed families were asked about the extent of their participation in various activities when they were in town. In most cases, perhaps, some business is

TABLE 40. ACTIVITIES IN TRADE CENTERS REPORTED BY CUBAN FAMILIES, 1946

| | Number of Times Mentioned | | | |
| | Male | | Female | |
Activity	Adult	Youth	Adult	Youth
Visiting friends and relatives	380	121	253	70
Attending political meetings	154	59	20	9
Listening to radio	106	62	54	34
Attending movies	76	99	44	51
Cockfights	75	34	3	2
Meetings at the club	89	15	7	5
Dancing	51	110	31	68
Playing ball	46	44	4	8
Drinking	56	37	9	6
Dominoes, cards, and checkers	48	19	3	1
General amusement*	97	149	52	95

SOURCE: Special Surveys.

* *Divertirse*, or general amusement, covers a "multitude of sins." It means having a rip-roaring good time.

transacted on the part of the adults, but young and old alike aim to have some enjoyment out of the trip to town. As Table 40 indicates, visiting is most often mentioned. Since most of the families have no radios, they often take the opportunity to listen to a radio in a coffee shop or tavern. Attending political meetings would not be called "recreation" in the United States, but in Cuba it is a diversion which is greatly enjoyed. Cockfights are important affairs and draw large crowds, and baseball is a very popular sport throughout the island.

The club is one of the most important social institutions in Cuba. In practically every small town there is a relatively imposing building, the club, where men gather to talk, play dominoes, or hold meetings. The men go to town more often than women, and the mores sanction much greater freedom in their behavior. Except for visiting, listening to the radio, attending movies, and dancing, women participate little in the other activities reported by the men.

READING MATTER IN FARM HOMES

Rural Cubans do very little reading, but apparently more would like to read if the material were provided. Of the 742 households represented in the Surveys, 515 or 69.4 per cent reported receiving no newspapers or magazines, and 498 or 65.9 per cent had no books in the home. An additional 129 or 17.4 per cent took one newspaper or magazine and reported the possession of "from one to four books," usually meaning one. Only 21 households reported having 25 or more books, while 95 had two or more newspapers and magazines.

In addition to these facts from the general survey, the author gathered information on this subject from 41 families in San Blas. Only seven families reported receiving newspapers or magazines. All were Havana publications: *Bohemia,* a weekly magazine had five subscribers; *Vanidades* and *Carteles,* monthly magazines, and *Siempre* and *Prensa Libre,* newspapers, had one subscriber each. Four of the San Blas families had receiver printed material from government offices. Two said they had received material from the Ministry of Agriculture, and one each reported material received from the Ministry of Communications and the Ministry

of National Defense. Four others said they received political fold-
ers during election time. Each of the San Blas farmers was invited
to make comments. Some of them wrote: "The government does
not remember that there are inhabitants living in this place, except
during elections." "They only visit us during elections." "In this
place we do not have mail service. We live 'incommunicado,'
separated completely from the rest of the Republic." "There is no
mail. We are without communication because of lack of roads and
public attention."

In San Blas every one of the 41 families wanted more reading
matter, especially on the following topics: agriculture, mentioned
28 times; general information on world affairs, etc., mentioned 11
times; social problems, sanitation, and "culture," 10 times; political matters, national and international, 9 times; and sports, mentioned 2 times.

While it is obvious that inability to read would account in large
measure for the small amount of reading matter in the homes of
rural Cuba, it is not the complete explanation by any means. The
problem is also related to poverty. People with incomes as low
as some of the Cuban families are not going to spend their money
for newspapers, magazines, or books. The point immediately occurs to an outsider that they might forgo some of the money they
spend on tobacco, liquor, and the lottery in order to provide a
little food for the mind. But the mind of rural Cuba is not hungry
enough for mental nourishment to make such a great sacrifice to
obtain it.

Although 594 of the 742 surveyed households expressed a desire for more reading matter, it is nevertheless fair to say that the
rural Cuban does not have the reading habit. He would much
rather spend his leisure in talking with his friends or his family
than in reading. Yet contact with Cuban farmers leads one to
think that if they were provided with reliable and informative
reading matter, they could easily be led to do much more reading
than they do. When the farmers of San Blas, gathered two nights
in succession at the home of one of the neighbors, asked the author
to tell them about farm life in the United States, it was not to
pay a compliment—gracious and hospitable though they were—

but because they were really hungry for information about the world outside. They were possessed of real intellectual curiosity. This is a trait that might well be exploited by Cuban educational leaders in developing a program of adult education.

PATTERNS OF EXPENDITURE

In asking the 742 Cuban families to estimate the amount of their expenditures for various items, we realized that the results would be only rough approximations. No budgetary studies have previously been made in Cuba, and it is an understatement to say that Cubans are not budget conscious. The Puritan economic virtues of thrift and frugality with which many generations of Americans have been indoctrinated are by no means as important in Cuban culture. Cubans spend their money freely, when they have it, and are not given to saving for the proverbial "rainy day." A corollary is that they do not keep family accounts. What matters to them is the cash in hand. With most people everywhere, superior value is placed upon what they have and get today, rather than at some future time, but this seems to be more characteristic of Cuban than of American families.

Extravagance is a rather minor problem, however, with so many Cubans living in poverty or on its margins. The struggle for mere survival is for many the chief preoccupation. This has been true for many generations of rural Cubans, and as long as this situation continues, talk about developing habits of saving is academic. For the Cuban economy in general, however, the war brought prosperity. The demand for its main product, sugar, was insatiable; and unemployment fell to low levels, although it by no means disappeared. Wages rose to the highest levels in history. Prices also increased rapidly, because the island imports so many of its necessities, including much of its food supply. It is doubtful if wages kept pace with the rising cost of living, although the indices for comparison of wage and price series are not available.

Table 41 presents the estimated percentages of family income spent in different areas for a number of major items. Food costs amount to about half the total expenditures. Clothing ranks second in importance, with tobacco and liquor next, followed by medical

TABLE 41. PERCENTAGE DISTRIBUTION OF AVERAGE EXPENDITURES OF 567 CUBAN FARM FAMILIES FOR VARIOUS ITEMS IN FAMILY LIVING, BY AREAS, 1945

Item	Total (N = 567)	Trinidad (N = 82)	Manguito (N = 78)	Florida (N = 62)	San Juan y Martínez (N = 56)	Cabaiguán (N = 74)	Sancti-Spíritus (N = 36)	Bayamo (N = 31)	Florencia (N = 68)	Güines (N = 80)
Total	100.0	100.0	100.0	100.0	100.0	100.0	100.0	100.0	100.0	100.0
Food	49.1	49.9	48.2	69.5	70.6	42.4	28.8	39.5	47.1	51.9
Rent	5.4	2.6	2.9	..*	..*	13.8	8.6	3.6	5.2	7.4
Clothing	18.4	18.8	14.6	11.1	15.9	22.7	18.7	15.8	19.0	18.4
Gifts	0.9	0.0	0.2	0.0	0.0	2.3	1.0	2.0	1.0	1.6
Medical care	7.9	9.4	6.6	6.0	0.2	9.0	7.5	16.9	9.5	7.7
Church	..†	0.0	0.0	0.0	0.3	0.2	0.0	0.0	0.0	0.0
Tobacco and liquor	9.0	5.6	17.5	6.2	3.8	2.2	19.4	13.6	5.4	4.8
Recreation	2.7	4.4	3.5	0.0	0.9	1.3	4.9	1.4	4.9	2.4
Lottery	2.8	1.6	2.1	5.1	0.7	3.9	5.3	2.2	1.9	1.5
Others	4.8	7.6	4.3	2.0	7.2	2.4	5.8	4.9	5.9	4.2
Average yearly expenditure per household	$934	$549	$499	$859	$1,638	$980	$1,745	$1,304	$895	$810

* Housing furnished by company.
† Less than .1 per cent.

care. Shelter is much less costly than in northern climates, and in two of the areas it was furnished by the companies. No attempt was made to place a value on this perquisite, which would be necessary in a careful budgetary study. Expenditures for the church did not appear at all in seven of the nine areas, and in the other two, there were only a few families reporting this item. The church has only occasional contacts with rural people. The priest appears only about once a year, when infants are baptised—usually at $3 per head—and that is about the extent of his ministry.

The lottery is a national weekly affair, and tickets are purchased by a large part of the population, even in remote areas. During past periods in Cuban history, it has been associated with political corruption in high places, but today it is regarded as being operated with at least minimum safeguards against scandal and chicanery, although there are those who question that it is strictly honest. Nevertheless, it is a long-established practice, in which both poor and rich participate. Whether or not they plan in advance for other expenditures, there is no doubt that many people on small incomes regularly devote a specified portion of their earnings to lottery tickets. It is useless to argue with them that the same amount placed in a savings account would in time provide a competence for old age or for a possible emergency. The remote chance of winning as much as $100,000 with an investment of 20 cents has too strong a pull on the imagination.

The net result of the lottery is probably the further economic degradation of the poor. More than that, it is the most potent enemy of any program designed to promote thrift among the population. It encourages a sort of chronic boom psychosis or speculative mania, where everyone lives in a bubble which, for most "investors," bursts every Saturday evening. For the limited few, of course, it brings various degrees of fortune. But win or lose, on Monday hopes rise anew and build up to feverish anticipation as the week advances toward another Saturday that will bring an answer to their hopes. The most that can be said for the lottery is that, besides rewarding a few, it constitutes an experience-continuum for the many that brings a modicum of excitement to lives that otherwise are drab.

In summary then, it must be said that a very large part of Cuba's population is ill fed, ill housed, ill clothed, and provided with few of the amenities of modern civilization. But changes are in progress; desires for better things have been aroused, in some communities more than in others, and there is definitely room for hope that such desires will not go unsatisfied much longer.

CHAPTER XII

Education and the Schools

Enrique José Varona, one of the great intellectuals of Cuba, reported on October 23, 1895, that the Cuban budget for that year provided $182,000 for education. "All of the countries of America excepting Bolivia," he said, "all of them, including Haiti, Jamaica, Trinidad, and Guadeloupe, where the colored race predominates, spend a great deal more than the Cuban Government for the education of the people. On the other hand, only Chile spends as much as Cuba for the support of an army. In view of this it is easily explained why 76 per cent of such an intelligent and wide-awake people as that of Cuba cannot read and write . . . The State in Cuba does not support a single library."[1] This was an indication of the condition of Cuban education under the colonial regime. What educational activity did exist during that period was the result of the work of private initiative, and opportunities for education were largely limited to those able and willing to pay for it.

The first real stimulus to educational and cultural activity during the colonial period came during the regime of Don Luís de las Casas (1790–1796). He founded the famous *Sociedad Económica*

---

[1] *Compilation of Reports of Committee on Foreign Relations*, United States Senate, 56th Congress, 2d. Session, Document No. 231, Part 7, p. 367. Although the amount spent on education was undoubtedly small at that time, Varona's figures do not correspond to those reported by the Department of Public Instruction, which reported a budget of $1,015,927 for schools of all kinds in the island, two-thirds of the amount coming from matriculation fees. See *Report of the Census of Cuba, 1899*, p. 585.

de Amigos del País, which was charged by royal order with the sponsorship of education in Cuba. One of its first acts after its organization was to make an inventory of schools in 1793. It found but thirty-nine schools in Havana, thirty-two of them for girls. The few schools that were functioning were offering instruction only in reading. In cooperation with religious orders, and even with the opposition of the bishop of the island, the society was able to establish a few schools and give considerable impetus to higher education. In the course of the following two decades, some progress was made toward securing funds for the operation of free elementary schools, but this movement received a setback when a royal order of 1825 withdrew some $32,000 which had previously been appropriated for this purpose.

In 1842 more positive steps toward the secularization of education were taken, and this date really marks the beginning of public education. However, progress was slow throughout the remainder of the century. As late as 1883 there were only 535 public and 184 private schools in the entire island. Excellent plans for a system of public education had been provided by legislation in 1865, modified by that of 1880; but failure to provide the necessary funds to carry them out meant that application of the plans was seriously impeded. Nevertheless, by 1895 the number of public schools had increased to 904 and the private to 740. Even so, the combined enrollment in both amounted to less than 62,000 pupils. By the time of the census of 1899, there were 755 public and 726 private schools in operation, with a total of 87,936 children reported attending. The law of 1880 specified that there were to be 1,870 schools, but more than half of them remained to be created.

The war period from 1895 to 1899 was one of almost complete disorganization and interruption of the normal functions of all social institutions, including education. Then followed the American military occupation, which was a period of rehabilitation.[2] By a civil decree published June 30, 1900, in Havana, General Leonard

---

[2] A good review of the history of education in Cuba previous to the period of the Republic will be found in the *Report of the Census of Cuba, 1899,* pp. 565–620. Most of this historical review is based upon the report of Mr. R. L. Packard, then Commissioner of Education of the United States. The reader will also find a brief resumé of the history of Cuban education in a recent publication by Severin K. Turosienski entitled *Education in Cuba* (Washington: Government Printing Office, 1943).

Wood, Military Governor, ordered the reorganization of the Cuban school system. The decree provided for the creation of the office of Commissioner of Public Instruction, to be assisted in each province by a provincial superintendent who together constituted a board of superintendents. The island was divided into school districts, each presided over by a board of education, the members of which were elected by popular vote. Composition of these boards varied according to the class of the school district— whether it was a city of the first class, a city of the second class, or a county. School affairs were almost entirely under the direction of these school boards. They were charged with the responsibility of establishing and maintaining schools, appointing teachers and other employees, and fixing their salaries, subject to certain maximum amounts indicated in the decree. The decree also made school attendance compulsory from the ages of six to fourteen. Under the Military Governor, education made rapid strides. Numerous schools were established and school attendance increased.

This was essentially the pattern of organization which was turned over to the Republic in 1902. Subsequently, the system has become highly centralized, with responsibility for educational affairs resting upon the National Secretary of Education, or Minister of Education, as he has been called since the Constitution of 1940. The educational provisions of the Constitution of 1940 are pertinent to note here and they read in part as follows:

Art. 48. Primary instruction is obligatory for minors of school age and it shall be furnished by the Nation, without prejudice to the cooperation entrusted to municipal initiative.

Both this instruction and preprimary and vocational instruction shall be gratis when given by the Nation, Province, or Municipality. The necessary school supplies shall also be gratis.

Lower secondary instruction and all higher instruction furnished by the Nation or the Municipality shall be gratis, excluding specialized pre-university and university study.

At the institutes now created, or which may be created in the future, having a pre-university status, there can be maintained or established by law the payment of a modest matriculation fee by way of cooperation which shall be devoted to the requirements of each establishment.

So far as possible, the Republic shall offer scholarships for the enjoyment of official instruction that is not gratis, to youths who, having shown outstanding vocation and aptitude, are prevented by insufficient resources from taking such studies for their own account.

Art. 49. The Nation shall maintain a system of schools for adults devoted particularly to the elimination and prevention of illiteracy; predominantly practical rural schools, organized with a view to the interests of the small agricultural, maritime, or other communities, and schools of arts and trades and of agricultural, industrial and commercial techniques so oriented that they will meet the needs of the national economy. All of this instruction shall be gratis, and the Provinces and Municipalities, to the extent of their abilities, shall collaborate in their maintenance.

Art. 50. The nation shall maintain the normal schools indispensable for the technical preparation of the teachers charged with the primary instruction in the public schools. No other institution can issue titles to primary teachers, with the exception of the Schools of Pedagogy of the Universities.

The foregoing provision is no bar to the right of schools created by law to issue teaching titles in connection with the special matters which they teach.

The teaching titles of special capacity shall carry the right to preferential appointment to positions that are vacant or are created in the respective schools and specialties.

In order to teach domestic science, cutting and fitting, and industries for women, it is necessary to possess the title of teacher of economy, arts, domestic sciences and industries, issued by the "Escuela del Hogar" (Domestic Science School).

Art. 52. The budget of the Ministry of Education shall not be less than the ordinary budget of any other Ministry, except in case of an emergency declared by law.

The monthly salary of primary teachers must not in any case be less than one-millionth of the total budget of the Nation.

With the exception of the provincial agricultural schools operated by the Ministry of Agriculture, the schools of Cuba are under the direction of the Minister of Education, a cabinet officer. In each of the six provinces there is a provincial superintendent of schools. Under the provinces are the 126 municipios, each of which constitutes a school district. The latter are nominally under the supervision of a board of education consisting of three members selected by the provincial school superintendent and appointed by the Minister of Education. One authority compares the Cuban system to that of France. He says:

It is highly centralized, with local boards of education almost completely lacking in administrative responsibility. Unlike the French system, and somewhat like that of North America, it has an end-to-end organization of schools, the elementary schools leading directly to the secondary and these in turn, except for special and technical schools, leading directly to the university. The elementary school has a six-year program; the secondary school, *Instituto,* a four-year course. A new type recently organized, called the Higher Primary School, represents a variant of this organization. These resemble, in their relation to other schools, the English higher primary and central schools. They parallel three years of secondary instruction, but are not an integral part of a primary-secondary-university series. Twenty-nine of these higher primary schools are now functioning.

The Cuban system resembles the French, again, more than the North American, in that secondary education is not provided for any large number of students, nor is it free, although tuition is low and many scholarships are offered at public expense. Moreover, the secondary schools are degree-granting institutions, although this similarity is purely superficial, since in Cuba the title is granted after a total of but ten years of schooling beyond the kindergarten.[3]

Another similarity with the European system is the scant attention which has been paid to the development of a system of instruction suitable to the rural environment. Undoubtedly changes for the better have come in this respect in at least some schools. The school in Florencia, in which the schoolmaster, Sr. Jiménez, has provided a small room for instruction in shop work and directs the pupils in the growing of a school garden with appropriate instruction in agriculture, is in marked contrast to the typical school of a few decades ago. More important than the facilities which this teacher has provided, largely out of his own and local resources rather than from the central government, is the fact that he has an appreciation of the possibilities as well as the responsibilities of the school in preparing rural boys and girls for a more satisfactory and useful life in the rural community.

[3] Buell, ed., *Problems of the New Cuba,* pp. 131-32.

TYPES OF RURAL SCHOOLS

There are a number of schools of particular significance to rural areas. The most important naturally, is the primary elementary school (*Escuela Primaria Elemental*). This school is supposed to provide instruction from the first to the sixth grades inclusive. Upon completion of the primary school, the rural child may, if his parents are able to make arrangements, attend the advanced primary school (*Escuela Primaria Superior*). This school offers a three-year course, including the seventh, eighth, and ninth grades, and prepares the student for entrance to the normal schools and vocational schools. Not many rural pupils are likely to have an opportunity to attend advanced primary schools, since they are quite generally located in the towns and transportation is not provided at public expense.

Completion of primary school also opens the possibility of attending one of the rural children's homes (*Hogares Infantiles Campesinos*). These are boarding schools, all expenses being paid by the government. The children are housed, fed, and clothed at public expense during the period of their attendance. In 1946 there were thirty-nine of these boarding schools, three of which were still under construction. Each school has two teachers resident with the students. The average enrollment is about thirty pupils. Attached to each school is a plot of agricultural land on which vegetables are grown for the school's own use. The pupils are selected from the rural schools in the municipios, or counties, assigned to the particular school; that is to say, each boarding school serves an area consisting usually of several counties. The instruction covers eight subjects—reading, writing, arithmetic, geography, language, history, agriculture, and shop work.

Upon finishing the course provided in the rural children's home, the student may be admitted to the Rural Normal School José Martí, at Rancho Boyeros, subject to passing a satisfactory examination. Here also the expenses are paid by the government. The purpose of the rural normal school is to prepare teachers, especially for service in rural areas.[4]

[4] During the school year 1945–46 an attempt was made to close this school, or rather to merge it with the provincial normal school of Havana. This was the signal for a strike on the part of the students of the school, who finally won at least tem-

In each of the provinces there is a school of agriculture under the direction of the Ministry of Agriculture. In order to be admitted to this school, a student is expected to have completed at least five grades of the primary school and passed a successful competitive examination. It offers a three-year course leading to the degree of Master Farmer (*Maestro Agrícola*). This degree is required of all personnel employed as agricultural inspectors in a county—a position roughly equivalent to that of county agricultural agent in the United States. Each of the six provincial agricultural schools follows the same curriculum and has about the same budget and the same number of pupils. During the winter of 1945–46, for example, the school of agriculture of Pinar del Río Province had thirty-three pupils and a budget of $34,818. The total staff consisted of twenty-three persons, six of whom were *profesores*. There were two technicians, one in charge of farm crops and the other in charge of the livestock. Of the total budget, $25,500 was for personnel and the balance for supplies and materials, including feed for livestock, maintenance and repair of buildings, vehicles, and implements, purchase of new implements and livestock, medical care, clothing and uniforms for the students, supplies for the dormitory, and so forth. All expenses of attending the school are paid by the government.

In addition to these major types of rural schools, there are the School of Forestry located in Havana, open to graduates of the provincial agricultural schools, and several schools of domestic science and rural economics. Naturally, a rural pupil who wishes to attend the University of Havana will need to take the pre-university course offered in the institutes of secondary instruction.

In addition to the scheme of formal instruction just described, the Ministry of Agriculture, through its provincial and municipal inspectors, carries on a program of adult education for farmers. This work has been very much handicapped for lack of transportation facilities. Up until 1946 none of the municipal inspectors had transportation provided them, although each of the provincial inspectors was furnished a pick-up truck.[5] Correspondence courses

porary victory and the school continued operation. It exists only under a decree law rather than a law of the national Congress.

[5] During the summer of 1946 the ministry announced its intention to purchase a number of "jeeps" for its agricultural inspectors.

are also offered in the fields of agriculture, livestock, and home economics. Up to 1945 the cumulative enrollment in these courses was as follows: agriculture, 7,452 pupils; livestock, 7,286; and home economics, 10,087.

Finally, the work of the 5-C Clubs must be mentioned in connection with rural education. Patterned after the 4-H Clubs of the United States, this organization began operation in 1940. As of 1945 there were 350 clubs in the island reporting 12,000 members, about 7,000 boys and 5,000 girls. The work was carried on entirely from Havana and largely by correspondence. Although no local club agents are employed, the government follows the practice of securing the cooperation of some public-spirited local adult to act as the club leader and to assume responsibility for making the reports required by the Ministry of Agriculture.

SCHOOL ATTENDANCE

School attendance in Cuba is extremely low for a country that has made marked advances in other aspects of its culture. In fact, if the data can be relied upon, the country is retrogressing in this respect, since the number of pupils who attended school in 1942–43 constituted a smaller percentage of the school population than in 1907. According to the census of the latter year, 39 per cent of children 5 to 14 years of age were attending school. The comparable figure for 1919 was 35.4 per cent. The data for the 1931 census are not comparable, since it reported school attendance for those "under 10" and those "10 years or older."

The figures for 1943 do not indicate any improvement. These are summarized by provinces in Tables 42 and 43. The figure of 35 per cent is about the same as that for 1919 and less than that for 1907. In other words, upward of two-thirds of Cuba's one million children of primary school age were not attending school during the year 1942–43. It was impossible to secure a report comparing the rural and urban populations, but the fact that the most urbanized provinces, Havana and Matanzas, rank highest indicates somewhat the rural-urban difference. It is well known in Cuba that there are extensive rural areas where no schools exist and where the children grow up without benefit of any education.

TABLE 42. POPULATION 5–13 YEARS OF AGE AND NUMBER AND PER CENT WHO
ATTENDED PRIMARY SCHOOL IN 1942–43*

Province and Sex	Population Aged 5–13 (1943)	Attending School 1942–43	
		Number†	Per Cent
All provinces	1,008,254	353,947	35.1
Male	518,009	143,875	27.8
Female	490,244	153,820	31.4
Pinar del Río	95,670	31,063	32.5
Male	49,309	14,460	29.3
Female	46,361	14,316	30.9
Havana	189,987	130,275	68.6
Male	97,522	49,327	50.6
Female	92,465	50,733	54.9
Matanzas	73,708	43,531	59.0
Male	37,595	18,638	49.6
Female	36,113	19,195	53.2
Las Villas	203,995	50,434	24.7
Male	104,810	21,210	20.2
Female	99,185	22,116	22.3
Camagüey	103,420	29,139	28.2
Male	53,270	11,729	22.0
Female	50,150	13,310	26.6
Oriente	341,474	69,505	20.4
Male	175,503	28,511	16.2
Female	165,971	34,150	20.6

*School attendance data supplied by the Ministry of Education.

†Total attendance for Cuba and provinces includes private school figures which were not available by sex. The figures for male and female include only public school pupils, and therefore do not add up to the totals as given. The breakdown by sex for the group for which this could be done was regarded as useful in indicating what sex differences tend to prevail.

TABLE 43. CHILDREN OF PRIMARY SCHOOL AGE WHO ATTENDED SCHOOL IN 1942–43
AND NUMBER WHO DID NOT, BY PROVINCE

Province	Population Aged 5–13 (1943)*					
	Total		In School†		Not in School	
	Number	Per Cent	Number	Per Cent	Number	Per Cent
All provinces	1,008,254	100.0	353,947	100.0	654,307	100.0
Pinar del Río ...	95,670	9.5	31,063	8.8	64,607	9.9
Havana	189,987	18.8	130,275	36.8	59,712	9.1
Matanzas	73,708	7.3	43,531	12.3	30,177	4.6
Las Villas	203,995	20.2	50,434	14.2	153,561	23.5
Camagüey	103,420	10.3	29,139	8.2	74,281	11.4
Oriente	341,474	33.9	69,505	19.7	271,969	41.5

*Censo de 1943.

†Number who attended, according to figures furnished by the Ministry of Education, includes those in public (297,695) and in private (59,253) schools.

The maldistribution of schools in Cuba is revealed indirectly in Table 42. Oriente Province is the most heavily populated and has the lowest attendance rate. It contains over one-third of Cuba's children in the age group 5–13, but has less than 20 per cent of the nation's children reported in school (Table 43). Havana, on the other hand, has only about 19 per cent of all children in the age group under consideration, but claims nearly 37 per cent of all those attending school. Las Villas is next lowest after Oriente when provincial school attendance figures are compared.

In the Special Surveys of eleven rural localities, it was found that of 720 children aged 6 to 12 years, 60.6 per cent were attending school. There was wide variation among the different regions, the percentages being as follows: Pinar del Río, 70.5; Cabaiguán, 78.6; Cienfuegos-Trinidad area, 35.7; Alto Songo, 59.5; Florida, 75.0; Manguito, 54.0; Sancti-Spíritus, 19.0; Bayamo, 48.8; San Antonio de las Vegas, 77.4; Florencia, 45.6; and Güines, 80.3. If these figures are any indication of more recent developments, there has been some improvement since 1942–43.

While the province of Havana may consider itself fortunate in being able to claim such a relatively high proportion of children attending school, it should not be under any illusion that it is unaffected by the poor conditions in the other provinces. As is true in every modern country, a migration of population from rural to urban areas is constantly taking place in Cuba. If these migrants have been denied the advantage of schooling in the provinces from which they come, Havana reaps the harvest in the lowered quality of its citizenship. In other words, what happens in one part of the island is the concern of all the provinces, not merely the particular one in which poor conditions exist.

The official figures do not tell the entire story. On the one hand is the important fact that many children who go to school attend only half a day, part of them coming in the morning and part in the afternoon. On the other side, however, is the consideration that a certain amount of private teaching or tutoring is done in the rural areas. For example, the writer met a young man in Ti-Arriba, an isolated coffee-growing area of Oriente Province, who was teaching a class of thirty pupils privately at a charge of twenty-five cents per week. Some of them were adults, some were children.

The children came during the day and the adults at night. The public school in this settlement, incidentally, had one teacher and ninety pupils. Similarly, in the tobacco-growing area near Cabaiguán, such instruction as the children received was arranged for by the parents' employing an itinerant private teacher. He charged one dollar per student per month and spent two hours at each of three different homes in the area during the day, the children coming from neighboring places to attend the classes. What is important to note in these instances is that there is more "education" going on in the country than is indicated by the official figures, and that this is due to the determination of farm people to see that their children receive instruction, even if they have to provide it entirely from their own resources.

THE TEACHING PERSONNEL

In the occupational census of 1943, data are available which reveal certain characteristics of the teachers in Cuba. In this connection, reference is made only to the primary school teachers (*Maestros de Instrucción Primaria*). According to this source, there were nearly 20,000 individuals in Cuba at the time of the census who regarded teaching primary school as their occupation. Elsewhere in the same volume, however, it is reported that only 9,711 were so employed.[6] This figure is about equal to that reported by the Ministry of Education for teachers in the public schools. There are probably an additional 2,000 primary teachers in private schools, besides an unknown number of private teachers like those just mentioned in Ti-Arriba and Cabaiguán.

However, if the census figures can be relied upon, it appears that there are more teachers available to the people of the Republic than are being used. If all of the teachers reported in the census were utilized, the island could take care of its school population without serious difficulty. The average number of children per enumerated teacher is fifty-one (see Table 44). On the basis of the number of public school teachers reported by the Ministry of Education, however, the picture is quite different, as will be discussed presently.

[6] Since the census enumeration was as of July 25, 1943, there was undoubtedly a larger figure for "unemployed" reported than was in reality the case.

TABLE 44. CUBAN POPULATION 5–13 YEARS OF AGE PER PRIMARY TEACHER, BY PROVINCES, 1943

Province	Population Aged 5–13	Number of Teachers	Number of Children per Teacher	Teachers' Median Monthly Income in Dollars
All provinces ...	1,008,254	19,758	51	78.90
Pinar del Río ...	95,670	1,417	68	82.67
Havana	189,987	8,166	23	97.76
Matanzas	73,708	1,616	46	80.56
Las Villas	203,995	3,906	52	78.50
Camagüey	103,420	1,385	75	77.00
Oriente	341,474	3,268	104	78.00

SOURCE: *Censo de 1943*, Tables 1 and 5.

There are, of course, wide differences among the provinces in the number of teachers and especially in the proportion of teachers to children of school age. At the two extremes are Havana and Oriente—so often found at opposite poles in the realm of social phenomena. With 104 children per teacher reported in the occupation census, Oriente is four times as badly off as Havana with 23 children per teacher. (It must be borne in mind that we are not here discussing the teachers in practice, but rather those who gave "primary school teacher" as their occupation.)

Training requirements. The requirements for certification as a primary teacher include graduation from the four-year course provided by the provincial normal schools. Requirements for admission to the normal schools include the completion of eight years of primary school training and the successful passage of an entrance examination. At the completion of the four-year course, a title of normal teacher (*maestra normal*) is granted.

Income. The income of teachers in Cuba is rather uniform when compared with the variation found in the United States. This is due to the centralized system of administration. The figures on income are likewise derived from the 1943 census and refer to all teachers, not merely those in the public service. The fact that private school teachers are included probably accounts for such variations as do exist among the provinces, although not all the differences can be credited to this factor. While teachers are heavily concentrated around the median, there are small numbers with very low and very high incomes. For instance, there are

TABLE 45. PERCENTAGE DISTRIBUTION OF TEACHERS FOR VARIOUS PROVINCES, BY INCOME CLASS, 1943

Monthly Income in Dollars	Cuba	Pinar del Río	Havana	Matanzas	Las Villas	Camagüey	Oriente
Total	100.0	100.0	100.0	100.0	100.0	100.0	100.0
Under 30	7.7	4.8	6.7	5.7	10.0	9.3	8.8
30–59	15.5	7.1	20.0	11.2	12.8	18.1	15.7
60–99	70.5	84.1	63.7	80.5	73.3	65.6	70.8
100–199	4.8	3.5	7.6	2.3	2.8	4.9	4.0
200–299	0.6	0.2	1.1	0.2	0.3	0.8	0.3
300 or more	0.6	0.3	0.9	0.2	0.6	1.2	0.4

SOURCE: *Censo de 1943*, p. 1203, Table 5.

some teachers earning under $30 a month, and a few get $300 or more (Table 45). Those who get less than $70–$100 are quite likely itinerant, private instructors. Moreover, while the median incomes for all provinces except Havana fluctuate around $80, there is a great deal of difference in the actual distribution among the various income classes. For instance, while only 4.8 per cent of the teachers in Pinar del Río receive less than $30 per month, in Las Villas 10 per cent were in this class.[7]

Color and income. Table 46 shows little difference in the median incomes of colored and white teachers. The white group has a slight advantage in the provinces of Havana, Camagüey, and Oriente, while the median of the colored group is higher in Pinar del Río and Las Villas. The two groups are practically equal in Matanzas. Incidentally, the proportion of colored people in the occupation of primary teacher does not equal the proportion of

[7] According to a remarkable provision of the Constitution of 1940 (Article 52), "the monthly salary of primary teachers must not in any case be less than one-millionth of the total budget of the Nation." The provision had not been fully implemented up to February 1946, although the teachers had staged a street parade and demonstration before the Presidential Palace and leading newspapers had plumped for the cause of a $114 monthly salary. The budget recommended by the executive branch of the government called for 114 million dollars of "ordinary" expenditures, although total expenditures were estimated at something over 170 million. Congress, however, did not approve the budget, although it decided that the teachers' minimum wages should be based upon the "ordinary" and not on the "extraordinary" budget. Thus, there is the technical question involved as to what is the "budget of the nation"—that which the president proposes (and spends in spite of congressional inaction), or the budget which Congress formally approves. Meanwhile, the teachers were promised an increase, although it may not in the end bring their minimum salaries up to $114.

TABLE 46. MEDIAN MONTHLY SALARY OF CUBAN TEACHERS FOR VARIOUS
PROVINCES, BY COLOR, 1943

Province	Median Monthly Salary		Per Cent of Those Reporting Who Are Colored*
	White	Colored	
All provinces 79.00		77.70	18.1
Pinar del Río 81.45		84.10	44.2
Havana 79.30		71.75	14.2
Matanzas 80.71		80.20	13.6
Las Villas 78.10		80.80	13.3
Camagüey 77.75		73.70	13.2
Oriente 79.10		74.65	25.1

SOURCE: *Censo de 1943*, p. 1203, Table 5.

*Only 11,437 of the 19,758 teachers reported on the income question.
Of these, 2,066 were colored. The proportion of colored teachers among
the total teacher population is 17.9. Colored people constitute 25.6 per cent
of Cuba's population.

TABLE 47. DISTRIBUTION OF WHITE AND COLORED CUBAN TEACHERS
BY INCOME CLASS, 1943

Monthly Income in Dollars	White		Colored	
	Number	Per Cent	Number	Per Cent
Total *9,371*		*100.0*	*2,066*	*100.0*
Under 30 682		7.3	202	9.8
30–59 1,479		15.8	305	14.8
60–99 6,584		70.3	1,489	72.1
100–199 496		5.3	57	2.8
200–299 67		0.7	4	0.2
300 or more 63		0.7	9	0.4

SOURCE: *Censo de 1943*, p. 1203, Table 5.

colored people in the total population, which indicates some
"selectivity" on the basis of color. The colored population is about
one-fourth of the total in Cuba, while the colored teachers constitute less than one-fifth of the teacher group. In Oriente, colored
teachers constitute one-fourth of the total group, however, and in
Pinar del Río, surprisingly enough, 44.2 per cent. Table 47 con-
firms the absence of any major difference in income between the
white and colored teachers.

Age and sex. The teachers of Cuba are predominantly young.
According to Table 48, about 63 per cent of them are under forty

TABLE 48. PERCENTAGE OF CUBAN TEACHERS IN VARIOUS AGE GROUPS,
BY PROVINCE, 1943

Age Group	All Provinces	Pinar del Río	Havana	Matanzas	Las Villas	Camagüey	Oriente
Total *100.0*		*100.0*	*100.0*	*100.0*	*100.0*	*100.0*	*100.0*
13–19 .... 3.7		4.1	3.9	2.5	3.8	5.2	2.7
20–29 .... 29.3		35.3	29.7	23.6	30.5	33.4	25.5
30–39 .... 30.1		30.7	30.0	34.1	27.8	29.4	31.4
40–49 .... 15.6		15.2	15.4	16.7	16.1	11.8	16.9
50–59 .... 13.8		10.5	12.7	14.6	14.7	13.6	17.1
60 and over 7.4		4.2	8.4	8.5	7.2	6.6	6.5

SOURCE: *Censo de 1943*, p. 1182, Table 4.

years of age. In this respect the country is comparable to the
United States, where the profession of teaching is also predominantly youthful. In Cuba, there are considerable differences among
the provinces, Havana and Matanzas, the most urban provinces,
having higher proportions of teachers in the upper age groups—
as is also true in urban areas of the United States. There are several well-known reasons for this condition. In the first place, the
tendency is for the teacher to begin his or her career in rural areas,
and for the cities to fill their schools with the experienced and
therefore older teachers from the villages, towns, and open country. Moreover, in the rural areas, where there is usually a surplus
of men of marriageable age, a young woman is likely to marry
after only one, two, or three years as a teacher. Her position is
then filled by another youthful person. Primary school teaching
in Cuba is largely a woman's world, with men constituting only
about 20 per cent of the total group.

Tenure. The tenure of teachers in Cuba is for life, unless removed for cause. An extraordinary condition exists in this respect,
which allows a teacher to draw pay whether he or she is teaching
or not. There are said to be a great many teachers drawing their
regular monthly pay checks who are not actually teaching. Sometimes this is due to the failure of the government to provide a
schoolhouse. Sometimes a teacher who is assigned to a rural school
simply fails to report for duty. Great sums of money are reputedly
spent on personnel which is not in fact performing any important
duties in connection with the educational system. Under such
conditions, the meaning of the census figures—which reveal a

comparatively adequate supply of primary teachers, but a very low school-attendance figure—becomes clear. The money that the Cuban people are paying in taxes for education is being spent— and in larger amounts than ever before—but the children are not being educated.[8]

SCHOOL BUILDINGS

Comparatively few publicly owned rural schoolhouses exist in Cuba. The number of school buildings owned by the state in 1943 amounted to 198. An additional 49 belonged to municipalities, 1,249 were granted free by individuals for school purposes, and 1,603 more were rented. The majority of the structures in which school is held in rural areas, therefore, have been designed and built for other purposes, usually to serve as a rural dwelling or other farm structure.[9]

The number of schoolrooms reported by the Ministry of Education for the year 1943 clearly falls far short of the needs of the children of the country. There were, according to the data reported, about 134 children of school age per room (Table 49). Of course, as we have already seen, about two-thirds of these children did not attend school, so that in terms of actual attendance there were only about 45 per room. Even this figure is high as an average. It means that there are many rooms with more than that number. As already indicated, in most schools it is the common practice to have some of the students come in the forenoon and some in the afternoon. This means that the pupils have only a half-day of school, but obviously it is better than not attending at all. According to the reported figures on the number of schoolrooms at various periods, the most favorable conditions in this respect existed during and immediately after the United States military occupation. There was apparently a serious deterioration from 1907 to 1919, and little improvement since that time.

[8] In ten years, 1935 to 1945, the amount budgeted (1934–35) or spent (1944–45) for education increased from $10,105,631 to $35,453,054. The former figure was 18.3 per cent of the national budget, the latter, 26.9 per cent of national expenditures.

[9] During the summer of 1946, the government decided to appropriate to its own use the "profits" accruing from the sale of 250,000 tons of sugar in the world market, the profit arising from the difference between the price for which most of the crop was sold to the United States and that received from sales to other countries. With part of this money, the government proposed to build 1,500 rural schools at an average cost estimated at $8,500.

TABLE 49. SCHOOLROOMS IN RELATION TO SCHOOL POPULATION
FOR VARIOUS CENSUS PERIODS

Census Period	School-Aged Children	School-rooms*	Children per Room
1899	446,158	541	825
U.S. military government.	425,000 (est.)	3,494	118
1907	405,541	3,841	105
1919	813,781	5,652†	144
1931	883,371	...‡	...‡
1943	1,008,253	7,516§	134

* *Censo de 1943*, p. 482.
†1920.
‡Data not available.
§198 belong to the state, 49 belong to municipalities, 1,249 to individuals who granted them free to be used for this purpose, 1,603 are rented. (In this case figures refer to school buildings, not to rooms.)

SUMMARY OF THE RURAL SCHOOL PROBLEM IN CUBA

The most obvious fact about Cuban education is the lack of opportunity for rural children to attend school. In some places there are school buildings, but no teachers, in other places there are teachers, but no school buildings. There has been no systematic plan of school-building construction for rural areas. In some cases, where the local interest in schools is sufficiently strong, parents have constructed school buildings at their own expense, contributing money, labor, or materials for this purpose. In still other cases, buildings have been constructed but have not been furnished with desks and other necessary equipment, and no books have been provided for the pupils. It is not unusual to see two children sitting in desks which were designed to accommodate but one.

One of the reasons for the present somewhat chaotic situation is the fact that responsibility has been centralized in the national government. The sense of local responsibility for education is at present very weak, as might well be expected. The Constitution of 1940 in Article 48 states: "Primary instruction is obligatory for minors of school age, and it shall be furnished by the Nation, without prejudice to the cooperation entrusted to municipal initiative." It will be noted that this reverses the order of responsibility provided in the United States constitution. In Cuba, some "cooperation" may be "entrusted to municipal initiative"; in the United States, the national government has only such responsibilities as may be granted to it by the states. In a later section of the Constitution of 1940, however, appears an injunction to the municipalities which, on the face of it, would appear to give them some responsibility for education. Article 213 states: "The municipal government shall especially: . . . (c) create and manage public schools, museums and libraries, physical training and recreation grounds . . ."

It appears, therefore, that there is no clear-cut responsibility for schools as between the national and the municipal governments. As a matter of official arrangement and practice, however, all schools are under the control of the Ministry of Education except for those specifically designated as the responsibility of other ministries, particularly the Ministry of Agriculture. Even such schools as are maintained by the municipalities are under the ultimate control and regulation of the Ministry of Education. But as long as initiative in school matters remains with the central government, the local units of government are not likely to do much on their own account. In recent years, the central government has apparently been slow to exercise its initiative in behalf of education, although increasing amounts of money are annually made available to the ministry.

Maldistribution of teachers. The latest reports available on the distribution of teachers are for the year 1942–43, when there were 9,515 employed teachers. Their distribution by provinces in relation to the number of children aged 5 to 13 years, inclusive (1943), is shown in Table 50. Havana again is revealed as the favored province. When it is realized that there are many more private schools in Havana than in the remainder of the island—and that the data presented refer only to public school teachers—the differential is even more pronounced. The generalization appears justified that the farther removed the area is from Havana, the worse the school situation appears to be. Dr. Ramiro Guerra, one of the best-informed individuals in the Republic on school matters and director of the newspaper *Diario de la Marina*, after presenting the facts regarding distribution of teachers, makes the following editorial comment:

The explanation of this fact [the poor distribution of teachers]: administrative centralization, that smooths the way for those aspirants

TABLE 50. CHILDREN AGED 5 TO 13 IN RELATION TO EMPLOYED TEACHERS,
BY PROVINCES

Province	Number of Children Aged 5–13 (1943)	Number of Teachers 1942–43	School Children per Teacher
All provinces	1,008,254	9,515	106
Pinar del Río	95,670	1,046	91
Havana	189,987	3,100	61
Matanzas	73,708	1,106	67
Las Villas	203,995	1,954	104
Camagüey	103,420	612	169
Oriente	341,474	1,697	201

SOURCE: *Censo de 1943*, p. 862, Table 9, and letter from the Ministry of Education to the author.

to attend schools where it is most convenient to provide them, not where they are most needed according to the pupil population. Until that centralization is remedied, and until school statistics are brought up to date with exactitude, so that the provinces and municipalities may know their respective situation and are able to demand it, the evil will not be remedied.[10]

Dr. Guerra comments further on the misfortune that there are not accurate statistics for the more recent years, but has no doubt that if they were known, they would manifest little or no improvement in the situation since 1942–43, and that "the terrible injustice that has been committed and is being committed against the majority and the most needy portion of the Cuban children would be manifest and would produce indignation, demands, and protests against the maladministration of the schools."[11]

Inadequate number of teachers. Not only are the teachers poorly distributed among the provinces in relation to the school population, but the total number of teachers is woefully inadequate. Even assuming that all of the teachers were engaged throughout the year in active teaching, and assuming further that the compulsory school-attendance laws were enforced, there would be over 100 pupils per teacher—an impossible situation for adequate

[10] *Diario de la Marina*, January 8, 1946. In the same article, Dr. Guerra reports that in an interview with President Grau San Martín on school problems, he called the attention of the president to the fact that in the municipio of the president's birth there was in 1944–45 a pupil population of 6,380, of whom 5,017 were not attending school.

[11] *Ibid.*

instruction. Even 50 pupils per teacher would be too many, but to achieve that ratio, it would be necessary to more than double the number of primary school teachers for the country as a whole. In the province of Camagüey, the number would have to be more than tripled, and in Oriente quadrupled.

The conclusion appears warranted that little if any progress has been made since 1907 in providing school opportunities for the nation's children. The impetus to education provided in the early years of the Republic has barely been maintained. Rural children, especially, are the victims of poor schools or the absence of any schools at all. Conditions vary throughout the island, getting relatively worse as the distance from Havana increases. This situation is not due to opposition to education among the rural people. On the contrary, the author is convinced that the *campesinos* are anxious for better educational facilities for their children, in many cases taking the unusual—for Cuba—step of assuming local initiative in building schoolhouses and hiring teachers. The fault would appear to lie in ineffective administration at the national level.

LITERACY

The literacy of a population constitutes an ultimate test of the adequacy of its educational system. For this reason it seems worthwhile to analyze the data concerning Cuban literacy. As might be expected, these data support our previous generalizations as to the inadequacy of Cuba's school system. The number of literate persons in Cuba was reported in the census of 1899, and in the four subsequent enumerations of 1907, 1919, 1931, and 1943. For the years 1931 and 1943, the number of illiterates and those unknown or not reported are also given. These data on literacy are available for each province, for white (native-born and foreign) and colored, and by sex and age. In addition, in the two later censuses it is possible to make some approximate rural-urban comparisons. Because the major part of the analysis to follow is based on the census of 1943, it is important to point out that the tabulation shows a grave statistical weakness in that the percentage marked "unknown" is unusually high, 6.6 per cent. The nature of the data with which we have to deal, as regards the literacy status, is set forth in Table 51.

TABLE 51. POPULATION OF CUBA 10 YEARS OF AGE AND OVER ACCORDING TO LITERACY
STATUS, BY NATIVITY AND COLOR, 1943

Literacy Status	Total		Native White		Foreign White		Colored	
	Number	Per Cent	Number	Per Cent	Number	Per Cent	Number	Per Cent
Total	3,575,434	100.0	2,532,942	100.0	139,963	100.0	902,530	100.0
Able to read ...	2,550,847	71.3	1,840,033	72.6	102,605	73.3	608,209	67.4
Not able to read .	789,301	22.1	530,129	20.9	29,587	21.1	229,585	25.4
Unknown .	235,286	6.6	162,780	6.5	7,770	5.6	64,736	7.2

SOURCE: *Censo de 1943*, Tables 15 and 16.

The census of 1931 showed only .01 per cent "not reported."[12]
It is possible, therefore, that the percentage of literate persons
reported in 1943 does not include all who are in reality literate,
although it is conceded by well-informed Cubans that the true
figure would not greatly exceed the one reported.

In Table 52 the figures are given by provinces and color for the
various census years. Several points of significance are immediately apparent:

1. There was a steady increase in the literacy rate in Cuba from
the beginning of independence to 1931.

2. There was no gain in literacy, so far as the total population
was concerned, from 1931 to 1943, although there was a slight
gain in the case of the native white and the colored groups.

3. The colored population has made the most marked advance
in literacy in the 45-year period, and is now approaching the white
rate.

4. In two provinces, Matanzas and Las Villas, the literacy of the
colored population was higher than that of the whites in 1943. It
was also higher in Las Villas in 1931, but in all other years and
provinces, the colored rate was less than the white.

5. Pinar del Río and Oriente are the provinces with lowest

[12]In the 1931 census the phrase *sin informe* was used to designate the group on
which information was lacking. In 1943 the phrase *se ignora* (to be ignorant of) was
used. Some persons who are familiar with the 1943 census regard this difference as
significant; they feel that actually, in many cases the question was "ignored," and that
a large proportion of those who fall in this category in the final tabulation are in
reality illiterate, but were not so classed because of attempts to increase the number
of possible voters.

TABLE 52. TRENDS IN LITERACY RATES IN CUBA SINCE 1899 OF THE POPULATION
AGED 10 YEARS AND OVER, BY PROVINCE AND COLOR

Province and Color	Percentage Literate				
	1899	1907	1919	1931	1943
All provinces 43.2		56.6	61.6	71.7	71.3
Native white 46.7		58.6	62.7	72.0	72.6
Foreign white 70.8		74.4	75.3	81.9	73.3
Colored 28.0		45.0	53.1	64.7	67.4
Pinar del Río 22.9		39.0	46.4	60.3	62.7
Native white 23.7		38.9	46.6	59.9	63.1
Foreign white 58.5		61.8	72.5	72.3	74.3
Colored 10.2		43.2	40.4	55.8	60.4
Havana 61.3		72.7	76.3	85.8	81.0
Native white 64.6		74.8	76.2	84.8	81.5
Foreign white 80.3		82.6	85.0	90.8	78.0
Colored 40.5		58.5	68.2	82.0	80.0
Matanzas 39.7		52.9	58.8	72.3	75.9
Native white 50.8		60.9	60.4	72.4	75.7
Foreign white 63.4		66.2	67.3	75.0	67.0
Colored 21.5		39.3	53.1	70.6	77.6
Las Villas 38.7		52.0	59.6	68.5	71.0
Native white 42.1		54.3	59.5	67.7	70.9
Foreign white 58.7		61.8	63.4	69.8	64.0
Colored 25.9		43.2	57.5	69.7	72.9
Camagüey 49.1		62.1	64.3	67.6	70.7
Native white 49.4		61.9	64.4	72.7	73.1
Foreign white 67.7		76.1	70.4	79.2	72.1
Colored 42.9		56.4	58.4	51.3	61.7
Oriente 34.2		49.6	53.3	64.4	62.6
Native white 37.1		51.6	57.6	66.8	65.2
Foreign white 67.7		71.8	76.6	84.5	76.3
Colored 26.8		43.0	44.8	57.5	57.9

SOURCE: Census reports for 1899, 1907, 1919, 1931, and 1943.

literacy rates. Havana ranks highest, followed by Matanzas, Las
Villas, and Camagüey in that order.

6. While the foreign white population has been consistently
higher than the other groups, it was very little higher than the
native white in 1943, having suffered a marked decline from 1931.

The failure of Cuba to make any gain in literacy during the
twelve-year period from 1931 to 1943 is a somewhat startling
revelation in view of the expressed ideals of the revolution which
overthrew Machado, and the lofty statements regarding education in the Constitution of 1940. The latter reiterates the dictum
that school attendance is compulsory for children from six to
thirteen years of age, provides that education shall be gratis when

furnished by the state, province, or municipality, and that school supplies shall also be free (Article 48). It sets forth, moreover, that the "nation shall maintain a system of schools for adults devoted particularly to the elimination and prevention of illiteracy; predominantly practical rural schools, organized with a view to the interests of small agricultural, maritime or other communities . . ." (Article 49). The apparent devotion to education is further indicated by Article 52, which states that the "budget of the Ministry of Education shall not be less than the ordinary budget of any other Ministry, except in the case of an emergency declared by law."

It is clear from the census data, however, that the actual implementation of these provisions of the constitution have been delayed. During the early part of the intercensal period, there was naturally a good deal of disorganization as a consequence of the revolution itself, not to mention the severe economic depression which prevailed at that time. However, there appears to be little rational explanation for the apparent neglect of education in more recent years.

The failure to provide for the education of Cuban children is shown by the literacy figures according to age (Table 53). Although the data were not reported comparably by age-groups for 1931 to 1943, rough comparisons can be made. For the population under twenty years of age, the literacy rate was somewhat lower in 1943 than in 1931. For the native white and colored groups, the younger the age, the lower the rate of literacy reported. This is highly significant, for it indicates that the condition has been getting progressively worse for several years. To state it another way, if conditions had been improving in 1943, the children ten years of age would have shown a higher rate of literacy than those eleven, and so on. If the country had been holding its own in the struggle against illiteracy, there would have been little difference among the different ages.

Without strenuous efforts at teaching adults to read and write, the literacy rate for the total population will grow steadily worse as the cumulative effect of the neglect of education of younger children manifests itself. The reason that adults over twenty in 1943 exceeded in literacy those in 1931 was obviously the passage

TABLE 53. PERCENTAGES OF CUBAN POPULATION IN VARIOUS AGE GROUPS
WHO WERE ABLE TO READ, BY COLOR, 1943

Age	All Classes		Native White		Foreign White		Colored	
	1931	1943	1931	1943	1931	1943	1931	1943
10–13 ....70.5			69.7		79.0		67.4	
10		50.2		51.7		76.5		46.1
11		57.6		59.0		76.3		53.6
12		61.8		63.0		76.9		58.2
13		66.8		68.1		82.5		62.8
14–19 ....76.3*		73.0	75.4	74.1	85.0	82.2	73.7	69.5
20 and over ...70.4†		73.1	71.3	74.5	81.5	73.2	61.7	69.1

* Ages 14–20.
† Age 21 and over.

into the adult group during the twelve-year period of the children
from ten to twenty in 1931 who had comparatively high literacy
rates. The next census will reveal the opposite effect.

The fact that the literacy rate of the colored population is so
near that of the white may be explained largely on the basis of
the greater proportions of colored people in urban centers where
educational opportunities are more abundant. It is in rural areas
that education is notoriously neglected, and the rural population
of Cuba is predominantly white. That is, a larger proportion of
the nation's whites than Negroes live in rural areas where schools
are poor or do not exist at all.

A word of explanation is in order regarding the foreign white
population, which showed a marked decline in literacy from 1931
to 1943. This statistical change is, in a sense, fictitious, because it
no doubt results in large measure from the change in definition
of citizenship which took place during the interim between the
two enumerations. The Constitution of 1940 declared everyone
born of foreign parents in Cuba to be of Cuban citizenship unless
a contrary declaration was made upon reaching twenty-one years
of age. This reversed the previous policy, which held children born
in Cuba of foreign parents to be of the same citizenship as the
parents. Thus the anomaly of the census of 1931 reporting that
over 50 per cent of the "foreign white" population was born in
Cuba. Moreover, there was considerable emigration of foreigners
from the island during the 1930's, which was probably selective
of the upper-class elements who could afford to return to their

native lands. No data are at hand to enable us to say more precisely how these factors—the change in definition of citizenship and emigration from the island—have influenced the literacy rate, except to cause it to decline.

The most highly rural provinces, Pinar del Río and Oriente, show the lowest literacy rates, and there can be no doubt that if a strict analysis could be made on the basis of rural and urban segments of the population, a consistently lower rate would be found among the rural group. In 1931 the literacy rate for the ten largest cities of Cuba was 91.1, while that for the remainder of the population was 64.4. The corresponding percentages for 1943 were 83.7 for the cities and 68 for the remainder of the population.

The province of Oriente on the eastern extremity of the island is the "problem" province in the matter of illiteracy. It contains 28.4 per cent of the total population—the most populous of the six provinces—but had 35 per cent of the reported illiterates in 1943. The other province with a major proportion (21.4 per cent) of the island's illiterates is Las Villas, containing 19.6 per cent of the total population. Havana is the most favorably situated, for with 26 per cent of the population, it has only 14.6 per cent of the illiterates.

Although Cuba has a considerable distance to go in eradicating illiteracy, it has made rather remarkable progress since the establishment of the Republic. According to one tabulation, it had the lowest rate of illiteracy of any Latin-American country except Argentina.[13] It is quite clear from the previous discussion, however, that Cuba may easily lose its present favorable ranking in the course of the next few years unless efforts are made immediately to improve the school attendance of children and to provide opportunities for adults to learn to read and write.

[13] *Estadistica: Journal of the Inter-American Institute*, Mexico, D.F., September 1945, p. 335.

CHAPTER XIII

The Rural Prospect

In making a few concluding generalizations about rural Cuba, the author is aware that within the broad framework of Cuban society there are many variations and diversities; and that although there are here, as in all societies, some common elements which provide a certain homogeneity, there is always a measure of heterogeneity as well. The student of a culture must attempt to see both the likenesses and the differences.

As we have seen, Cuban culture of today is derived predominantly from the heritage of Spain. The conquistadores who overran the island in the early sixteenth century founded the first settlements, established the forms of government and religion, and promulgated legal institutions to govern all aspects of life in the new colony. Family life, moral codes, and rights to property were fundamentally the same in Cuba as in the Spanish homeland. Indigenous culture was not an important factor in the Cuban heritage, since the natives were practically annihilated in a little more than a generation. Thus, unlike some of the other Spanish colonies, there are very few traces of the native culture discernible.

There was, however, another cultural stream which influenced historical developments—namely, that which came from Africa with the importation of Negro slaves. But since the African immigrants occupied a subordinate position vis-à-vis the Spanish masters, they influenced the total culture less than they were influenced by it. Nevertheless, their assimilation by the dominant culture was by no means complete, nor is it so today. For example, although the Negroes have been incorporated into the dominant form of religious organization—the Roman Catholic Church— vestiges of their traditional religions remain, even though mixed with Christian forms and beliefs. Family relations among the descendants of the slaves show some evidence of being less formalized and perhaps less stable.

The heritage of social status, whether it be the survival of the feudal structure which characterized Spain at the time of Cuba's settlement, or that of the master and slave tradition, where skin color became an identifying badge of servitude, influences contemporary life in many ways. The people are very much aware of class, particularly of "upper" and "lower," rich and poor. Farmers, for instance, may vote in an election—voting is compulsory by law—but they do not run for office. Government is the business of people who do not work with their hands—the professional groups, notably the legal profession, and persons of wealth. Farmers may complain a great deal about what the government does or does not do—mostly the latter—but they do not seek redress by getting themselves or their associates elected to office.

Again, the feudal heritage manifests itself in political life. The pattern of centralized government, as opposed to that of local autonomy, leads the people to expect too much from the capitol and too little from their own efforts. If roads are poor and schools are lacking, complaints are made against the national government which has the responsibility for providing both. Only in rare instances does one discover local groups taking matters into their own hands and providing facilities by themselves. When one asks why farmers in a certain locality do not spend their time during the "dead season" in cooperative effort to improve their roads, or in building a schoolhouse, the reply may be similar to that of a woman leader in one community, who said: "Cubans will not work together; they don't trust each other; they are afraid someone will get more benefit from such a project than they will. While they can comfortably sit and smoke, as long as the house does not fall on their heads, they do nothing."

While this particular individual was perhaps exaggerating the situation, and voicing her own feelings of frustration arising from the failures of her industrious efforts to improve conditions in her community, one cannot but feel that she has a valid point. It is easy to generalize that farmers are always individualistic, a trait commonly attributed to the American farmer by various writers; but there can be little question that in Cuba, farmers have not yet developed a sense of local initiative or of responsibility to work cooperatively to achieve solutions to problems of which they may be generally aware, but which they think are the responsibility of the government. The poor roads common in many rural sections of Cuba could be improved and kept in condition by only partial mobilization of the unused labor resources of the community; but the people will tolerate poor facilities indefinitely, contenting themselves with criticism of the central government and the sending of petitions or delegations to the *Presidente*, rather than spend their efforts at improving conditions by themselves. This lack of community cohesion at the local level derives, in part, from the centralized pattern of government, from the paternalistic tradition inherent in the feudal and slave societies, and from the fact that the family and the larger kinship group remain extremely strong as units of Cuban society.

SPECIFIC RURAL PROBLEMS

It is not difficult to see clearly some outstanding problems confronting the rural population of Cuba, some of which can be summarized briefly.

Low income. While insufficient income is a problem of most farmers the world over, it is particularly serious in Cuba. For a great many rural families, the struggle for mere survival is a daily concern. The average per capita income for all people in the nation for the years 1941–44 was estimated at $129.[1] This compares with an average per capita income in the United States of $949. The figures include all classes, urban as well as rural. If the rural figure alone were available for Cuba, it would probably be even lower than that for the nation as a whole. The per capita net

[1] See Clarence Senior, "The Puerto Ricans of New York City," *Economic Review,* Puerto Rico, June 1945, p. 12, for comparative income figures on various countries of the Caribbean.

farm income in the United States in 1946 was $779.[2] Nor must the reader assume that a corresponding differential in costs of living exists between the two countries. Food costs are relatively high in Cuba, as are those for clothing, medical care, transportation, and many other items. The cost of housing and fuel is less, because of the favorable climate, but if modern types of home construction, furnishings, and equipment were utilized, housing costs would also be high.

It is easy to remark in this connection that granting the low incomes, it would be possible for the people to vastly improve their living level by more home production of the proper kinds of food for an adequate diet, by building even simple latrines where none now exist, and otherwise adding to their general well-being by the expenditure of little beyond their own labor. But where a blanket of poverty has rested upon a people for many generations, initiative to do these things dries up, and they succumb to the inertia of habits and ways of living long established. The vicious circle of "poor ways—poor people" is not easily broken.

What the rural people themselves regard as their most urgent problems are shown in Table 54. Naturally there was a great deal of variation in the replies according to sections of the country, but in the totals, roads and highways—especially field roads—get the highest ranking in importance, followed by education. Housing also is a problem of great concern. The high importance which rural people ascribe to these items could have been foretold after a few casual interviews with farm families.

Roads and communication. The isolation of families resulting from the scattered farmstead pattern of settlement makes roads and other communication facilities especially important. In the Special Surveys, 392 of the 742 families were located on roads which were passable only in the dry season. Not only are people denied access to many social advantages by the lack of passable roads, but it is impossible for them to reach the market with products harvested during the wet season. Their production is therefore limited to supplying only local demand. More facilities must be provided if people are to have easy contact with each

[2] *How Families Use Their Incomes* (Washington: U.S. Department of Agriculture, Miscellaneous Publication No. 653), p. 53.

TABLE 54. NUMBER OF TIMES SPECIFIC PROBLEMS WERE MENTIONED IN THE
SPECIAL SURVEY OF CUBAN FARMERS

Problem	Times Mentioned
Farming:	
More land	66
Machinery	68
Irrigation	90
Better seed	9
Fertilizer	2
Better prices	23
Rent reduction	52
Rural credit	32
Roads and highways	250
More schools	188
Night schools	6
Health and hygiene:	
Sanitation	64
Medical care	4
Better diets	8
Housing:	
Larger or better homes	72
Electricity	20
Wells	9
Running water	3

other and with the trade centers. The cost of constructing and maintaining roads becomes a major problem in a country with such low per capita wealth as Cuba possesses.

Housing and sanitation. As we have seen from data presented earlier, the housing of rural Cubans leaves much to be desired. The simple bohío, with its dirt floors and cheap construction, cannot be called a fit habitation for a family. Only the salubrious climate makes it possible for such a structure to serve at all as the family shelter. Most of them are not only inadequate from the standpoint of providing mere shelter, but they are too small to accommodate at a level of decency the large families which live in them.

Perhaps the most serious aspect of housing, however, is the absence of sanitary facilities. The fact that a large proportion of the families in the Special Surveys reported no latrine at all indicates a wide neglect of even rudimentary sanitation. The very high incidence of intestinal parasites in the Cuban population is a direct consequence of this neglect. This general attitude of indifference in matters of sanitation is by no means confined to the rural areas. One needs only to enter a so-called "sanitary" toilet in one of the towns to see a similar negligence manifested.

The water burden. In any area of scattered farmsteads, the provision of water for domestic purposes is a major problem. In the Caribbean generally, a visitor is impressed with the magnitude of the task of procuring this vital necessity. Farm people in Cuba for the most part depend on wells for their supply. However, many of them do not have wells of their own, but haul or carry water from the neighbors. A gravity system, piped into the house, is a rarity. When a family has to haul water from a distance, a barrel or tank is used, frequently a section of a variety of palm which is characterized by a bulge in one part of the trunk. When this is hollowed out, it makes a convenient receptacle, holding several gallons of water. If the time and energy involved in procuring culinary water could be carefully measured, it would undoubtedly amount to a large fraction of the time and labor expenditures of the population. Even in the city of Havana, where the water supply is inadequate to serve the growing population, numerous households are supplied by hauling and carrying from taps where pressure is still sufficient to produce a flow. Under such conditions of scarcity it is hardly to be expected that water would be used freely for bathing or for frequent washing of clothing and bed linen.

Inadequate educational facilities. Leaders in Cuba are well aware of the deficiency of their schools. As we have seen in Chapter XII, the educational level is low and illiteracy is high. Failure in this important respect must be placed largely at the door of the central government, which has primary responsibility. While much progress has been made since Cuba gained its independence, it is not unfair to say that much greater advancement could have been achieved if the funds available for schools had been wisely and efficiently spent. For example, nearly a third of the national budget for 1946 was designated for education, but the general criticism is made that too much of it is spent on the needless expansion of the bureaucracy in Havana, and all too little finds its way into the hinterland. As of 1945, school teachers were not poorly paid, even by American standards, but often they draw their

salaries whether they teach school or not. One also sees teachers
in the countryside with no place to hold school, unless a farmer
has an extra building or an extra room in his home which can be
used for school purposes. Then again, there may be a perfectly
good schoolhouse with no teacher available. In the meantime,
children grow up without contact with formal education, even
though the law makes attendance compulsory. Needless to say, the
law is not enforced, nor can it be so long as the schools are not
available. Again, the fact that the rural population is scattered
means that many children do not have ready access even to such
schools as do exist, and no transportation is provided at public
expense.

FACTORS FAVORABLE TO IMPROVEMENT

The fact that Cuba has a number of outstanding rural problems
does not mean that the situation is hopeless. There are several
reasons for thinking that improvements can be expected. One of
the most encouraging factors is the capacity of Cubans for self-
analysis and self-criticism. If the comments in the preceding pages
seem presumptuous for an "outsider" to make, the author offers
the defense that these criticisms are but the statements, in effect,
of many Cuban leaders. The best evidence that Cuba is an emerging democracy is the fact that there is the fullest freedom of expression and criticism on the part of the individual. There is running criticism of the government and of general conditions in
Cuban periodicals, in books, on the radio, and in the lecture halls.
When it was proposed that the Cuban government participate in
the Special Surveys of a number of rural communities, the president of the Republic himself enthusiastically approved the project,
and reportedly said: "We ought to make a hundred such surveys."
The first step in bringing to realization some improvements in
Cuban rural life is the ability and the willingness to face facts. The
Cuban people have both of these traits.

One of the main difficulties in translating this self-criticism into
action for improvement lies in the present nature of the governmental structure, which minimizes local autonomy and initiative.
Moreover, leaders in government have not yet become imbued
with the doctrine that the government should be a servant of the

people. Too often government office-holders regard the government as an enterprise to be operated for their private benefit. Nepotism is not regarded as politically sinful but is a recognized and established practice. One hastens to add that there are notable exceptions to this attitude on the part of Cuban politicians, but these exceptions only emphasize the rule. All governments suffer more or less from the temptation on the part of office-holders to exploit their positions for their own aggrandizement, but at least it should not become the norm of political behavior, and when corruption is found out, the evildoers should not go unpunished.

Cuban farm people, influenced by the elaborate promises of office-seekers to do something about roads and schools, have repeatedly voted for candidates to high office, only to be disappointed in the end as the promises fail to be carried into effect. Although the investigator finds a rather widespread cynicism among Cuban farmers toward the government, nevertheless he also finds a persisting desire for better schools, better roads, and a better life in general. And this is true in spite of a large measure of apathy on the part of the very poor. The wonder is that such ideals persist in the face of repeated frustrations. But as long as ideals for better things persist, there is reason to expect that there will come a time when leaders can no longer ignore their promises to satisfy the people's wants.

Meanwhile, voluntary organizations of farmers are steadily coming into existence which should provide a means for the rural people to become more articulate and to influence the course of social and political life. All such organizations in their constitutions express the aspirations of the farmer for a better income and improved transportation, schools, and community services. They want, perhaps more strongly than anything else, ownership of their land and the security that is assumed to go with it. Agrarian reform, as they call it, is already provided for in the Constitution of 1940; but again, as in so many aspects of government, implementation lags behind the written law.

In recent years also a number of so-called "cooperatives" have been formed for purposes of buying and selling, providing further evidence of a growing tendency of farmers to realize that they must to a large extent solve their problems by their own joint efforts without relying on government to do it for them. While these enterprises are not cooperatives according to the usually accepted criteria, they provide some of the experience in leadership and organization at the local level which is a necessary prerequisite to action on a broader scale.

STEPS TOWARD A BETTER FUTURE

With favorable attitudes toward community action and growing experience in community-wide organization, Cuban farmers have the basic resources with which to bring about desired improvements in rural living. It may be useful to suggest some immediate steps that might be taken by leaders in and out of government to accelerate the movement.

Enlarge and emphasize the field service of the Ministry of Agriculture. There already exists in the Ministry of Agriculture an extension service for farm people, with a staff in Havana and an inspector (county agent) in each of the municipios, as well as a supervisor in each of the six provinces. The personnel, both in the national capital and in the field, should be more adequately protected in their tenure by a strict adherence to civil service standards. Here, as in other aspects of government, there are too many employees in Havana in relation to the field staff, and too large a proportion of them do not have adequate qualifications for their jobs. A small staff of technical experts in various aspects of Cuban agriculture and livestock production, carefully selected for their competence and training, would be worth much more than a building full of people whose only interest in government service is in getting on the payroll, whether they do any work or not. This headquarters staff should have a liberal allowance for travel and should be expected to spend most of their time in the field. As it is now, to cite one example, the director of the boys' and girls' club work has to do most of his work by correspondence because he has such a limited allowance for travel.

The "inspectors," as of 1946, were not provided with transportation.[3] The more faithful and energetic of them managed to get into the field occasionally by bus or other means provided by themselves, but lacking automobiles, their direct contact with farmers

[3] Some of them were furnished with "jeeps" in 1947.

was infrequent. Moreover, their salaries were not sufficient to justify the more competent in remaining on the job, or in any case, in carrying on their work with enthusiasm. Another difficulty is that regulatory and educational work are combined, in that the same person attempts to perform both functions. The inspector who has police functions is not likely to be an effective educator. Both the field and the central staff should be augmented by women trained in home economics and social work, who could carry information on homemaking to the farm women of the island. Meetings of farmers for the purpose of receiving instruction from the local agents should be more frequently held, and because many farmers are not able to read, wide use should be made of the demonstration method. Visual aids—the motion picture, charts, and slides—should be very effective devices.

Promote the organization of farmers. The extension service of the Ministry of Agriculture could greatly enlarge its service to the farm population by organizing local groups into associations for educational and social purposes. Local clubs, composed of neighboring families electing their own officers, conducting regular meetings for discussion of agricultural and social problems, and providing opportunity for visiting and recreational activity, would be helpful in developing community spirit, and in giving badly needed experience in self-help. Such associations should be dedicated primarily to educational and social objectives, rather than toward political action. Projects looking toward improving schools, roads, and sanitation could well be undertaken by such groups.

The government should also encourage the formation of *true* cooperatives among farmers for buying and selling. There are many cooperatives in Cuba, but almost all of them are nothing more than ordinary stock companies using the name *cooperativa*. The true cooperative is based on the democratic principles of one man, one vote; distribution of dividends on the basis of patronage; and the payment of a fixed rate of interest on the stock subscribed. There is no law in Cuba to govern the organization of cooperatives, and such legislation is an essential first step. Once the cooperative movement gets established, it should be a function of the government to provide short training courses for leaders in the techniques of management. There should, of course, be a continuous program carried on by the cooperatives themselves to educate their members in the privileges and responsibilities of membership.

Establish a definite plan for road construction and maintenance. Mitigation of the geographic isolation to which so many Cuban farm people are subjected should constitute an immediate objective of the government. Equally important is the necessity of providing for continuous maintenance of roads after they are constructed. Too often in the past, goods roads built at great cost have been allowed to deteriorate through lack of any attention to their upkeep. The cost of road construction is said to be higher than necessary, due to the corrupt practices of politicians in league with contractors. This problem—by no means peculiar to Cuba— can be eliminated only as the citizens become enlightened and eternally vigilant. It is a pity, indeed, that in a relatively poor country so much of the money appropriated for road construction should dribble into the pockets of unscrupulous politicians and contractors.

Continue research in social and economic problems. Conditions such as we have tried to describe in these pages call for continuous study by competent students. It is not enough to make a survey or a census now and then. These economic and social problems should be given major attention by a well-trained staff in the Ministry of Agriculture. It goes without saying that such a staff should be protected by civil service regulations from the caprice of politicians.

Initiate agrarian reform. Political unrest, arising from the frustration of the desire of peasants to obtain possession of and security on the land, will be chronic in Cuba until more positive action is taken in this respect. Admittedly the problem is a difficult one, with the existing rights of large landholders to consider; but it is not a question that can be continually postponed. It is likely that continued delay in carrying out the law may result in serious political consequences.

It is not the purpose of this writer to judge the merits of the peasants' point of view. They want a general redistribution of the land. This would involve the breaking up of many large holdings and their subdivision into small farms. It may be appropriate to suggest, however, that the experiences of other countries in this respect might be assembled and made available to farmers and policy-makers. It should be apparent from such experience that breaking up large holdings in favor of many small farms does not per se bring economic salvation to the people on the land. Cuba's major products meet strong competition in the world market, and any program that impairs the island's productive efficiency would bring worse rather than better conditions. Small farms are not easily and economically mechanized. Yet mechanization in competing areas will in time compel mechanization in Cuba, or else the further degradation of the land workers.

However, there is a great deal of land in Cuba that is now either not used at all or not used intensively, which might well be utilized for family-size farms for some of the landless people. This use, with appropriate facilities provided for equipping and stocking the farms, should help to increase the national production, particularly of diversified crops. A land policy is badly needed which will provide the broadest practical distribution of the land and at the same time assure that it will be wisely and efficiently used.

In summary, the major problems that weigh heavily on rural Cuba are poverty, ignorance, isolation, and lack of local initiative and responsibility. There exists in many farm people a full awareness of these problems and a desire to do something about them. The leaders in and out of government know the problems also, and are being driven—by their own humanitarian impulses or by pressures from the people themselves—to do something about them. The way is already open for such leaders to develop and carry through a constructive program. Some progress has been and is being made. The task is great, but the surge of public demand is making rapid action increasingly urgent.

Reference Material

Brief Description of Areas Covered
by the Special Surveys

Pinar del Río. The families surveyed in Pinar del Río are located in two sections. San Juan y Martínez is located near the south coast about twenty miles southwest of the city of Pinar del Río, capital of the province of the same name. It represents some of the richest tobacco land of Cuba. The other area is east of the city a few miles, on much less fertile soil but still in tobacco-growing country. In these areas farmers grow few crops other than tobacco. The San Juan y Martínez families were tenants or laborers on land owned by the Cuban Land and Leaf Tobacco Company. The others were largely independent growers of various tenure classes.

Cabaiguán. This area is located in the central part of the island, but also in tobacco-growing territory. Family farms—tenant and owner—predominate. The farmers are mostly renters, however. Landowner-ship is concentrated in a few hands. Like the Pinar del Río sample, the families here are near towns of some size. Geographic isolation is not characteristic of our tobacco-growing samples.

Cienfuegos-Trinidad. This area is devoted to coffee-growing and was chosen to represent that farming type. The country is mountainous and poorly provided with roads. Through the rainy season it is almost inaccessible. The nearest town of importance is about thirty miles away. The land, to the extent of several hundred square miles, is owned by Casa de Castaña, a wealthy Cuban family firm. The coffee growers are tenants of this concern. The coffee-processing equipment main-tained by the firm near the coffee plantations is among the most

259

modern in the island. The population is mostly, but not all, white. The level of living is fairly high considering the isolation.

Alto Songo. Located in the mountains of Oriente Province in the eastern part of the island, this area is also devoted to coffee production. It, too, is characterized by concentrated landownership, high proportion of tenants, and poor roads and communication. The families are predominantly colored, and the level of living extremely low.

Florida. One of two areas chosen to represent sugar cane production, this plantation is one of the largest in the island. Most of the land is under lease to colonos, and the families interviewed were all wage laborers working for colonos and living in bateyes on the colonias. It is located in the east central part of the island of Camagüey Province. The plantation is owned by an American company.

Manguito. In contrast with Florida, this sugar-producing area is characterized by small colonos, most of whom owned their farms or rented from individuals other than the company. The location is in the central part of the country.

Sancti-Spíritus. This is one of three dairy areas included in the Surveys. It is located a few miles out from the city of Sancti-Spíritus and is supplied with some hard-surfaced and other all-weather roads. A condensed milk factory recently constructed here serves a wide area. Dual-purpose cattle are common, combining milk and beef production. Milk production per cow is low. Farms are large but ownership by the operator is common.

Bayamo. This region is similar in type of operation to Sancti-Spíritus, combining beef and milk production, but with somewhat greater attention given to the latter. Cheese and butter manufacturing are important in this area.

San Antonio de las Vegas. This area near Havana specializes in supplying market milk for the metropolis. Here one finds the dairy industry more highly developed than in any other part of the country. The dairy breeds—Jerseys, Holsteins, Guernseys, and others—are the rule, although various crosses with breeds better suited to the climate are being attempted. Some farms are equipped with milking machines and other modern equipment. The dairy industry is largely a development of the last forty years and there is much still to be done to bring it to a high state of efficiency. Although some farms are modern and are producing sanitary milk, the majority would not pass a very rigid inspection. Most of the dairy farms are owned by the operators.

Florencia. This area in the north central part of the country is one of two areas representing mixed or diversified farming. In addition to supplying several canning factories, the community specializes in growing and packing tomatoes for the United States market.

Güines. Located in Havana Province, this area also represents mixed farming. It has the good fortune to be able to irrigate much of the land, thus adding to the assurance of good yields. Irrigation has also made Güines one of the most important rice-producing sections of the island. Small farms and relatively high rates of ownership prevail.

APPENDIX B

General Social and Economic Conditions in the Cienfuegos-Trinidad Survey Area

by

ALEJANDRO FERNÁNDEZ DE CUETO[1]

In this short account are found my personal observations regarding the life of the rural population of this zone—perhaps the most difficult in the province because of its having been so little studied and having scarcely had even its geographical boundaries determined. The inconveniences of this country, mountainous and far removed from important urban centers, together with the lack of means of communication, make this region the antithesis of places favorable to the development of culture. Only three factors can be set down as propitious in this sense, and they are: the fertility of the soil in which every seed germinates; the state of protection (against potable germs) of the farmers, who always enjoy good health in spite of their not very hygienic life; and the natural beauty of the landscape, which is perhaps the principal element of influence upon the peaceable character of the people and their hospitable and brotherly feelings.

[1] Agricultural inspector of the municipality of Cienfuegos, a position roughly equivalent to that of county agricultural agent in the United States. Sr. de Cueto interviewed the families in the Cienfuegos-Trinidad survey area, and in addition wrote this interesting account of his observations of life in the area. The translation, made with the assistance of my son, is printed here with Sr. de Cueto's permission, and with the thought that it will convey something additional regarding the area and illustrate the capacity for self-analysis which is so characteristic of the intelligent Cuban. While by no means all of the agricultural inspectors in Cuba would be able to write accounts of their respective areas which would equal this in quality, there can be no doubt that such an effort would be worth while. For those who might wish to undertake it, this report would serve as a useful model.

262

GEOGRAPHICAL DESCRIPTION

The zone made up of the districts of Cabagán, Aguacate, and Guaniquical encloses within its boundaries to the north the heights which, in the mountainous group called Guamuhaya, correspond to those to the south of Trinidad, where the Sierra de Siguanea rises, and the Cabeza del Muerto and, more toward the south, the valley of Yaguanabo, which extends some distance from the Loma de Myará and Piedra Blanca to the Loma del Burro in an oblique line from west to east and from north to south, flanked by great elevations. South of this imaginary line are the heights and escarpments of Las Canas, Las Campanillas, La Yava, and Muñoz. Right on the coast or very near it is the valley of San Juan de Baullua and El Inglés, where there is a virgin beach of considerable dimensions, great beauty, and great tourist possibilities. The boundaries of these theoretical and confused districts are described below.

Cabagán. Cabagán is bounded on the north, with the district of Aguacate; on the south, with the ocean; on the west, with the districts of Gavilán and La Sierra, which belong to the municipality of Cienfuegos; on the east, with the district of Táyaba in the municipality of Trinidad. In this district we find that the principal sources of wealth are coffee, livestock, and lumber; and on a minor scale, bee-culture, garden products, and hogs, all of which are consumed almost totally by the farmers themselves. The garden products, which are produced in large quantity by the fertility of the land, are used mostly as feed for the animals, a lesser part for the consumption of the family, and, on a very small scale, for selling; in the last category it is unavoidable that there be a very high price on the consumer market, since the handling and the freight are of greater cost in most operations.

There is considerable raising of cattle, and at the present time, because of difficult communications, it is the principal means of exploitation, since fattening or the transportation of milk to the market is impossible. But on a small scale there exists a fresh cheese industry, which is carried on mostly in order to tame the stock, because the great extent of pasture land would cause them to go wild. This, in times past, used to bring about great losses, for once the cattle were brought into the corrals, they would die on account of the domestication, or "dogification" as the farmers say.

The principal kinds of wood exploited are cedar, mahogany, yava, ocuge, majagua, and many others. The exploitation is recent, since transportation was always the obstacle which the owners of fincas encountered. Now, owing to the improvement of private roads into the interior of the fincas of this coffee zone (carried out by the Casa Castaño), sawed lumber is being taken out in trucks which haul it to the boat. Until a year ago the lumber was sawed by hand, but at the present time there exists a sawmill in El Naranjo, which is driven by the motors used in the processing of coffee. Another factor in the production of wood has been the high price reached due to present economic conditions.

Coffee is the principal source of wealth in this district. It is planted now on a moderate scale; but, considering that the plantings go back to the year 1895, it is certain that the majority are old plots, like those of Mayarí, Las Vegas, and Río Chiquito, whose plantings date from before the War for Independence. The handling of the coffee is done mostly in a primitive fashion, but there exists now on the Finca El Naranjo a modern plant, where the coffee, washed of the effects of fermentation, dried, shelled, and classified, is technically processed. The Casa Castaño, owner of the plant, carries out the processing of the coffee which it buys from the harvesters. This system of processing has benefited the zone a great deal since roads have been constructed for transportation by truck; the same means is used for getting out the lumber; and the Casa Castaño has the exclusive right to use the roads.

Aguacate. In this district also coffee is the only source of wealth, since livestock is found on a small scale and garden products in less proportion. It is expected in this zone that the installation of the sawmill on the Finca El Naranjo, in the district of Cabagán, will permit the exploitation of its woods, of which that called mantequero exists in great quantity. There are coffee zones in the district, which, because of deforestation, the effect of erosion, or owing to some disease unknown to the farmers, are in a state of decadence. This alarming condition has not yet been taken into consideration; it is reported here so that the Ministry of Agriculture may take cognizance of it.

Guaniquical. The chief sources of wealth of the district are coffee and lumber (which in recent years has greatly increased). The importance of lumber is such that private concerns have carried into effect the construction of a road from Siguanea to Manicaragua, for the purpose of taking it out in trucks—after the sawing, since there are several sawmills in the vicinity.

Cows and hogs are raised on a moderate scale. In the valley of Siguanea garden products are sown for selling. The principal products are black beans, rallados, yellow malangas, white malangas (*guagüí*), and cabbage, which this year has been planted in considerable quantity. The valley of Siguanea, in spite of being the zone in which the most garden products are sown, also forms part of the zone which produces the most coffee, because on the Finca El Nicho there are the extensive plots of coffee and, for its processing, a plant which works on a larger scale than that on the Finca El Naranjo, since almost 12,000 *quintales* have been handled. This development has recently brought about improvements in the means of transportation; roads have been constructed which span the whole finca and extend as far as the town of Cumanayagua, for more than thirty-eight kilometers; they were built by the Casa Castaño, owner of the Finca El Nicho.

POPULATION

The population throughout the whole zone is rather scanty. The great expanse of land, in relation to the small number of inhabitants, causes the farmers to have their dwellings a great distance from their nearest neighbor. This makes social intercourse difficult, and is an important factor in their infrequent quarrels, since their fowl and other animals do not get mixed up, and, if this happens, they settle their differences without the intervention of the law. Nevertheless, it is common to find places where the increase in children has caused successive divisions of a finca, and in time a small settlement is formed with neighboring houses; usually all the neighbors there are relatives. Thus, such places have the characteristics of the original families, and usually the inhabitants are all white or Negro rather than mixed. The population has increased in these last years, but not at as rapid a rate as has the population of the province or of the island as a whole.

HISTORICAL SKETCH

The city of Trinidad was from its foundation the center of the zone; but its progress and brilliant epoch had very little influence upon the colonization of these lands, which remained almost unoccupied until the foundation and rapid development of the city of Cienfuegos. The development of these districts is really owing to the increase in the population of the latter city, with which almost all commercial intercourse takes place. The founders of Cienfuegos were families of French origin, and so it is certain that those Frenchmen were the ones who introduced the cultivation of coffee about the year 1820. However, the inhabitants of this region are mainly the descendants of Canary Islanders and peninsular Spaniards, who, coming as laborers, have remained as landowners. The Negro population has its origin among the early slaves.

The origin of many farms goes back to the end of the last century, where their development began. On the farms of Las Canas and Río Chiquito, district of Cabagán, people say the first coffee was planted by a Chinese, obeying the orders of a Frenchman. When the woods had been removed, coffee was planted between plots of bananas and cacao, which still exist and, in spite of being of very good quality, are not utilized. The farm Las Canas has passed into the hands of successive owners, who have had it rented or sharecropped; at present, one of its owners has kept the property for his own use.

In the section of Buenos Aires, district of Aguacate, we find a novel form of development: the owner of a finca, obtained by dollar purchase, used to pay his workers in land, which they tilled on their days off, that is, Sundays and holidays. The work which they carried out for the owner was the planting of coffee within the woods.

From the earliest times coffee was the first plant exploited in these zones, and its cultivation has evolved little, though in some places certain improvements have been introduced in recent years. The reason for the improvements is the necessity of protection against great losses in yield. One improvement consists in the pruning and planting of special shade trees, such as *búcaro* in mountainous places and *algarrobo* (carob) in lowlands. Until a short time ago, the seedlings were gathered from under the plants or in natural seedbeds formed when the seeds are carried down by water to lower ground. Today most coffee growers reject this sort of practice, choosing only those seeds which have all the requisites of good germination. The cultivating tools which have always been used are hatchet, machete, hoe, *guaña*, pickax, and recently a small saw for pruning; the hoe is being discarded for the guaña.

DIVISION OF THE LAND

The land was originally granted by the rulers of Spain to men of great power, many of whom did not so much as visit the island; and they in turn granted *peso de posesión,* which was registered without being measured, without fixing the boundaries, without establishing to which municipality the land really belonged. Thus we encounter the strange instance of the Finca El Naranjo, which is recorded in the property registry of Cienfuegos, while all the surrounding fincas are recorded in the property registry of Trinidad; El Naranjo is also recorded there, its owners acquiring property rights in both places.

There has been much litigation, producing two consequences, one advantageous, the other disadvantageous. The first is that all the owners have now been obliged to fix their boundaries and clarify their titles, making possible a better knowledge of the zone; and the second, that litigation has caused many quarrels among owners, and has aroused hatred among farm families, although this is becoming less and less serious. The way in which the present owners acquired the fincas was almost always the following: they would rent the finca from the owner, who had it recorded in the property registry of Trinidad or Cienfuegos, and, once in possession of it, would buy the title conflicting with that of the owner in actual possession, who would bring suit when they refused to pay the rent; they also claimed to be owners and ended up with absolute ownership by acquiring both titles. It is to be noted that the titles of Cienfuegos are older than those of Trinidad, and that there are still lawsuits, and fincas without clarified titles.

In the district of Guaniquical there is a suit for the ownership of lands being exploited for lumber. At present this battle is for the sake of fixing boundaries, since many of these lands belonged to owners who were killed in the War for Independence, leaving their fincas abandoned; they had them through *peso de posesión*. When they disappeared, others took possession of the lands, enlarging the boundaries by night, building houses and planting bananas so that they could claim their ownership dated from a long time back. These battles are directed by the great landowners, who pay people in their confidence for this work, employing even the farmers themselves. They have reached an alarming state of affairs: houses have been burned, shots have been exchanged, machete attacks have been made, so that the authorities have had to intervene.

SCHOOLS

The farmers are frankly in favor of adequate instruction for their children, and it is really interesting to see among these country people the live desire they feel for progress; they are thus disposed to favor any governmental project for the creation of schools. The chief obstacle is the teachers, who are so young when called upon to teach in these places. They maneuver in order to be transferred, or abandon the schools for military service, since poor communication prevents them from going to town as frequently as they wish and they do not care to take up the rustic life of the farmers. It is possible that this failing is due to the lack of normal schools, which would prepare the farm youth themselves for the task. The present instruction is limited to the primary grades, since the teachers are incapable of helping the farmer improve his means of cultivation and mode of life through vocational education.

There are very few official schools, so that the percentage of children attending school is insignificant. The most well-to-do farmers solve this problem by paying a person to come and live in their houses for the purpose of teaching their children the rudiments of knowledge. In all these districts there are approximately six schools, with a teacher for each. These schools are maintained by the government. Private persons do not maintain schools, but the farmers in their eagerness to facilitate matters for the teachers have constructed at their own expense schoolhouses which are not functioning; they are always ready to construct such houses; and the schools that are functioning have been built by the farmers.

THE CHURCH

The most widespread religion is Catholicism. In all this region there exists no church. The nearest ones are those of the towns La Sierra and Cumanayagua, many leagues distant. Every so often, when the feast of some patron saint is commemorated, the farmers go in considerable numbers to have their children baptized by a priest who comes to the district from La Sierra. This priest is himself from the town of Cumanayagua; he does the baptizing in bulk, charging three dollars for every child baptized. In other instances, the priest is brought to the house of some well-to-do farmer, where a group of children receive the baptismal sacrament at the same price. This "exploitation," as the farmers say, together with the rare exposure to religious ideas, accounts for the lack of religious faith and the introduction and progress in some zones of new sects, like that called Jehovah's Witnesses.

The most well-to-do farmers are the ones who have church weddings, for in these regions concubinage is most common. A young lover abducts his beloved, brings her to his parents' house until a bohío can be built not far from the paternal dwelling within the boundaries of the finca. Legal matrimony is all the rarer since usually those who get married do so through the intervention of some politician, whose candidates take advantage of the event as an act of propaganda. Nevertheless, the children are registered in the civil registry, being thus officially recognized by their parents.

LIFE, CUSTOMS, AND ORGANIZATIONS

Among these farmers, what establishes the greatest difference is not economic position or cultural level, since these are almost the same for all. Owners take part in the chores, the same as their sons and em-

ployees. Race is usually the source of discrimination, though there is
no great tyranny, and the farmer is quite fraternal.

In this zone, where the people are very trusting, robberies are not
committed by local persons but by strangers. Nevertheless, they have
the custom of providing food and sleeping quarters for the strangers
who come to work. The latter come during the time of coffee harvesting—the months of September, October, November, and December.
Their wages depend upon their ability (being paid on a piecework
basis), and there are some places which have benefited from certain
social laws, such as those concerning workers' insurance. On each
finca there is ordinarily a number of individuals who come to work
year after year. Notice is sent to them when there is work; likewise,
other workers who bring the recommendation of neighbors are accepted. The life of these men is very rough. While the sun shines, they
continue working. At night they rest in barracks which are not hygienic; they use hammocks and clean themselves once a week. The
food is plentiful, because of the quantity of vegetables harvested and
some pork and beef. It is characteristic of the descendants of Spaniards
to make bread at home. There is no social life among them, but there
is mutual aid. In the whole region there is no society at present which
carries on an active life, except in the zone of Mayarí, district of
Cabagán or of La Sierra; in the place known for *sopapo,* there is a
society for recreation called the Asociación de Caficultores, which has
its meeting place made of stucco and tile and, for furnishings, a few
folding chairs and some rustic benches. The society is sponsored by
various coffee farmers who use the meeting place for gatherings of
any sort related to their labors.

In places where there are several houses, usually there are general
stores, a barbershop, a blacksmith's shop, a small café, a small drug-
store where medicines are sold, and a ring for cockfighting. The principal amusements of the farmers are cockfights, for which they gather
in great numbers and for which they lay bets with all their passion.
The size of the bets depends upon economic position and the sym-
pathies felt for the cock, to which various qualities are attributed.

Also the *guajiro* songs are a means of entertainment, especially the
décima guajira, accompanied by the guitar or the *tres* and rosewood
sticks. They also have dance festivals, the music being played on the
guitar, the *tres,* rosewood sticks, *maracas,* a drum called the *bongó,*
and, on some occasions, accompanied by the cornet (*cornetín*). The
most common dance is the *són.*

In these districts there are no public facilities. The people have never known libraries, or public parks, or amusements. Today the most well-to-do farmers are buying radios, for which they have their own electric plants which also provide light. They usually are powered with gasoline, although in some places waterfalls are utilized for the production for electrical energy. In the whole region there is no doctor, no nurse, no lawyer, no newspapers, no banks, no telegraph; there are only post offices, though in most cases letters and newspapers are brought by private individuals from the city. The telephone has penetrated somewhat into the country in the region of Siguanea, district of Guaniquical, at the station for the improvement of coffee. There is another line which reaches the farms of Mayarí, because of the hydroelectric plant in that place. These telephones are used in urgent matters by the neighbors of the region. In case of illness, the sick are helped by persons who have more knowledge of these matters, using home remedies—neither faith healing nor spiritualism is practiced. In serious cases, the sick are carried to the city, this being very costly since they have to stop at hotels.

In this zone the organization of the 5-C clubs has turned out to be very difficult, for there are very few schools. Nevertheless, two clubs have recently been founded, both in the district of Guaniquical. One of them, named Martí, has for its co-worker Señora Clara Villafaña; it is devoted to horticulture and was founded November 15, 1944. The other club, called America, whose co-worker is Señora Matilde Martínez, is devoted to horticulture, sericulture, aviculture, and home economics; it was founded September 24, 1945.

MEANS OF TRANSPORTATION

Communication is the chief obstacle to all progress here. The principal means is the mule train, which carries their products to the seacoast where they can be sent by sea (district of Cabagán and section of Aguacate), or to points where they are sent by truck (district of Guaniquical and Aguacate) to Cienfuegos. The most effective communication is found in the district of Guaniquical, since it is by truck. In the region of Cabagán, it is very difficult, since transport is carried on by sea, on two sailing ships with auxiliary motors which leave from various docks along the coast. The official dock is that in El Inglés, making four departures a week, two by each ship.

GOVERNMENTAL ORGANIZATION

The municipal government is represented by the district mayors who are persons in the confidence of the municipal mayor. Their function is to keep the livestock registry and cooperate with the Ministry of Agriculture. Some mayors collect the municipal taxes. Policing is very meager. The *Guardia Rural* is in charge, and its officers make the rounds of the different fincas. In these three districts there is no barracks (*cuartel*) of the Guardia Rural, though there are some permanent posts, with one or two soldiers in charge.

The other functionary who exercises direct influence over the farmers is the municipal inspector of agriculture, who, besides keeping the Ministry of Agriculture informed of the progress in the muncipality under his jurisdiction, advises the farmers concerning crops and distribution of seed, and tries to introduce all the improved methods in agriculture.

THE POOR

There is no asylum for the aged or for poor children. The aged are cared for at home; they reach an advanced age. Beggars do not exist. The poorest families are helped by those neighbors who have obtained better harvests; they give them vegetables and in some cases milk for the children. Such cases are observed particularly in time of great drouth. The children, owing to the very bad hygienic condition in which they are raised in direct contact with the soil, show a high percentage of parasitism, in spite of which they appear to be healthy and strong.

DELINQUENCY

Delinquency is even rarer among the young people, since obedience to parents is a custom which is never slighted. This obedience lasts until the death of the parents. Robbery and theft are observed on a larger scale than homicide. Robbery is most frequent at the time of coffee harvest, because it is then that people always come from other zones, and these are the ones, as noted above, who commit robberies.

RESUMÉ

In the life of the coffee farmer what has struck me most is the abandoned condition of the roads, the lack of schools, the lack of medical protection, and the ineptitude and carelessness which some farmers have in their system of cultivation. An example of the latter is the sharecropper contract, which can be classified into two varieties: the one in which the sharecropper, besides cultivating the coffee, is able to secure other lands for planting vegetables for his sustenance, and also for raising cows, pigs, and chickens. These sharecroppers are found in the zone of Las Lomas. In Río Chiquito, among other places, sharecroppers use their land exclusively for the growing of coffee, while the lands of owners which could be devoted to vegetables and livestock are rented to other individuals.

In the sharecropper contract, the 33⅓ or 40 per cent of the coffee crop which goes to pay for a caballería of land amounts to as much as eight hundred dollars and sometimes more, although the cost of these lands is some five hundred dollars. In the case of a rent contract this does not happen, for there the cost of rent is from eighty to eight-five dollars per caballería on lands suitable for coffee; and from sixty to forty or less when the finca can be devoted to livestock or the growing of vegetables. This sort of contract exists in the zone of Siguanea.

The coffee farmer-owner has also been a victim of warehouses which are veritable usurers. After charging an enormous sum in interest, which is 20 per cent, they demand as a guarantee for their capital the transference of the property to the name of the warehouse or its representative. Besides, the warehouses make it necessary for the farmers to buy their groceries from them, selling them at a very high price. In all these cases, the deal is made so difficult for the coffee farmers that they gradually lose their fincas. In the case of the sharecropper or the renter, these lawbreakers keep the crops, since they manufacture documents in quantity which cover double the amount loaned.

The development of coffee groves is carried on in the following manner. The owner of the finca hands over the wooded land to the tenant coffee farmer for eight years; the latter plants coffee trees in the woods and nurtures them to maturity, but after the eight years, he has to leave all the benefits to the owner. The only benefit the coffee farmer receives consists in three harvests, two moderately good and one good, since coffee takes four or five years to reach the bearing age, during which time the tenant farmer lives a wretched life and, if he has any money, invests it in sustenance. When eight years have passed, the owner, if he likes, makes him a new contract as a sharecropper, the tenant farmer having to hand over the 33 or 40 per cent of the crop.

Glossary

agricultare. An agriculturist, either an operator or wageworker.

alcaldes. Mayors of cities and other local political divisions.

arrendatario. A renter, usually a cash renter.

arroba. A measurement of weight equaling twenty-five pounds.

arroyo. A small stream.

baldíos. Refers to public lands which are barren, wild, and not susceptible to cultivation.

barracones. Barracks for laborers.

barrio. A local unit of government roughly equivalent to a township.

batey. The premises of a sugar mill; also refers to a cluster of workers' dwellings on a sugar cane plantation.

besana. A unit of land measurement a little over six-tenths of an acre in size.

bohío. A peasant dwelling.

bongó. A small drum, about six inches in diameter, held between the knees and "played" with the bare hands.

boniato. The sweet potato.

caballería. A unit of land measurement equal to 33.16 acres.

caballero. A gentleman; originally a mounted knight.

cabildo. A municipal council.

cafetal. A coffee farm.

caja. A box, or case.

campesino. A farmer; a peasant.

caro. One-tenth of a caballería, or 3.32 acres.

caserío. A hamlet.

central. A sugar mill.

centro. Literally "center," but in Cuba refers to a club; thus, the *Centro Asturiano, Centro Gallego,* etc.

chófer. An automobile driver; the Spanish spelling of "chauffeur."

ciudad. A city.

claves. Two hardwood sticks, about eight inches long, which a member of an orchestra clacks to the musical rhythm.

cobíja. A sort of "bee" for the thatching of a *bohío* with *guano* (palmetto).

colonia. A sugar cane field operated by a *colono.*

colono. A sugar cane grower; may be either an owner or renter.

conquistadores. Conquerors.

cordel. About one-tenth of an acre.

corral. A grant of land usually one league in radius from a given center; used for small livestock, mostly sheep and goats. See *hato.*

criada. A maidservant.

cuartario. A tenant farmer who pays one-fourth of the crop for the use of the land.

dansón. A popular Cuban ballroom dance, slightly faster in tempo than the *són* (see *són*).

décima. Literally, a poem or song with ten verses; but in Cuba, it refers to a folk song sung to the accompaniment of a guitar and the claves. The words are composed by the singer as he sings and are appropriate to the situation.

desalojos. Persons evicted from land which they had been occupying without the consent of the owner.

encomienda. The right to use Indians for labor, granted to Spanish colonists in the New World. The colonist was supposed to assume responsibility for their physical welfare and to convert them to Christianity.

finca. A farm.

ganado mayor. Cattle.

ganado minor. Small livestock; usually refers to sheep and goats.

guajiro. A peasant.

guano. The leaf of the palm or palmetto.

guaracha. A ballroom dance somewhat faster in tempo than the *dansón,* but similar to it.

guardarrayas. Strips of idle land which separate the cane fields of a plantation.

hacendado. A landowner, usually on a large scale.

hacienda comunera. A communal ranch which developed as a result of the practice of not subdividing the circular grants when the owner died or sold portions of it.

hato. A circular grant of land used for cattle raising; usually two or three leagues in radius from a central headquarters.

ingenio. A sugar mill.

jornalero. A day laborer.

la seca. The dry season.

lata. Literally means "can"; a commonly used measure for coffee. Originally the five-gallon oil can came into use as a unit of measure in the coffee areas, and although a basket has been substituted for the can, the basket is still called a *lata.*

limones. Lemons.

malangos. A common vegetable plant in Cuba, the tubers of which provide a popular starchy food.

marabú. A tough shrub of little economic value, which spreads both by seed and by underground rootstock; a serious problem for Cuban farmers.

maracas. Gourds fitted with handles and containing shot or seeds; used in orchestras to accentuate the rhythm of the music. The performer holds one in each hand and shakes them to the beat of the music.

mayoral. The local representative of a landowner; a manager.

merced. A gift or grant of land.

mestizo. As used in Cuba, a person of mixed white and Negro blood.

municipio. A local unit of government; a county.

partidario. A share renter or sharecropper.

paseo. A walk.

peso de posesión or *peso de tierras.* A certificate of ownership of rights in a communal ranch.

plátano. Plantain; belongs to the banana family.

poblado. A small village.

prado. A walk down the center of a main street.

precaristas. Unauthorized settlers on land; squatters.

pueblo. A small town.

quintal. One hundred kilograms.

realenga. Unappropriated lands held by the Crown; public domain.

repartimiento. Usually refers to division of land (*repartimiento de tierras*) but may also apply to distribution of Indians (*repartimiento de Indios*).

roza. A unit of land measurement equivalent to about 1.8 acres.

solar. Generally means a building lot, but in Cuba it usually designates an urban slum.

són. The most popular ballroom dance in Cuba. A rather slow tempo characterizes the dance, and the couple may move over only a few square yards of floor space during the dance.

tabla de palma. Slabs sawed from the trunk of the royal palm.

tercedario. A tenant farmer who pays one-third of the crop for the use of the land.

tiempo muerto. The dead season.

trapiche. A small sugar mill.

vara española. A unit of linear measurement, about 2.78 feet.

vega. A fruitful plain, but used almost exclusively in Cuba to refer to a tobacco field.

villa. A town.

yuca. The cassava root.

zafra. The sugar cane harvest.

Bibliography

Books and articles about Cuba are numerous. Not only have Cuban writers produced a voluminous literature concerning their beloved island, but because of the close ties which have linked Cuba and the United States, many American students have also interested themselves in the subject. The following list of titles is not exhaustive but includes at least most of the works relevant to the social and economic backgrounds and conditions of the country.

Not listed here are the numerous documents relating to hearings of investigating committees of the United States Congress concerning Cuba, or the official reports and military orders of the provisional American governors (Wood, Magoon, Crowder), where were valuable sources of information on several aspects of the problems discussed in this volume. With few exceptions, articles in periodicals are not included, although several are cited in footnotes throughout the volume.

There are several bibliographies on various aspects of Cuban life. These have recently been brought together by Fermin Peraza Surausa, *Bibligrafías cubanas*, Washington: Library of Congress Latin American Series No. 7, 1945. The general reader interested in a selected list of books (annotated) will find John T. Reid's article useful, "Knowing Cuba through Books," *Hispania*, November 1946.

CENSUSES OF CUBA

In the preparation of this volume, the author has relied heavily on the five censuses which have been taken since Cuba gained its independence. These enumerations were made in 1899, 1907, 1919, 1931, and 1943.

Report of the Census of Cuba, 1899. Washington: Government Printing Office, 1900. The census of 1899 was taken under the auspices of the United States Army of Occupation, with the United States Bureau of the Census providing the technical supervision. Field work was done by Cuban enumerators. Since President McKinley had stressed the importance of the census as a first step in the establishment of a system of self-government, some incentive existed for making it as complete as possible. The final report contains interesting accounts of the hazards faced by field enumerators in their attempts to reach remote and almost inaccessible parts of the island. The census followed closely the form of the United States census. The published volume contains not only the statistical tables and appropriate text on the census itself, but also a description of the island, a brief history, a statement of economic and social conditions, form of government, and so forth. There is a short history of education in the island and the complete text of the military order of Governor Wood setting up a new educational system. An appendix gives a review of earlier (colonial) censuses of the island.

Cuba: Population, History, Resources, 1907. Washington: United States Bureau of the Census, 1909. Also taken during military occupation of the island by the United States, when Charles E. Magoon was provisional governor. Again the enumeration and analysis was under the technical supervision of the United States Bureau of the Census. The chief motivation of this census was the registration of eligible voters as one step in the holding of fair elections to select the government that was to follow the intervention. Perhaps this emphasis accounts for the fact that the tabulations and analyses are less extensive than in the 1899 census. It follows the latter in general form, including the incorporation of much general information about the country. No information is given regarding agriculture.

Census of the Republic of Cuba, 1919. Published in Havana in both English and Spanish. No date appears on the title page; probably 1922. The United States also participated in this census, and as in 1907 the goal was to purge the voting lists of fraudulent names. It follows essentially the form developed in the previous enumerations, with such improvements and changes as had been developed in the United States Bureau of the Census.

The *Census of 1931* was taken under Cuban auspices but during a critical period of the country's politics. It included questions regarding the agriculture of the country, but it is generally regarded as of doubtful reliability on this point. The revolution incident to the overthrow of Machado in 1932 no doubt accounts for the fact that the tables were not published until 1938–39, and then by a private printer and without any explanatory text.

Censo de 1943. Havana: P. Fernandez y Cia. No date of publication given; probably 1945. This census was taken under Cuban auspices entirely, and planned and executed by Cuban technicians. It follows the pattern established in the earlier censuses with some modifications and improvements. It contains 700 pages of general information regarding Cuba in addition to the population data. About 80 pages of textual analysis of the data are incorporated.

The National Agricultural Census, 1946. This is the first comprehensive census of agriculture in the history of Cuba. It follows somewhat the form and content of the United States census of agriculture. A volume is in preparation for publication at the time of this writing. The author has had access to the preliminary mimeographed releases.

BOOKS AND ARTICLES

Abbot, Rev. Abiel. *Letters Written in the Interior of Cuba between the Mountains of Arcana to the East and of Cuzco to the West.* Boston, 1829.

Arredondo, Alberto. *Cuba: tierra indefensa.* (Prologo de Ramiro Guerra.) Havana: Editorial Lex, 1945.

Bacardí y Moreau, Emilio. *Crónicas de Santiago de Cuba.* (Recopiladas por E.B.M.) Barcelona: Tipografía de Carbonell y Esteva, 1908–24.

Ballou, M. M. *History of Cuba.* Boston: Phillips, Sampson, and Co., 1854.

Barbour, Thomas. *A Naturalist in Cuba.* Boston: Little, 1945.

Beals, Carleton. *The Crime of Cuba.* New York: Lippincott, 1934.

Bradley, Hugh. *Havana, Cinderella's City.* New York: Doubleday, 1941.

Bremer, Fredrika. *Homes of the New World.* New York, 1853.

Buell, Raymond Leslie, ed. *Problems of the New Cuba.* New York: Foreign Policy Association, 1935.

Cardona, Juan M. Chailloux. *Sintesis histórica de la vivienda popular.* Havana: Jesús Montero, 1945.

Casas, Cadilla Rogelio. *El problema económico de Cuba.* (Pamphlet.) Havana: Companía Editoria, 1944.

Celorio, B. *Las haciendas comuneras.* Havana, 1914.

Chapman, C. E. *History of the Cuban Republic.* New York: Macmillan, 1927.

Compilación estadística sobre café, años 1935–36, 1936–37, y estimado de la cosecha de 1938. Havana: República de Cuba, Secretaría de Agricultura, 1938.

Dana, Henry. *To Cuba and Back.* London, 1859.

Davis, J. Merle. *The Cuban Church in a Sugar Economy.* New York: International Missionary Council, 1942.

de Acosta y Albear, Francisco. *Compendio histórico del pasado y presente de Cuba y de su guerra insurreccional hasta et el de marzo, 1875.* New York: Imprenta y librería de N. Ponce de León.

Ewart, F. C. *Cuba y las costumbres cubanas.* Boston, 1919.

Ferragút León, Casto. *Lineamientos generales para una política agrícola nacional.* Havana, 1948.

FitzGibbon, Russell Humke. *Cuba and the United States, 1900–1935.* Menasha, Wis.: George Banta Publishing Co., 1935.

Forbes-Lindsay, Charles Harcourt Ainslie. *Cuba and Her People of Today.* Boston: L. C. Paige and Co., 1928.

García de Arboleya, José. *Manual de la isla de Cuba.* Havana, 1852. (2nd ed., 1859.)

Guerra y Sánchez, Ramiro. *La defensa nacional y la escuela.* Havana: La Moderna Poesía, 1923.

———. *La industria azucarera de Cuba.* Havana: Cultural S. A., 1940.

———. *Manual de historia de Cuba: económica, social, y política.* Havana: Cultural S. A., 1938.

Hazard, Samuel. *Cuba with Pen and Pencil.* Hartford: The Hartford Publishing Co., 1871.

Huber, B. *Aperçu statistique de l'île de Cuba.* Paris: P. Dufart, 1826.

Humboldt, Baron Alexander von. *Ensayo político sobre la isla de Cuba.* (Tr. al castellano por D.H.B. y V.M.) Paris: En casa de Jules Renouard, 1827.

———. *Ensayo político sobre la isla de Cuba.* (Introdución por Fernando Ortiz.) 2 Vols. Havana: Cultural S. A., 1930.

Jenks, Leland H. *Our Cuban Colony.* New York: Vanguard, 1928.

Johnson, Willis Fletcher. *The History of Cuba.* 5 Vols. New York: B. F. Buck and Co., 1920.

Laws, Ordinances, Decrees, and Military Orders Having the Force of Law, Effective in Porto Rico, May 1, 1900. H. R. Document No. 1484, 60th Congress, 2nd Session. GPO, 1909. Part I.

Leyes de las Indias. Madrid, 1847.

Lobingier, Charles S. *Recent Legislation and Law Reform.* New York, 1926.

Lockmiller, David A. *Magoon in Cuba.* Chapel Hill: University of North Carolina Press, 1938.

Marrero, Levi. *Elementos de geografía de Cuba.* Havana: Editorial Minerva, 1946.

Martínez Escobar, Manuel. *Historia de remedios: colonización y desenvolvimiento de Cuba.* Havana: Jesús Montero, 1944.

Massé, E. M. *L'île de Cuba et la Havane.* Paris: Lebegue, 1825.

Menocal y Cueto, Raimundo. *Origen y desarrollo del pensomiento cubano.* Vol. I. Havana: Editorial Lex, 1945.

Moreno, Francisco. *Cuba y su gente: apuntes para la historia.* Madrid, 1887.

———. *El país de chocolate: la immoralidad de Cuba.* Madrid, 1887.

Ortiz, Fernando. *Las fases de la evolución religiosa.* Havana: Tip Moderna, 1919.

———. *La fiesta afrocubana de dia de reyes.* Havana: Emp. El Siglo XX, 1925.

———. *Contrapunteo cubano del tabaco y el azúcar.* Havana: Jesús Montero, 1940.

———. *La decadencia cubana.* Havana, 1924. (32 pp.)

———. *Los negros brujos: apuntes para un estudio de etnología criminal.* Madrid: Editorial-America, 1921.

———. "Los negros esclavos," *Revista bimestre cubana.* Havana, 1916.

Osgood, Cornelius. *The Ciboney Culture of Cayo Redondo.* New Haven: Yale University Press, 1942.

Parker, W. B., ed. *Cubans of Today.* New York: Putnam, 1919.

Pazos y Roque, Felipe. *La economía cubana en el siglo XIX.* Havana: Molina y Compañía, 1941.

Pepper, Charles M. *Tomorrow in Cuba.* New York: Harper, 1899.

Pérez de la Riva, Francisco. *El café, historia de su cultivo y explotación en Cuba.* Havana: Jesús Montero, 1944.

Pezuela y Lobo, Don Jacobo de la. *Diccionario geográfico, estadistico, historico de la isla de Cuba.* Madrid: Imprenta del establecimiento de Mellado, 1863–66.

———. *Ensayo histórico de la isla de Cuba.* New York: Imprenta española de R. Rafael, 1842.

———. *Historia de la isla de Cuba.* Madrid: C. Bailly-Baillière, 1868–78.

———. *Necesidades de Cuba.* Madrid, 1865.

Pichardo y Jiménez, Esteben. *Agrimensura legal de la isla de Cuba.* (2d. ed.) Havana: Imprenta y libreria antigua de Valdepares, 1902.

Pichardo y Tapia, Esteben. *Geografía de la isla de Cuba.* 4 Vols. Havana: Establecimiento topográfico de D. M. Soler, 1854–55.

Portell Vilá, Herminio. *Historia de Cuba, en sus relaciones con los Estados Unidos y España.* Havana: Jesús Montero, 1938–39.

———. "La indústria azúcarera y su futuro," *Revista bimestre cubana.* Vol. L, No. 2 (September–October 1942). Havana, Molina y Compañía.

Portunondo, José Antonio. *Curso de introducción a la historia de Cuba.* Havana, 1938.

Raggi Ageo, Carlos M. *Cuba, oficina de estudios del plan de seguridad social.* Havana: Editorial Lex, 1944.

Reed, W. W. "Climatological Data for the West Indian Islands," *Monthly Weather Review,* Vol. LIV (1926). U.S.D.A., pp. 133–60.

Robinson, Albert G. *Cuba and the Intervention.* New York: Longmans, 1905.

Rodríguez-Ferrer, Miguel. *Naturaleza y civilización de la grandiosa isla de Cuba.* 2 Vols. Madrid: J. Noguera, 1876–87.

Rodríguez, Francisco de Paula. *Sociología cubana.* Havana, 1919.

Roldá Oliarto, Esteban, compiler. *Cuba en la mano: enciclopedia popular ilustrada.* Havana, 1940.

Rosemond de Beauvallon, J. B. *L'île de Cuba.* Paris: Dauvin et Fontain, 1844.

Sagra, Ramón de la. *Historia económico-política y estadística de la isla de Cuba, o sea de sus progresos en la población, la agricultura, el comercio y las rentas.* Havana: Imprenta de las viudas de Arizoza y Soler, 1831.

———. *Historia física, económica-política, intelectual y moral de la isla de Cuba.* Paris: Librería de L. Hachette y Cia, 1861.

Simpson, Lesley Byrd. *The Encomienda in New Spain.* Berkeley: University of California Press, 1929.

Soule, George, David Efron, and Norman T. Ness. *Latin America in the Future World.* New York: Farrar and Rinehart, 1945.

Strode, Hudson. *The Pageant of Cuba.* New York: Smith and Haas, 1934.

Thomson, Charles A. *The Cuban Revolution: Reform and Reaction.* New York: Foreign Policy Association, 1936.

———. *The Cuban Revolution: The Fall of Machado.* New York: Foreign Policy Association, 1935.

Turnbull, David. *Travels in the West: Cuba, with Notices of Porto Rico and the Slave Trade.* London: Longman, Orme, Brown, Green, and Longmans, 1840.

Turosienski, Severin K. *Education in Cuba*. Washington: U.S. Office of Education, Bulletin No. 1, 1943.

Varona, Enrique José. *De la colonia a la república, selección de trabajos políticos, ordenada por su autor*. Havana: Cuba Contemporánea, 1919.

Walker, W. "Timeless Village of Cuba," *Travel*, February 1938.

Whitbeck, R. H. "Geographical Relations in the Development of Cuban Agriculture," *Geographical Revue*, Vol. XII (1922), pp. 223–40.

——. "The Lesser Antilles—Past and Present," *Annals* of the Association of American Geographers, Vol. XXIII (1933), pp. 21–26.

Williams, Eric. *The Negro in the Caribbean*. Washington, D.C.: Associates in Negro Folk Education, 1942.

Wilson, Charles Morrow. "The Heart of Rural Cuba," *Travel*, December 1939.

Wright, Irene Aloha. *Cuba*. New York: Macmillan, 1912.

——. *The Early History of Cuba (1492–1586)*. New York: Macmillan, 1916.

Wright, Phillip Green. *The Cuban Situation and Our Treaty Relations*. Washington, D.C.: Brookings Institution, 1931.

Zayas y Alfonso, Alfredo. *Lexicografía antillana*. Havana: Tipos-Molina y Cia, 1931.

Subject Index

Acculturation of Spanish and Cubans, 152

Batey (premises of a sugar mill), *see* Locality groups

Cafetal (coffee farm), 122–30: methods of establishing, 129–30
Chinese in Cuba, 10, 27–29
Church: status of, in rural Cuba, 174–75; expenditure for, 217; in Cienfuegos-Trinidad area, 268
Cienfuegos-Trinidad area, social and economic conditions of, 262–72
Class, *see* Social classes, Social stratification
Climate, *see* Geography
Clothing, expenditures for, 217
Coffee: processing, 16, 128; production encouraged by tariff, 51; farm organization in production of, 122–30; picking, 128
Color, *see* Negroes, Social classes
Colono (sugar cane grower), 120ff

Dead season, 57
Diet, *see* Food
Divorce, 196–98
Dry season, 56–59

Encomiendas (rights to use Indians for labor), 80–84
Education, *see* Schools

Family, 174–200: historical background of, 175ff; male dominance in, 176–78; children in, 178–79, 183–85, 187; decline of aristocratic, 179; Negro, 179; upper-class, 182–85; lower-class, 185; farm, 187; composition and size of, 189ff
Farmers: small, 10; large, 92–97; mobility of, 132, 170–73; organization of, 158, 173, 252, 254; level of living of, 201–19; income of, 202
Farming, systems of, 114–38
Farm laborers: migratory, 65, 171; number of, 166; social status of, 166–67, 171–72
Farms: naming of, 109; defined, 114; early types of, 116–27, 134–38; size of, 134–35, 167–68; family, 134–38; number of, 168
Food, 15, 208–12: expenditures for, 217
Foreigners, in various industries, 152–54
Forest resources, 45

Geography, 47ff: map of, 5; topography, 5; climate, 47ff; seasonal rhythms, 52–53
Government: corruption in, 5–8, 20; able public servants in, 21–22; intervention in sugar production, 98–103; nepotism in, 184–85, 252; in Cienfuegos-Trinidad area, 270–71

Haciendas comuneras (communal ranches), 87–90, 109
Harvard Botanical Garden, 19
Housing: condition of, 15, 121, 204–5; among the Havana lower class, 186; farms, 202–5; construction materials used in, 203–4; cost of, 204; sanitation, 249–50

Illegitimacy, 198–99
Illiteracy, 239–44

281

Index of Names